# DIVERSITY IN COLLEGE SETTINGS

# DIVERSITY IN COLLEGE SETTINGS
## DIRECTIVES FOR HELPING PROFESSIONALS

Edited by
Yvonne M. Jenkins

Routledge
Taylor & Francis Group
New York   London

Published in 1999 by
Routledge
711 Third Avenue
New York, NY 10017

Published in Great Britain by
Routledge
2 Park Square, Milton Park
Abingdon, Oxon, OX14 4RN

*Routledge is an imprint of the Taylor & Francis Group, an informa business*

Copyright ©1999 by Routledge

All rights reserved. No part of this book may be reprinted or reproduced or utilized in any form or by any electronic, mechanical, or other means, now known or hereafter invented, including photocopying and recording, or in any information storage or retrieval system, without permission in writing from the publishers.

Library of Congress Cataloging-in-Publication Data

Diversity in college settings: directives for helping professionals / edited by Yvonne M. Jenkins.
    p. cm.
    Includes index.
    ISBN 0-415-91305-5—ISBN 0-415-91306-3 (pbk.: alk. paper)
    1. Minority college students—Mental health services. 2. Minority college students—Mental health. 3. College students—Mental health services. 4. College students—Mental health. I. Jenkins. Yvonne M., 1952–
RC451.4.S7D59 1999
362.2'089'00973—dc21                                                                                                       98-5920
                                                                                                                                              CIP

# DEDICATION AND ACKNOWLEDGMENTS

This book is dedicated to my daughter, Ylana Janét, whose sweet and energetic spirit was a daily source of affirmation and inspiration while I worked on this project. It is my hope that her educational experiences will somehow be enhanced by the contents of this book toward a bright and happy future in which every aspect of her identity shall be embraced.

*Special thanks* are extended to each one of the contributors, whose interest, knowledge, experience, and diligence made my dream a reality. Without this very gifted, enthusiastic, and encouraging group of professionals, this project would not have been possible. *Special thanks* are also extended to Dora Wang, M.D. and Beverly Greene, Ph.D., whose feedback and support were especially helpful in the early stages of this project, and to Professor Elaine B. Pinderhughes for her extremely valuable suggestions concerning the manuscript. I am also particularly grateful to the college students with whom I have had the privilege to work over the years for their role in making the worth of this project unquestionable.

Finally, I would like to thank my mother, Esther Jenkins, Janet Surrey, and several other close friends for their consistent expressions of interest and support along the way.

# TABLE OF CONTENTS

**FOREWORD**    Chester M. Pierce    ix

**PREFACE**    Yvonne M. Jenkins    xi

**PART I**    **COUNSELING AND PSYCHOTHERAPY WITH STUDENTS OF COLOR**    1

**1**    DIVERSITY IN COLLEGE SETTINGS
The Challenge for Helping Professionals    5
Yvonne M. Jenkins

**2**    THE NATIVE AMERICAN INDIAN CLIENT
A Tale of Two Cultures    21
Winona F. Simms

**3**    THERAPEUTIC CONSIDERATIONS FOR AFRICAN AMERICAN STUDENTS AT PREDOMINANTLY WHITE INSTITUTIONS    37
Irving M. Allen

**4**    DUAL TRAUMATIZATION
A Sociocultural Perspective    51
M. Maureen Walker

**5**    ENGAGEMENT OF AN ASIAN AMERICAN WOMAN
Cultural and Psychological Issues    67
Jenai Wu

**6**    CULTURE, SEXUALITY, AND SHAME
A Korean American Woman's Experience    77
Connie S. Chan

**7**    CULTURE SHOCK AND CROSS-CULTURAL THERAPY WITH A JAPANESE STUDENT    87
Suzanne H. Vogel

**8**    DIVERSITY AMONG LATINAS
Implications for College Mental Health    99
Margarita Alvarez

**9**    THE BIRACIAL BIND
An Identity Dilemma    117
Diane Hart-Webb

| | | |
|---|---|---|
| **10** | COLLEGE ENROLLMENT AND ACADEMIC SUCCESS AMONG PUERTO RICAN WOMEN<br>Brunilda De Leon, Michelle C. Stefanisko, and Belinda Lopez Corteza | 129 |
| **11** | GROUP SERVICES FOR STUDENTS OF COLOR<br>Doris J. Wright | 149 |

| **PART II** | **UNDERRECOGNIZED AND EMERGING CHALLENGES** | 169 |
|---|---|---|
| **12** | THE WORLD OF THE SO-CALLED "LEARNING DISABLED" STUDENT<br>Kenneth T. Dinklage | 171 |
| **13** | KEY FACTORS THAT DIFFERENTIATE NONTRADITIONAL FROM TRADITIONAL STUDENTS<br>Diane G. Hansen | 191 |
| **14** | CONTEXTUALIZING CAREER CONCERNS OF ASIAN AMERICAN STUDENTS<br>SungLim A. Shin | 201 |
| **15** | PSYCHOTHERAPY IN THE SHADOW OF DEATH<br>A Graduate Student with AIDS<br>Nadja B. Gould | 211 |
| **16** | SALIENT THEMES AND DIRECTIVES FOR COLLEGE HELPING PROFESSIONALS<br>Yvonne M. Jenkins | 217 |

| | | |
|---|---|---|
| **AFTERWORD** | Thomas A. Parham | 239 |
| **CONTRIBUTORS** | | 247 |
| **INDEX** | | 253 |

# FOREWORD

## Chester M. Pierce

This splendid volume speaks to a wide readership. It presents valuable theoretical and practical information to anyone engaged in or concerned about *diversity* in our society. The book is of value for college counselors and mental health specialists as well as for anyone else who wishes to become informed on the intersection between diversity and counseling/mental health issues.

The chapters that follow reflect a surpassing depth and breadth of knowledge about *who* seeks treatment in college settings, *how* they present, *why* they present, and *what* issues need resolution. Furthermore, the contributors provide examples from a variety of individual and group therapy approaches to address neglected or understudied areas. Those who read this volume may become more aware of requirements for cultural and social competence and sensitivity, as well as flexibility and adaptability in approaching diverse populations, especially when such persons are in marginalized status. To achieve competence in the case management of such clients, counselors and psychotherapists are invited to appreciate when and how to use less traditional or less orthodox methods, as well as how to mobilize all sorts of formal and informal support from the college setting and even appropriate resources in the surrounding community.

The subject matter in this book encompasses a wide range of human diversity. For example, attention is paid to race and color, ethnicity (i.e., nationality, religion), culture, social class, and gender. In addition, the voices of a young single mother, immigrants and international students, including survivors of war and political unrest, students challenged by dyslexia, and a young man who is challenged by HIV infection, then AIDS, are included among the case studies. This display of diversity extends to the contributing authors themselves who come from various clinical, counseling, and administrative disciplines. Thus, an important strength of this book is its inclusion of diverse viewpoints. It becomes apparent through reading the case studies that despite disciplinary background and ideology, indeed there are useful, common approaches to solving some overarching problems associated with diversity. Readers discover important clinical hints, are made privy to valuable administrative applications, and are encouraged to design and to evaluate critically the outcomes of research from a position of cultural and social competence.

In the past 65 years, save time as a naval officer, I, an African-American, have been a full-time student or faculty member at predominantly White education institutions. Most of these years have been spent at Harvard. So I can claim unusual experience in *diversity* in academic settings. Had I read this book, say 50 years ago, my life would have been enhanced. There is no doubt that material in this book would have helped me to be a better student, clinician, faculty member, and member of the general society. I hope all readers will use this book to enrich their lives.

# PREFACE

## Yvonne M. Jenkins

Based upon the belief that everyone benefits when diversity is embraced, this book was written to enhance the quality of life for *all* students in college and university communities. Traditional counseling and mental health perspectives on college life often ignore vital social, cultural, and political realities that influence the daily experiences of marginalized and underserved populations. Therefore, this book reveals the importance of acknowledging these realities to competent intervention. This book also reveals how diversity frames world views and contextualizes some of the issues that students of color and other marginalized groups at predominantly White colleges and universities present in counseling and psychotherapy. Its emphasis on case material is of tremendous value to counselors and mental health professionals. The authors' perspectives serve as useful guides for building rapport, assessment, intervention planning and implementation, and outcome evaluation.

Particular attention is paid to how diversity affects counseling and therapeutic processes from the initial stages of intervention until termination. Of special importance from a relational perspective is how work with these clients has stimulated the growth of practitioners, personally and professionally. Attention is also paid to how culture and other salient sources of social diversity (e.g., race, ethnicity, gender, social class) influence the self-image, identity, and relational development, as well as the ways that students respond to various difficulties encountered in college settings. The benefits of acknowledging, appreciating, and responding to diversity in helping relationships are also highlighted. Moreover, each case study suggests that effective intervention with diverse populations requires more of practitioners than competence in standard intervention skills.

At a personal level, effective intervention requires the practitioner to be aware of his or her internal experience of sameness, diversity, the status of his/her own social esteem (Chin et al., 1993), and accurate, rather than distorted, perceptions of difference. These requirements can only be satisfied through ongoing introspection and dialogue with others who seek to embrace diversity. It is also important for practitioners to learn about the social history, social stratification, and ethnocultural values of his or her reference group, as well as those reference groups of clients they serve.

## THE IMPETUS FOR THIS BOOK

*Diversity in College Settings* was conceived out of my search for such a book several years ago upon beginning my career at a college counseling and testing center. To my disappointment, only a few journal articles on relevant topics were available at that time. At another level, this book was also conceived out of my past experiences as a college student, several years of professional training and experience in the areas of college counseling and college mental health, as well as private practice where I have enjoyed the privilege of treating many college students. Each of these experiences has enabled me to develop an increasing awareness of how powerfully diversity influences identity and relational development.

As an undergraduate at a historically Black university, and thereafter as a graduate student at two predominantly White universities, I found counseling and mental health resources at those institutions unprepared to support African American students effectively. Just as these institutions differed considerably from one another, there were very different explanations for their inadequacies in addressing the counseling and mental health needs of this population. Modest state and federal funding, tuition fees to accommodate a low- to middle-income student population, and private contributions from a primarily middle-income alumni association permitted the Black university to hire only one part-time African American psychiatrist, whose primary responsibility was to do crisis intervention within the confines of a small infirmary.

Although the counseling centers and mental health service for the predominantly White universities had more staff available, none was a person of color. Furthermore, neither of the predominantly White institutions seemed particularly interested nor competent in addressing the concerns of students of color. Yet, at the historically Black university, a common culture and the supportive influence of African American professors and administrators, the alumni association, Black sororities and fraternities, the Black church, and a strong extended family network compensated for limited mental health staffing and nurtured students' academic and psychosocial well-being. Students were affirmed and empowered daily through supportive relationships, affirming curricula, continuous exposure to African American scholars and celebrities who were invited to participate in campus programs, and the availability of various culturally based extracurricular activities.

Unlike many current students from pluralistic populations, I was fortunate enough to have supportive professors at one of the predominantly

White universities I attended. Without culturally competent and politically astute counseling and mental health services, many students struggle in isolation, give in to loneliness and despair, achieve academic goals much later than hoped for, withdraw prematurely or simply drop out with no confidence in their abilities, a poor self-image, and an embittered view of the world. Obviously many of these students "fall through the cracks" without the attention they deserve. Many are students of color and others from marginalized populations. Because these populations continue to be relatively neglected by much of the literature, they have been chosen to be the primary focus of this book. For some, diversity is a highly visible matter; for others it is relatively invisible.

Even though students of color are the primary focus of this book, *Diversity in College Settings* also attends to other marginalized populations. These include dyslexics, students with significant responsibilities outside of the college setting, and a young man who has contracted AIDS and approaches the end of his life. While the inclusion of these cases is not representative of the entire population of students that embody less obvious sources of diversity, their inclusion is intended to acknowledge that such groups do exist and to highlight the commonalities of human experience when any key dimension of diversity is embraced.

As I mentioned, another factor that influenced my decision to edit this book was my graduate training in psychology. That training was traditional and embedded in the dominant culture perspective. However, my experiences as a woman of African ancestry and as an intern at the Center for Multicultural Training in Psychology, Boston, enabled me to know the importance of: (a) understanding the cultural world view of the client as well as social and political contexts for life experiences, (b) critically evaluating traditional theoretical and standard practice paradigms, and (c) developing relevant paradigms that respond effectively to the needs of marginalized and underserved populations.

Over the years, my professional work and continuing education experiences have enabled me to recognize that these challenges are essential to transform counseling and mental health practice from mechanisms of social control to ones that promote advocacy, mutuality, empowerment, and social change. Only then can the healing and recovery of many of those at the margins of this society be realized.

Finally, my decision to edit this book was influenced most by the privilege I have enjoyed of working with college students. This very promising and challenging population has been a source of inspiration and renewal, continuous learning, and much joy.

**THE CASE STUDIES**

The case material that follows is based on many hours of counseling and psychotherapy conducted with college students of color as well as others affected by less visible sources of diversity. To protect the confidentiality of these students, their names and other potential identifying information have been changed. Most chapters include case composites to achieve this purpose. Contributors to this book were asked to describe how diversity influenced the presenting problems and mental status of the clients presented as well as the intervention process. They were also invited to describe how they were affected by their work with the students they chose to write about. Some contributors follow a complete case study format focused on one client while others use excerpts from more than one case to define and explore relevant issues.

Part I, "Counseling and Psychotherapy with Students of Color," focuses on more visible and controversial sources of diversity. Case material is included from each one of the prominent racial and ethnic groups of color in the United States. In addition, attention is paid to how culture, social class, and gender contextualize the experiences of students. Part II, "Underrecognized and Emerging Challenges," includes case studies involving less visible sources of diversity. These include dyslexia, multiple roles in addition to that of student, sexuality and physical health status. One particular cutting edge challenge that is addressed in Part II is that of treating students with HIV infection and AIDS.

Contrary to earlier stereotypes and misconceptions, it is now well documented that persons from all walks of life contract these illnesses. College students are not excluded. As increasing numbers of students with HIV infection and AIDS and their loved ones seek the services of college counseling and mental health facilities, college helping professionals have an ethical responsibility to competently address the needs of this population.

The cases in Parts I and II highlight the reality that many students are challenged by key dimensions of diversity and significant circumstantial factors simultaneously. The latter include being the first from one's family to attend a college or university or to study abroad without mentors or role models to provide essential psychological support, family and work obligations, as well as lengthy commutes which limit access to peers, professors, and other academic personnel, limited economic resources, and the lack of other benefits of privilege. Unfortunately, some students struggle with these issues alone in silence. A potential request for help may be perceived as an indication of weakness or inadequacy since internalized oppression influences the belief that it is always necessary to manage all things perfectly without meaningful help from others. Therefore, in many instances, help is not sought until a relational or academic crisis or troublesome lifestyle has developed; or help is never sought at all.

In view of the presence of an increasingly diverse student population, *Diversity in College Settings* is a timely, practical, and essential contribution to college counseling and mental health. This book advances cross-cultural and developmental frameworks for intervention with students from all walks of life. It also highlights the reality that students' concerns cannot be effectively addressed in isolation from pertinent social, cultural, and historical factors. The contributors' perspectives provide valuable insights for counseling and mental health professionals. Trainees, students, and instructors in the fields of psychology, counseling, social work, and psychiatry may also benefit from these perspectives. In addition, these perspectives may offer college administrators, educators, residence staff, campus police, and other college personnel more insight into how diversity contextualizes the strengths and vulnerabilities of students from marginalized populations, and reveal some of the issues they struggle with prior to entrusting a helping professional.

This book also acknowledges the power of diversified staffing. Furthermore, it supports the value of effective administrative, counseling, and mental health outreach services since many students of color and others from marginalized populations are reluctant to seek help and so suffer in silence. It is my hope that this text will (a) inspire and reassure practitioners who have already accepted the challenge to provide culturally competent care to persevere, and (b) encourage those who have not to recognize that such care is needed, deserved, and required if students are to feel valued, successful, and able to thrive in college communities and ultimately society at large. I also hope that this book will inspire meaningful dialogue between professionals, trainees, and both groups on how various dimensions of diversity affect the lives of students and helping relationships.

## THE CONTRIBUTORS

The contributors are experienced counselors and mental health practitioners who are informed by professional and personal experience. This diverse group is inclusive of women and men from all races and several ethnic and cultural groups. More importantly, contributors share a commitment to culturally and socially competent[1] practice. Because their perspectives are informed, insightful, and instructive, the case studies that follow are quite useful to those who are interested in diverse student populations as well as college counseling and mental health services.

## NOTE

1. The term "socially competent" encompasses cultural competence and measurable proficiency in addressing the impact of social problems that are influenced by responses to diversity. These problems include oppression on the basis of race, ethnicity, socioeconomic status, gender and sexual preference, language, and immigration status. Therefore, this concept is also concerned with measurable proficiency in attending to the obvious and the subtle influences of race, ethnicity, socioeconomic status, gender, sexuality, linguistics, and immigration status that may surface in counseling or psychotherapeutic encounters.

## REFERENCE

Chin, J. L., De La Cancela, V., & Jenkins, Y. M. (1993). *Diversity in psychotherapy: The politics of race, ethnicity, and gender.* Westport, CT: Praeger.

PART I

# COUNSELING AND PSYCHOTHERAPY WITH STUDENTS OF COLOR
The Challenge of Intervention with Diverse Populations

**COMMENTARY**

With the influence of diversity in mind, Part I focuses on clinical and counseling issues in social and cultural contexts. That is, it emphasizes ways in which social identity (e.g., race, ethnicity, gender, social class) and culture influence the practitioner and the client in the helping process. The case studies in this section suggest that competent intervention is influenced by the practitioner's personal status with understanding and embracing his/her own social identity, as well as diversity-affirmative perspectives and capacities, and competencies that foster the psychosocial, academic, and career-related growth of clients. The latter include the capacity to arrive at culturally competent and politically astute formulations, to implement interventions that are syntonic with the client's cultural values, and to consider social realities that affect his or her concerns.

The practitioner's ability to understand and embrace his or her social identity enhances his or her capacity to be free of prejudice, racism, and other barriers to culturally competent intervention. Diversity-inclusive formulations and diversity-syntonic approaches are essential to healthy adjustment, healing and recovery. Both go beyond the capacity of traditional approaches to nontraditional populations via nurturing more open, growth-fostering relationships between clients and practitioners than traditional approaches have allowed.

Chapter 1 introduces basic but essential background and contextual information that frames the case studies that follow. In chapter 2, Simms discusses a Native American Indian undergraduate. The author highlights complexities of biculturality in a world where diversity is not embraced, the importance of Native American Indian practitioners for Native American Indian college students, and the value of culturally inspired intervention.

Simms also discusses the powerful impact that oppression may have on identity formation and relational development, access to resources, one's chances for exposure to trauma and loss prior to the college years, and how one generally moves and copes in the world. Toward actualizing ethical and competent practice, the author emphasizes the importance of ethno-specific formulations and cautions against relying on "packaged judgments," preconceived impressions of clients that are rooted in stereotypes or other distortions.

The focus then shifts to African American students. In chapter 3, Allen highlights essential but commonly neglected considerations concerning race and psychological development that need to guide evaluation and treatment planning. The vignettes this author includes also highlight the importance of understanding Black identity development to evaluate and treat African American students. Allen calls for attention to the reality that some African American students eventually recognize that they are not valued as much as Caucasian students, which can threaten psychosocial development and achievement. He also explains how clinical issues may be understood within powerful ethnocultural and intergenerational familial contexts that can aid with enhancing the student's psychological and academic development.

In chapter 4, Walker's presentation of an African Caribbean woman graduate student is a poignant study in how early deprivation and loss, sexual trauma, immigration, and a strict religious upbringing influenced by culture, ethnicity, and oppression affect this client's identity development and relational style. Walker also uses this case as the basis for an insightful discussion of the interaction between race, gender oppression, and trauma as these affect women of African ancestry. In addition, she highlights the limitations of standard diagnostic classification for capturing the essence of the relationship between social trauma, identity formation, and relational development.

Case studies of Korean American students are offered by Wu and Chan. In chapter 5, Wu provides a useful example of how understanding the relationship between key sources of diversity and psychological experience can enhance the practitioner's understanding of a client. Yet, she argues that neither is a sufficient basis for definitive conclusions. Of particular interest in Wu's case study are her perspectives on the role of women and how this has an impact upon the expression and management of emotion and the ability to adapt to transition. This author focuses on the disturbing stance a young Asian American woman assumes in relationships. However, at a broader level, this case study also suggests that there is an important relationship between culture, women's gender roles, and individual coping styles.

In chapter 6, Chan presents the struggles of a young Korean immigrant to manage the pain of longing for the homeland she left behind while trying to do her best to acculturate to the United States. After already experiencing many losses, her life becomes even more complex as she becomes a victim of significant trauma and betrayal caused by someone she respected. Yet, this trauma was not the reason she sought treatment. The client's difficulties seem to reflect a fascinating blend of ethnocultural and gender role issues.

It is evident that Chan's empathy with this young woman's cultural values and world view, and the relationship that evolved between them, initiated the beginning of the client's recovery process. The artistry of the therapist is apparent in the therapist's ability to use herself both as a bicultural person and as an immigrant in the treatment process. Such artistry is also apparent in the therapist's decision to weigh the impact of both sides of the client's biculturality while evaluating how these influence her thinking and behavior.

In chapter 7, Vogel describes the powerful impact of culture shock on a young Japanese student's academic performance, along with other relevant adjustment and background issues. With an ethno-specific perspective, she prioritizes the importance of understanding Japanese culture over mastery of the Japanese language, accessibility to supportive culturally competent resources, and ethno-specific understanding over universalism in working effectively with this population. Her view of the complexities that Asian students encounter in managing parental expectations is shared by Shin in Part II.

In chapter 8, Alvarez focuses on the impact of shifting identifications on Latinas who study in the U.S. Via several interesting case vignettes, she discusses complex conditions typically endured by this population while transitioning to life in the United States. This often involves unresolved separation issues, loss, and trauma. The author emphasizes that separation from family, culture, and a familiar way of life during a period of study in the U.S. involves far more than meets the eye. Therefore, she challenges practitioners to be attuned to the strengths as well as vulnerabilities associated with identity shifts within this diverse population. Useful guidelines are offered for assessing the status of identity shifts for Latinas.

In chapter 9, Hart-Webb describes the identity, relational, and behavioral struggles of a young man of African American and Irish descents. This case study highlights the anger and resentment that is sometimes inevitable when inadequate attention is paid to being of mixed race heritage earlier in life. It also illustrates the alienation, marginalization, internalization of oppression, and a variety of other difficulties some mixed race students experience because of their heritage. Furthermore, Hart-Webb describes how internal conflict associated with this issue turned against the self may be experienced. Moreover, this case study illustrates how mixed race identity conflict may be used as a catalyst for growth and change.

In chapter 10, De Leon, Stefanisko, and Corteza present the findings of a study that examined factors that influence the educational and psychosocial development of Puerto Rican women college students. This is a particularly valuable chapter in view of low admissions and retention rates for this population and limited data on its strengths and determinants. The authors identify several factors linked to academic success in this diverse population. They echo Alvarez's perspective that the Latina's decision to attend college is not without important social and emotional costs. Even so, their findings support the reality that many young Puerto Rican women are still determined to succeed.

The final chapter of Part I highlights the usefulness of counseling and psychotherapy groups for diverse college populations. Wright discusses how practitioners can make use of and enhance the cultural relevance and specificity of these interventions and the ways in which culture and race affect group process. The author also suggests strategies for facilitating more participation and psychosocial growth among diverse college populations.

CHAPTER 1

# DIVERSITY IN COLLEGE SETTINGS
## The Challenge for Helping Professionals

Yvonne M. Jenkins

**INTRODUCTION**

In the United States, much of what determines how one is perceived and the overall quality of one's life are associated with race and color, gender, and social class. Until recently, perceptions of these realities have been primarily shaped by a dominant culture perspective and assumed to be true and relevant for everyone, even though the world views of people of color, the poor, immigrants, and other marginalized populations have not been included. Therefore, in many instances, myths, distortions, and other misperceptions have been accepted as unquestionable truths. Since mental health care systems have been primarily shaped by the same perspective, it is not surprising, then, that people of color, immigrants, the poor, and other marginalized groups are prevalent among those who are underserved by the helping professions. This reality has important implications for the fields of counseling and mental health in college settings.

Colleges and universities are becoming increasingly diverse as people from many different backgrounds and experiences come together to prepare to meet the challenges of a changing world. Of course, deliberate and conscientious efforts are made by some institutions of higher learning to diversify student populations, to develop curricula and teaching practices that prepare students to work in a diverse world, and to offer culturally and socially competent counseling and mental health services. Nevertheless, while the high visibility of diversity at some institutions may suggest that all is well in these areas, many still fall short in creating learning and psychosocial environments that genuinely embrace diversity beyond a surface level. Of course, it is easier to change the composition of the student body than to make changes at deeper systemic and practice levels that regulate power. Environments that embrace diversity would permit access to culturally and socially competent college counseling and mental health services by students from disenfranchised U.S. populations as well as international students.

Even though significant milestones toward fairness, equity, and the empowerment of these populations have been achieved through legislation, progressive and innovative education (e.g., diversity workshops, socially competent curricula), and goodwill, there is still considerable anxiety about race and skin color, culture, and other important aspects of human diversity. Furthermore, even though college counseling and mental health practitioners are more aware than ever before of the limitations of standard practice, oppressive mindsets and practices still too often influence professional formulations, interventions, and outcome appraisals. Therefore, much remains to be done toward understanding and responding effectively to cultural and social factors that contextualize the concerns of *all* students.

Johnson and Mapp's (1997) astute analysis of diversity issues at a prestigious graduate school of education supports the latter point. They contend that as diversity expands, shortcomings in the status quo will inevitably be revealed. Well-intended efforts to change may not initially be successful or even found adequate by marginalized populations, which can be unsettling and painful. Thus we are left with the probability that there is still much to learn and do.

College and university communities are microcosms of the larger society. Even though counseling and mental health services for students tend to be more accessible and comprehensive than those typically available to less educated underserved populations, students of color at predominantly White universities are still too often shortchanged in receiving culturally and socially competent care. In addition, international students and others marginalized by less visible differences are often neglected by college counseling and mental health resources.

Because mental status and current functioning, inclusive of academic performance, are influenced by diversity and how it is responded to, *a fundamental challenge for helping professionals is to provide culturally and socially competent intervention, supervision, and training.* This chapter defines and highlights some important considerations toward meeting this challenge.

## PERCEPTIONS OF DIFFERENCE

In her seminal work, *Understanding Race, Ethnicity, and Power*, Pinderhughes (1989) discusses how difference is primarily associated with negative feelings and images. Unfortunately, such constructs are learned as early as the toddler years and impede positive self-concept formation, while perpetuating ongoing distortions concerning those who are different. In addition, negative perceptions of difference interfere with positive identity development, healthy personality integration, and stable psychosocial functioning. At a broader level, the preponderance of negativity associated with sociopolitical and cultural differences have been integral to socialization and acculturation processes in the U.S. despite increasing awareness of the superficiality of the melting pot ethic. Negative perceptions of difference are associated with culture and color. Denial of such perceptions ranges from minimization to color blindness and a complete failure to recognize significant sources of diversity. Such denial aims to minimize anxiety about difference and is often viewed as evidence of unconditional acceptance.

Dimensions of difference have been rationalized as "something wrong," "something missing," or "less than" and "not as good as" on a comparative level. The standard yardstick that serves as the basis for such rationalizations is the dominant U.S. culture value orientation. By this yardstick, those in the numerical or psychological minority have either been viewed as not having anything of significance in common with the dominant culture or anything of value. As such, the consequences attendant to perceptions of difference have often included devaluation, demoralization, and perceived threats to acceptance, connection, and power. Then there have been instances when difference has been perceived as "unique," "special," or "an exception" to dominant culture perceptions of particular reference groups. The underlying assumption here has been that those who are different are inherently inferior to the dominant culture.

What, then, accounts for such negative feelings and images? Pinderhughes highlights the following hypotheses by Gehrie and Mahler as possible explanations. Gehrie suggests that difference represents a significant absence of connection to others which threatens the psychological wholeness or sense of intactness needed to relate to another. The child's natural sense of grandiosity and perfection is threatened by the feeling of exclusion this imposes.

Difference evokes a sense of aloneness and abandonment which means an absence of connection or relationship to another. This sense of disconnection and aloneness threatens the sense of psychological wholeness and intactness the child needs. This is because an experience of difference from others can trigger feelings of exclusion internalized as a result of early narcissistic injury. Such an injury occurs when a young child is not positively mirrored by loved ones with whom he or she seeks to identify. Thus, "[a] sense of injury that magnifies anxiety about differentness develops as a consequence of being unable to acquire that needed sense of belonging, inclusion, and value" (Gehrie, 1976, p. 31).

Mahler (1975) suggests that anxiety about difference results from:

> the young child's struggle to develop separateness and to master the task of separation-individuation. The struggle begins with painful awareness that the child is different and therefore separate from the mother. Successful mastery of this stage requires [the ability] to form a mental image of a separate self. The struggle to separate is marked by anxiety, rage, . . . helplessness, and intense ambivalence which diminish when mastery is achieved and there is comfort with the self as separate and . . . different. (p. 30)

Finally, Pinderhughes observes the tendency for the meaning of *different from* to imply comparison. She notes that power is implicit in the notion of difference as commonly used since we seem unable to view two objects as merely different from (i.e., not the same as) the other. Rather we seem compelled to place a value on that difference, meaning that one is viewed as "better than" or "less than" the other. All three explanations suggest that difference is commonly perceived as negative and threatening, and that one of the compared objects is perceived as inadequate or of less value. An unfortunate outcome is estrangement from one's own reference group(s) toward positive perceptions of difference.

Surrey's (1995) hypotheses concerning *relationship-differentiation* and the *self-in-diversity* appear central to transforming negative perceptions of difference. Associated with Kaplan's (1991) concept of *informed empathy*, these hypotheses emphasize:

1. the importance of the capacity to see oneself and others as individuals within a larger cultural and social frame of reference;
2. the capacity to *de-center* or to accept and be open to seeing the [cultural] embeddedness of one's own perceptions, assumptions, judgments, and to move away from seeing others through one's own culturally bound lenses;
3. that the capacity to see and to know oneself is inextricably relational; and
4. that self-acceptance is basic to a healthy psychological experience of difference and the processes of learning to live and grow with others in relationship.

These conditions transcend unclear or negative perceptions of one's own social identity and differences in others.[1] Furthermore, these conditions facilitate and support connection through mutually empowering interactions between individuals from the same *or* different reference groups (Jordan, 1991), particularly at more vulnerable moments like the initial stages of a crossracial relationship or at times of conflict and potential disconnection. Moreover, these conditions decrease anxiety related to *being with* difference.

The *self-in-diversity* hypothesis is syntonic with this author's stance: *Authenticity in the process of embracing diversity in others begins with intense self-reflection and self-activity intended to advance one's own social identity development through self-awareness, definition of a clear and positive social identity including social esteem.* Guidelines for implementing this process have been offered by Pinderhughes (1989). As I and others have stated elsewhere, ongoing attention to these areas facilitates readiness for authentic celebration of diversity, valorization of different lifestyles, and the building of relationships with those who are different that are free of exploitation, objectification, and other conditions which devalue diversity (De La Cancela, Jenkins, & Chin, 1993).

## EMBRACING DIVERSITY

The process of embracing diversity involves *a way of thinking and a way of relating or being.* The cognitive dimension of this process involves thoughtful movement toward increased social self-understanding and acceptance, empathy with those who are different, and gradual disintegration of personal barriers (e.g., prejudice, stereotypes) that block openness to human differences. This dimension also involves becoming aware of and knowledgeable about both local and world communities, and the unfolding of a flexible and socially contextualized perspective of human relational development.

The practice/behavioral dimension of this process is active. At an initial level it involves defining, clarifying, and appreciating one's own social identity (Jenkins, 1993), and an openness to opportunities for mutually valued interaction with those who are different from oneself. As such, both subject and object are enlarged by this process just as both are deprived of opportunities for growth and suffer indignity when diversity is devalued.

Another important aspect of the practice/behavioral dimension involves learning to cope with difference without diminishing it by universalizing or equalizing it with other kinds of difference. For example, the impact of homophobia is sometimes assumed to be the same as the impact of racial prejudice. Equalizing these experiences is a defense against anxiety about differences between the two experiences that may provide a sense of relief from fear of *an unknown*. Or this strategy may be indicative of the denial of trauma suffered in relation to culturalism, racism, and other dimensions of human diversity.

Experience based on race, ethnicity, culture, gender, and social class, and any interactions between these may vary from one individual or reference group to another.

## CHANGING TRENDS IN THE PSYCHOSOCIAL HEALTH OF COLLEGE POPULATIONS

College students constitute an exciting and promising population. Qualities like vitality, resilience, resistance, creativity, and motivation to succeed have enabled this population to benefit enormously from counseling and psychotherapy. Yet, in recent years the problems presented by college students appear to be more complex and severe than before. This is reflected by:

1. an increase in episodes of violence (e.g., rape, assault and battery, murder) involving students on campuses and in surrounding communities;
2. higher incidences of suicidal gestures, suicide completions, and serious psychological disorders;
3. a rise in the incidence of substance abuse; and
4. an increase in psychiatric hospitalizations, and academic leaves of absence and withdrawals for psychiatric reasons.

Knowledge of these disturbing changes in the complexity and severity of presenting problems appear to be influenced by:

1. effective outreach and advocacy services;
2. increasingly positive perceptions of help seeking;

The occurrence of such changes appear to be influenced by:

1. increasingly complex societal problems and health issues;
2. technological advances that facilitate rapid and efficient communication but, at times, compromise optimal relational development (e.g., ability to communicate effectively, vulnerable capacities for trust, intimacy, empathy, and frustration tolerance);
3. the changing structure of the family;

4. a growing population of students who express significant adjustment concerns associated with being (a) a student of color in a predominantly White academic setting; (b) the first in one's family to attend college; (c) from a background of limited financial resources in the midst of an affluent or privileged student population; (d) a transfer student from another institution; (e) one who returns, after a period of absence from an institution for personal or medical reasons, to complete an academic program; and
5. an increasing number of students whose social, cross-cultural. or developmental issues are exacerbated by previous exposure to immigration, war, sexual abuse, or other significant trauma.

## Anxiety About Help Seeking

In the initial stages of help seeking, some students of color feel particularly anxious about the possibility that practitioners might not understand, be interested in, or competent to address their concerns effectively. Anxiety about help seeking is commonly experienced in relation to stress and trauma associated with exposure to racism, sexism and other persistent societal problems, immigration, and culture shock. Such anxiety seems to be especially intense when relatively few or no practitioners from marginalized or underserved populations appear to be available. Even though the expectation of little understanding and empathy is more often assumed of Caucasian helping professionals, there are certainly instances when there are similar expectations of helping professionals of color.

Anxiety about help seeking also seems to influence some students to not seek help until a crisis develops, or increasing psychological/social discomfort progresses to the extent that these interfere with academic performance. Still there are others who never seek help at all because it appears unlikely that their concerns will be attended to with sensitivity and competence. Even though anxiety about help seeking is not limited to students of color, underlying contexts (e.g., shame, self-perceptions of inadequacy) for this dynamic within this population seems to differ in intensity from those contexts which underlie similar patterns for Caucasian, middle- to upper-class students.

In addition to the visibility of relatively few practitioners of color, differential ethnocultural perceptions of help seeking, and the rather troubling deficit-driven/pathology-based stance that has been assumed historically by helping professionals toward people of color in the U.S. also influence anxiety about help seeking. Of those who decide to seek help, cultural paranoia, an adaptive form of suspicion, is relied upon by some to detect any anxiety about difference on the part of the practitioner. It is also sensitive to cultural blindness and other defensive postures that are subject to compromise an empathic connection to their experiences.

Finally, some college training sites fall short on preparing trainees to meet the needs of diverse populations effectively because some supervising practitioners lack sufficient knowledge and understanding of the cultural and social backgrounds of clients served. Whether or not cultural and social competence is valued is largely determined by the social ambiance of the institution.

## SOCIAL AMBIANCE

Every college and university has a distinct social ambiance which involves how diversity is responded to at every level of campus life. This dynamic involves everything from the most subtle nuances of daily life to the most visible expressions of acceptance and rejection.

The social ambiance for predominantly White colleges and universities is influenced by the nature of an institution's relationship with people of color and marginalized populations since its inception. Answers to questions like the following are useful for clarifying the nature of that relationship: When was the institution founded? When were students of color and those from lower socioeconomic backgrounds first admitted? How enthusiastic has the institution been about recruiting qualified students and staff of color? During the past decade, how many students from specific racial and ethnocultural groups have applied and been accepted for admission? Of those, what percentage has graduated at the expected time? What percentage dropped out or transferred to other institutions? Why? Is there any past or current documentation of the experiences of former students that pertains to race relations? If so, what information is included? Have organized student protests related to institutional rejection of diversity ever taken place on campus? If so, when? What motivated these protests? How did the institution respond? What public image(s) does the institution have in relation to specific reference groups of color? Do students of color feel valued or devalued by the institution? Are students of color generally viewed as "*affirmative action quota-fillers*" or as competent and deserving? What campus organizations are available to students of color on the basis of racial or ethnocultural identity? Is this population adequately represented among elected or appointed officers of other student organizations? How involved are former students of color with alumni activities, particularly annual giving campaigns? What percentage of the faculty and administrators are people of color? What percentage of college counselors and mental health practitioners are people of color? How do these percentages compare with the percentages of students of color enrolled? Do students of color feel their needs are met adequately by campus counseling and mental health services?

The social ambiance of a college or university is vital to the sense of agency or empowerment felt by students. All people have social and ethnocultural origins that influence their ways of perceiving, responding to, and living in the world. Therefore, when the social ambiance of an institution is one which embraces and celebrates diversity, the university community as well as society at large have much to gain.

## WHEN DIVERSITY IS VALUED IN THE ACADEMY

When diversity is valued, *all* students feel valued and connected to the college or university community. They feel understood, accepted, cared about, supported and powerful. Confidence that their strengths are appreciated offers assurance that their presence matters. Students who feel valued also share a sense of camaraderie with their peers. School pride, reflected by a personal sense of belonging, ownership, and interest in school-related endeavors, is readily apparent. Discriminatory standards of behavior and academic performance do not exist. Therefore, students of color may comfortably sit together or alone in dining halls or other places on campus without automatically being perceived as threatening, suspicious, or alienating. Neither does their presence automatically make them targets of suspicion by security, residence staff, or others in authority. Instead, their need to spend time with others with whom they share much in common is recognized as part of the natural order of things just as other students fulfill similar needs for belonging, familiarity, and connection.

For those who feel uneasy when students of color express these needs by sitting together, considerable self-understanding and personal growth can be gained from clarifying and realistically examining the perceptions that underlie such anxiety. Furthermore, when diversity is valued, *all* students can trust that their best interests are taken to heart by those in authority. Administrators, professors, and student personnel and support services are open to progressive change and can, indeed, acknowledge that difference does matter. Furthermore, the strengths of different lifestyles as well as commonalities of human experiences are appreciated. A sense of mutual value exists among students, professors, and other authority figures despite obvious power differentials.

Students of color are not humiliated, ignored, or objectified through exoticism, fantasy, or tokenism. Course content reflects openness, a socially contextualized view of the world, and acknowledges the relationship between the current plights and histories of disenfranchised groups in the United States. Affirmative language is used to refer to marginalized groups rather than that which offends and perpetuates oppression. When diversity is valued, students are held reasonably accountable only for themselves rather than pressured to represent an entire racial, gender, or cultural group. Neither are they expected to educate their counselors, therapists, and professors on matters concerning diversity, or to provide comfort by relieving the tension and guilt of those from the dominant culture. Moreover, institutions that genuinely value diversity recognize the limitations of standardized admissions tests for accurate measurement of the skills and abilities of those whose backgrounds and social realities differ from traditional norm groups. Instead, there is an openness to including diversity-inclusive measures.

Finally, when diversity is valued, it is visible in staffing and the student body. Optimal efforts are expended to implement a successful model of "recruiting and training [qualified] people of color as students and faculty" and "to involve colleagues of color in shaping plans, goals, and agendas" for academic departments and services (Bowser, Auletta, & Jones, 1993). All of this mobilizes hope and facilitates the realization of dreams.

What enables diversity to be valued? Diversity is valued through:

1. resolution of one's personal barriers to embracing diversity, which can be achieved through self-definition and an appropriate level of self-activity, involving clarifying one's ethnicity, level of social esteem, and coming to terms with troublesome internalizations (e.g., prejudice, stereotypes, discrimination) concerning difference that impose barriers to embracing certain aspects of one's background (e.g., privilege, race, ethnicity);
2. cross-cultural and multicultural education;
3. knowledge of how history and sociopolitical processes presently affect different groups from within the United States as well as others from the global world community. Such knowledge facilitates empathy with different world views and social realities (e.g., oppression through domination, marginalization, colonialization, exclusion), and mutuality. Such awareness is also relevant to understanding differential accessibility of various resources to different groups, as well as how a particular reference group is perceived and responded to in the larger society; and
4. ongoing exposure to individuals from different reference groups through in-depth and meaningful personal relationships. Active, authentic, and ongoing engagement in such relationships over time influences accurate perceptions and a level of trust that

withstands any conflict resolution that might become necessary. With accurate knowledge of different world views, lifestyles, and cultural practices, devaluing misperceptions and actions are less likely to persist.

Although *valuing difference* seems to be a popular and at times even trendy concept within politically correct circles at institutions of higher learning, many students from marginalized groups are painfully aware of the difference in its use as rhetoric, and the reality of their daily experiences.

## WHEN DIVERSITY IS NOT VALUED

When diversity is not valued, students who do not primarily identify with the dominant culture feel unworthy, marginalized, and estranged from the larger college community. Feelings of alienation, isolation, and rejection are also common. Students often feel as though they are trespassing and do not "feel at home." Many of those who begin their studies with reasonably intact self-esteem feel robbed of this trait closer to the completion of their studies. Students of color who do not fit the stereotypes created by the dominant culture are often viewed as anomalies or exceptions to the rule, since negative images of their reference groups still tend to be prevalent.

The strong group/communal orientation of students of color is sometimes reflected by unrealistically high performance standards and exemplary conduct. One may feel undue pressure to represent an entire reference group, to fulfill the hopes and dreams of loved ones, or may perceive that it is necessary to protect faculty of color from shame or disappointment. Many of those driven by such pressure have a need to disprove stereotypes (positive *and* negative) about the abilities, moral character, and interests of their own reference groups.

Negative internalizations of one's own reference group may be turned against the self and projected onto others, thereby perpetuating the cycle of oppression through self-hate and estrangement from one's own and other reference groups. For some students, efforts to disprove stereotypes are at the cost of forgoing help seeking or of acknowledging vulnerability in any other way. Resulting silence can be destructive and may entrap the student in a spiral of loneliness, despair, and perpetual disconnection from the affirmation and validation that is so desperately needed.

The pressure of intense scrutiny, dual and discriminatory standards of accountability, and routine suspicion inevitably generate tension and insecurity. Therefore, instead of being the best years of a lifetime, the college years are sometimes the worst for students of color. This is evident in the following example. In retrospect, one African American woman, who had just finished her senior thesis, both questioned her choice to attend a predominantly White university and expressed regret that she had not attended a predominantly Black university near her home. Even though she had a record of outstanding achievement, this young woman unexpectedly recognized that at a psychosocial level, her education had considerable costs for her and many of her African American peers at the same institution.

In contrast to her own experience, her friends at the predominantly Black university seemed to feel much happier about their experiences. She found it unfortunate that she and her peers at the predominantly White institution could only feel happy that they would soon be leaving it rather than sad to leave a more pleasant experience behind. Also, she recalled that upon beginning therapy she was in "a state of emergency" that was perceived to be a cumulative outcome of the institution's inadequate attention to her experience as a woman of color since her first year of studies.

Some students of color have the appearance of a less vulnerable demeanor which may be interpreted as indifference, hostility, or aggression. What usually lies at the core, however, are unfulfilled needs for acceptance, affirmation, and connection. Inadequate attention to these needs compromises both psychosocial and career development.

## Professionals' Anxiety about Social and Cultural Diversity

Anxiety about social and cultural diversity interferes with the ability of some professionals to intervene effectively with students from marginalized and disenfranchised groups. This anxiety is often an outcome of negative societally embedded attitudes concerning differences that have influenced personal upbringing, an absence of personal relationships with individuals from marginalized and disenfranchised groups, and inadequate educational experiences, in view of the reality that some academic and training programs and continuing education programs have only recently begun to offer culturally competent curricula. Such anxiety often influences the preference to not treat students from these populations, the tendency to automatically pass them along to professionals of color, or intervention and case supervision that fails to consider the significance of social and cultural realities to psychosocial status and current functioning. Obviously, the latter is unethical and may have particularly destructive consequences.

## THE STRUGGLE TO NAME/DESCRIBE DIVERSE POPULATIONS

Just as society struggles to embrace diversity, the fields of counseling and mental health engage in a similar struggle. Nowhere is this struggle more evident than through efforts to use appropriate language to name/describe diverse populations. During the past three decades, descriptions of these populations have gradually progressed from highly negative concepts to more affirmative and socially contextualized ones (De La Cancela, Jenkins, & Chin, 1993).

This struggle is also evident in this text. Inasmuch as several terms might appear to be used relatively interchangeably to refer to diverse populations, this is not intended to universalize their experiences. Instead, this represents the continuing struggle to capture more accurately the myriad of social and cultural realities and experiences of individuals from these groups. It is in this spirit that the following terms are used: *students of color; diverse/diversified, different, disenfranchised, underserved, marginalized, indigenous, visible, invisible, oppressed, numerical and psychological minority, culturally different, nontraditional,* and *pluralistic populations.* Even though none of these terms seem to be completely adequate, each comes closer to capturing the true essence of the populations described than ones that have negated their experiences; *minority, culturally deprived, and culturally disadvantaged.* The struggle to find adequate language to describe these groups affirms the complexity of capturing the essence of diversity.

## WHO ARE STUDENTS OF COLOR?

In "Confronting Diversity on Campus," Bowser, Auletta, and Jones (1993) remind us that the United States and its colleges and universities are still stratified by color. Thus, *students of color* is used here to refer to students from the U.S. and other countries of African, Asian, Latin American, Native American Indian or mixed race ancestries. Obviously, this is an extremely heterogeneous group that encompasses all races, many ethnicities, cultures, lifestyles, and first languages other than English. There is also considerable diversity of physical characteristics both among and within these groups. Inasmuch as race and skin color are prominent determinants of social identity and social status in the United States, *students of color* is a highly political term in that it includes those for whom oppression is most intractable.

Given current college enrollment trends, it is expected that by the year 2000 more students of color than ever before will be attending colleges and universities in the United States. This has far-reaching implications for college counseling and mental health services as far as staffing, theoretical frameworks that influence practice, competence to intervene with diverse populations, outreach, advocacy and programming, methods of recruiting and supervising trainees, as well as the content of training.

## THE CENTRALITY OF THE HELPING RELATIONSHIP TO INTERVENTION WITH PLURALISTIC POPULATIONS

The helping relationship is central to all forms of intervention with pluralistic populations because affiliation and collateral relationships are valued highly by many of these groups. Personal warmth, approachability, and genuineness are central to establishing the types of growth-fostering relationships that facilitate prevention, healing, and recovery. In counseling and therapeutic contexts, these conditions are shaped by the practitioner's capacity to embrace diversity. Low expectations of achievement for students from some reference groups serve as a barrier to approaching counselors, therapists, and other authority figures for help with personal and academic difficulties at the time these surface. Those who do seek help are likely to terminate treatment prematurely if a positive connection to the practitioner is not developed early on in the intervention process.

Relational theorists suggest that growth-fostering relationships serve as catalysts for the release of personal power by enlarging the capacities of those involved *to see the self and the other* more clearly (Miller, 1986; Surrey, 1983, 1991). This enables the client and the practitioner to act more progressively as a result of the connection created. Such relationships are facilitated by engagement, mutuality, empathy, authenticity, and social esteem. However, in order for diversity to be embraced, these concepts must be expanded beyond their initial definitions to include those processes which value diversity that were mentioned earlier in this chapter.

According to relational theorists, engagement is the ability to pay attention to and to express interest in another (Surrey, 1991). Relative to pluralistic populations, this process requires openness, flexibility, and spontaneity. Mutuality involves

> both affecting the other and being affected by the other; one extends oneself . . . to the other and is also receptive to the impact of the other. There is openness to influence, emotional availability, and a constantly changing pattern of responding to and affecting the other's state. There is both receptivity and active initiative toward the other. (Jordan, 1991)

Mutuality is central to actualizing positive professional relationships with these populations, given the lack of reciprocity that many of these groups have been denied. Mutuality is open, unconditional, and reciprocal. Furthermore, mutuality facilitates active collaboration within culturally syntonic boundaries. Empathy involves feeling with the client and is dependent on openness and commonalities of human experience. Yet, Tyler, Brome, and Williams caution that "commonality of experience cannot always be achieved" (1991, p. 13). However, when achieved, the practice of mutuality does much to facilitate an empathic connection. Authenticity is the ongoing challenge to feel *real*, connected, vital, clear, and purposeful in relationship. To achieve this, risk taking and the willingness to challenge old images and practices are necessary. How engagement, mutuality, empathy, and authenticity are expressed may vary from one ethnocultural group to another. This is dictated by cultural world views, values, social stratification, and the social history of a particular group.

Miller (1986) contends that "no culture provides an optimal relational context for living and developing because once any group of people has been socially defined as dominant, and another as subordinate, there cannot be a full relational context" (p. 10). Therefore, the practice of valuing diversity challenges college helping professionals and the basic core of standard practice in the U.S. which has been shaped by the world view, values, and privilege of the dominant culture.

## CONCLUSION

Human diversity is as rich and fascinating as it is complex. As the range of diversity at colleges and universities expands, helping professionals are challenged to develop more flexibility and socially contextualized approaches to practice. A basic prerequisite is the practitioner's own social self-understanding and development, and an openness to acknowledge and to confront any personal barriers to embracing diversity that might exist. It is also important to understand how different social realities (e.g., race, ethnicity, socioeconomic status, gender) influence how students perceive and respond to the world. Therefore, knowledge of the self, the world, and competent professional skills that are applied within an affirmative, diversity-syntonic framework are basic to the delivery of culturally and socially competent services.

## NOTE

1. Social identity is that component of personal identity determined by social factors. The historical experiences of a particular group, how it is perceived and responded to on the basis of race, ethnicity, culture, gender, socioeconomic status, and linguistics figure prominently in shaping, integrating, and consolidating social identity.

## REFERENCES

Bowser, B. P., Auletta, G., & Jones, T. (1993). *Confronting diversity on campus.* Newbury Park, CA: Sage.

De La Cancela, V., Jenkins, Y. M., & Chin, J. L. (1993). Diversity in psychotherapy: Examination of racial, ethnic, gender, and political issues. In J. L. Chin, V. De La Cancela, & Y. M. Jenkins, *Diversity in psychotherapy: The politics of race, ethnicity, and gender* (pp. 5–16). Westport, CT: Praeger.

Gehrie, M. (1976). Aspects of the dynamics of prejudice. *Annual of Psychoanalysis, 4,* 423–446.

Jenkins, Y. M. (1993). Diversity and social esteem. In J. L. Chin, V. De La Cancela, & Y. M. Jenkins, *Diversity in psychotherapy: The politics of race, ethnicity, and gender* (pp. 45–64). Westport, CT: Praeger.

Johnson, S. M., & Mapp, K. L. (1997). A working paper on diversity at the Harvard Graduate School of Education. Unpublished manuscript.

Jordan, J. (1991). The meaning of mutuality. In J. Jordan, A. G. Kaplan, J. B. Miller, I. P. Stiver, & J. L. Surrey, *Women's growth in connection: Writings from the Stone Center* (pp. 82–96). New York: Guilford.

Kaplan, A. G. (1991). The "self-in-relation": Implications for depression in women. In J. Jordan, A. G. Kaplan, J. B. Miller, I. P. Stiver, & J. L. Surrey, *Women's growth in connection: Writings from the Stone Center* (pp. 206–222). New York: Guilford.

Mahler, M. (1975). *The psychological birth of the human infant.* New York: Basic Books.

Miller, J. B. (1986). What do we mean by relationships? *Work in progress, 22* (p. 10). Wellesley, MA: Wellesley College Stone Center Working Papers Series.

Pinderhughes, E. B. (1989). *Understanding race, ethnicity, and gender.* New York: The Free Press.

Surrey, J. L. (1983). Relationship and empowerment. In J. Jordan, A. G. Kaplan, J. B. Miller, I. P. Stiver, & J. L. Surrey, *Women's growth in connection: Writings from the Stone Center* (pp.162–180). New York: Guilford.

Surrey, J. L. (1991). The "self-in-relation": A theory of women's development. In J. Jordan, A. G. Kaplan, J. B. Miller, I. P. Stiver, & J. L. Surrey, *Women's growth in connection: Writings from the Stone Center* (pp. 51–66). New York: Guilford.

Surrey J. L. (1995). Diversity at the core: Implications for relational theory. In C. Garcia-Coll, R. Cook-Nobles, & J. L. Surrey, Building connection through diversity. *Work in progress, 64.* Wellesley, MA: Wellesley College Stone Center Working Papers Series.

Tyler, F. B., Brome, D. R., & Williams, J. E. (1991). *Ethnic validity, ecology, and psychotherapy.* New York: Plenum.

CHAPTER 2

# THE NATIVE AMERICAN INDIAN CLIENT
## A Tale of Two Cultures

Winona F. Simms

### INTRODUCTION

Although the Native American Indian population comprises a relatively small percentage of the U.S. population, it constitutes almost half of the cultural, racial, and ethnic diversity within the total population (Hodgkinson, Outtz, & Obarakpor, 1990). Unfortunately, the latter point is not yet realized in many college and university communities, since Native American Indian students comprise less than 1% of the total population of college students in the U.S. (Carter & Wilson, 1997). One-third to one-quarter of these students attend tribal community colleges (Gritts, 1997). Even though this percentage is higher than in the past, unfortunately, much of the intellectual talent within this population continues to be neglected. This neglect also includes the absence of culturally competent counseling and mental health care to Native American college students.

Although Native American Indians are an extremely heterogeneous population, the following case study highlights some of the social (e.g., culture, ethnic, socioeconomic, gender) and familial issues that have influenced a young woman's difficulties. It is hoped that this chapter will draw more attention to the counseling and mental health needs of the Native American Indian college student population. It is also my hope that this chapter will inspire counselors and psychotherapists to promote higher retention rates for this population by developing socially competent outreach, intervention, and outcome assessment strategies. Finally, it is my hope that this chapter will inspire more Native American Indians to pursue careers in college counseling or college mental health.

## ALITA
### Source of Referral

Alita was a 27-year-old Native American Indian woman undergraduate student of mixed tribe ancestries who was self-referred to her university counseling center. Her decision to seek help was influenced by her participation in a native women's talking circle support group. Members of the group encouraged her to seek help at the center when it was learned that there was a Native American Indian counselor on site. Another important consideration for Alita was the availability of services to students at little or no cost.

Although Alita had never participated in any form of counseling, she wanted to find help. She was grateful to the women in the group for not making judgments about her problems. She trusted them and found them helpful for influencing her to look differently at various issues in her life. After all, they too had achieved "hard" things. Some were in professional career tracks such as nursing, medicine, and law. Most of the women seemed to feel confident that they were going to finish their degrees. So Alita admired and wanted to be like them.

On the day of Alita's first counseling appointment she was nervous. She considered not keeping the appointment but knew she would do so because her grandmother had instructed her to always try to keep her word. Furthermore, her fear of not succeeding in graduate school, as well as loneliness, frustration, and the desire for confidence in herself as a Native American Indian woman surpassed her fears of trying this new way of "healing."

### Presenting Problems

Alita attended a two-year tribal community college before transferring to the university. She had not anticipated how this transfer would affect her. She complained of fatigue, a low energy level, poor concentration, frequent tardiness for assignments and appointments; she had even missed a few. She also felt "stressed" because she could not "seem to get things done as quickly as other students." Her enthusiasm about being a college student had diminished significantly recently, even though she had worked hard to meet college application deadlines, to move to the town where the university was located, and to find housing. Although Alita felt determined to do her best, she could not "seem to find the time to do everything." When various instructors suggested that she schedule an appointment with them to discuss her work, she hesitated.

### Relevant Background Information

Students were expected to interact with their advisors and professors, which Alita dreaded. She was afraid they might find out that she really didn't belong at the university. After all, Alita did not even know what "liberal arts education" meant. In addition, she reported several complaints. Alita's primary source of income was her Indian Health Service Scholarship. She was afraid of losing this and other scholarship awards if she failed or withdrew from her courses. Such a loss would impose a severe financial hardship that would end her dream to become "useful" to her community and surviving family members.

Because Alita had doubts about being "capable" of college work, she sometimes felt disillusioned with academia and her career goals. When self-doubt surfaced, she resorted to work as an alternative. Alita had "always worked" because a lifetime of financial stress had caused her to worry about being without a job. Therefore, to alleviate some of her emotional and financial distress, she had decided to take time out from her studies to work for a while to pay some of her debts. Yet, Alita recognized that her chances of finding a "good" job were nearly impossible without a college degree.

To make matters worse, Alita and her boyfriend of six years had recently ended their relationship. Although she initiated the breakup, she was unhappy about it and felt very lonely. Alita worried that she might have been "drinking too much" to ease her pain. This was particularly disturbing to her since her mother had died of complications caused by alcoholism three years earlier.

Alita's distress frequently led to sleepless nights and sleep-filled days. Things felt "out of control" and she would have "run home" if this had been possible. However, due to the loss of both of her biological parents in the last four years and the more recent death of the grandmother who had helped raise her, Alita felt as though she no longer had a "real home."

Alita was raised on a large north central reservation where she lived with her parents and various other relatives until the age of 10. Lakota, the language of her mother, was Alita's first language. Later, she was influenced by her father's relatives. Because her parents were from different tribes, they could not communicate with one another in their native languages. Instead, English became the language spoken in their home.

As the first born, Alita had many caretaking responsibilities in her extended family, both prior to and immediately following her placements in foster homes. Because of her mother's alcoholism and her father's diabetes and heart disease, common ailments among Native American Indian people, Alita was forced "to grow up fast" in that she inherited many of the household responsibilities at an early age.

When Alita was 10 years old, her parents divorced. This became a significant turning point in her life. Thereafter, she spent a short time attending a Catholic boarding school, which she recalls to have been "an unpleasant experience." Then, for reasons that were unknown to her, her parents lost custody and she was placed in a series of foster homes. This forced a separation from her younger brother and sister. Alita blames the divorce and a "harsh" court system for taking her away from the family she loved. The foster care system allowed her to see her family of origin and extended family on the reservation only two weeks out of the year. The remainder of the year Alita lived with wasicus (Caucasian families). Although she was not mistreated, she was unhappy.

Alita found the White middle-class lifestyle to be a tremendous culture shock. Once she entered the foster care system, she was expected to act "White" and to ignore everything associated with her "Indianness." Therefore, she felt forced to give up her "culture, language, and way of thinking." Eventually, through disuse, her native language skills slipped away. In the third grade at the boarding school, Alita quickly learned that Indian children who spoke their native tongue were severely punished. Therefore, as a matter of survival she learned to be "quiet and tried to become invisible." Although Alita did the best she could to survive, she never felt completely comfortable or at ease in any of the foster homes.

The adolescent years were especially difficult for Alita. She simply did not know who she was. With thick black hair, dark eyes, and tan skin, Alita knew she looked different from her foster siblings and schoolmates. She was told that her looks did not matter as long as she didn't "act like one of 'them'" (i.e., presumably Indian). Everything Alita had been prior to foster care, and everything that had been so important in her life was now challenged, devalued, or discounted. She began to learn that "time is important because it means money; if you don't have money there's something wrong with you." She longed for the time when she knew who she was and felt no shame for being Indian. She also longed for the days when happiness meant dancing at pow wows or sitting out on the bluffs all day.

Until the age of 18, Alita's visits with relatives were limited to two weeks a year. This regulation was enforced despite the protests of her father. Except for occasional birthday cards and letters she received, Alita felt lost and abandoned by her family. She resented them "for not trying hard enough" to get her back.

In her foster homes, Alita was taught to value work and required to earn her keep. Although she enjoyed and was talented in athletics and art, chores and a part-time job prohibited her from participating in these activities. Alita recalled feeling angry because she had so little control over her life at that time.

Alita had an enormous problem with her social life in high school. Dating was particularly difficult to do, since her foster parents were quite strict about her hours. In their view, she was "after all, Indian," which meant that Alita had a propensity for being wild, out of control, and untrustworthy. A part of her felt acceptable because she had achieved good grades and didn't get into trouble. Yet, the other part felt totally unacceptable because of who she "really" was.

To make matters worse, some Indians, who really did not know her, accused Alita of being an "apple," red on the outside, white on the inside, while some Caucasians who hardly knew her considered her to be "another Indian who gets money and free everything from the government." Alita was humiliated by these assumptions. She would respond with humor and minimization or would immerse herself in work activity. It was very important to her to not feel the pain. More recently, she had begun to drink alcohol, which caused her concern because of her mother's fate.

During the final years of Alita's father's life, he depended on her for a place to live. She also worked and helped to take care of her brother, sister, and their grandmother after graduating from high school. In fact, she developed a "keen knack" for finding many types of jobs. Alita's ability to keep her family financially secure was only hampered by her enrollment at a nearby tribal community college before transferring to a four-year college where the few jobs available paid low salaries.

Sometimes Alita believed she would meet the same fate as her mother, although she initially reported that her "drinking days" had begun and ended with her last relationship. However, this was later contradicted by the admission that she had been arrested several times for driving under the influence of alcohol; this had resulted in a suspended license and her participation in a mandatory driver's education program focused on alcohol-related misdemeanors. Alita never experienced blackouts, "just drank beer to be sociable," and to please her boyfriend. She worried that her use of alcohol might have damaged her brain and about her vulnerability to "partying" once she completed her degree and returned to the reservation. Therefore, she wanted to confront her problems before she left college, out of fear that she would not be supported on the reservation for abstaining from alcohol. This had motivated her to join the talking circle support group.

Alita did not date until she went to college. Her former boyfriend was the first man who expressed an interest in her. She was eager to please him and immediately worked to support him and his carefree lifestyle in less than a year. The relationship lasted while she attended the community college and began to fall apart when she informed him of her intent to transfer to the university. He abandoned her for a "woman with a better paying job." Alita sensed that she still had some "growing up to do about relationships." She wondered why she tended to assume a carefree role in relationships as well as why she chose "the wrong kind of men."

**Current Functioning**

Alita appeared easygoing and friendly. She was neatly groomed and usually dressed casually. She was also articulate and seemed to have no difficulty with talking about herself. However, she twirled strands of her long hair with her fingers and appeared restless. Sometimes her hands seemed to search for an object on a leather strap that was around her neck. Her gaze remained focused on the floor or on various objects in the room. Much of her affective expression was nonverbal, as evidenced through sad looks, silence, and stillness.

As part of the initial assessment, Alita was asked to complete an intellectual and personality evaluation, and a career interest inventory. She arrived breathless and apologetic, several minutes late for the appointment. Therefore, testing was postponed and light conversation was initiated until she could compose herself. Alita announced that she had never performed well on standardized tests and had always finished last. At the time of testing a few days later, her anxiety was evident through several false starts. She would look at her task, paraphrase the instructions, and would then ask, "Is that right?" after being instructed to begin. Alita also apologized profusely for each drop of a pen or other objects, and for her perception of having done something "wrong" even though she had been assured that there were no right or wrong answers. She reiterated that she never did well on tests and was always the last to finish.

The Global Assessment of Functioning Scale (GAF) score for Alita was 65, which indicated moderate difficulty in social and school functioning. DSM IV diagnoses were deferred on Axes I and II. However, on Axis III, a V-code for situational life stressors, was assigned due to Alita's school pressures and financial worries, the recent loss of her relationship, the losses of her parents, and separation from remaining family support systems. Alita appeared to have unresolved family of origin issues associated with grief, loss, and abandonment. Identity conflicts and a tendency to overfunction in relationships with men were also apparent. The difficulties were associated with low self-esteem. Initially, it was unclear whether Alita was alcohol dependent. She said she did not desire a drink and had no difficulty with abstaining from the intake of this substance after breaking up with her boyfriend. However, Alita attended Alcoholics Anonymous and Al Anon meetings and had engaged sponsors in both groups.

After several sessions, it was clearly determined that Alita experienced mild to moderate depression associated with unresolved childhood issues and the recent loss of a significant relationship. In addition, she had recently experienced her first panic attack.

## The Intervention

After exploring Alita's beliefs and cultural traditions, it was determined that she felt comfortable with an integrated relational, cognitive-behavioral, psychoeducational, and Native healing approach (Thin Elk & Thomas, 1996). Group options were also presented in the initial phase of her treatment and she chose the adult children of alcoholics group. However, Alita said she wanted to stay in the talking circle for a while longer. The talking circle allowed the importance of the Native American Indian community to take its proper place in her healing process. Having been placed in foster care and isolated from her cultural roots for many years did not diminish the importance of her culture in her everyday life. Alita needed to explore the missing pieces of her cultural belief system in order to reclaim her identity and to discover her strengths. The talking circle provided an opportunity for achieving both.

THE TALKING CIRCLE. An important value of the talking circle is its ability to offer safety and support via sharing thoughts and feelings. Usually a feather is passed around a circle of participants; the one holding the feather is allowed to speak. Everyone else listens until the speaker passes the feather to the next person. In this way, the speaker is validated and respected which allows her to be recognized and listened to without criticism or judgment. These conditions are considered "gifts" of the community and are essential to the healing process.

Eventually, Alita enjoyed the freedom of sharing when she felt like doing so and was quiet when she just needed to listen. More than anything, she enjoyed simply being accepted. Her discovery that "Indian people don't try to change you" was quite liberating from the inferiority she had felt many times as a Native American Indian in dominant culture settings. Alita participated in this group for several sessions. She found it very therapeutic in that she had begun to reconnect with other Indian women who shared freely about their own experiences. In addition to the talking circle, Alita scheduled an appointment with a Native American Indian counselor at the university she attended. A contract for individual and group sessions was agreed on in an effort to relieve her emotional distress.

INDIVIDUAL COUNSELING. Alita attended 16 individual counseling sessions which explored her fears, anger, and sadness. She and the counselor agreed that medication would not be used. Instead, Alita believed that she was capable of "walking with the pain" since she had "lived with sadness" much of her life. More importantly, she also believed that counseling could help her to "think better," so she could "walk in a good way."

Alita enjoyed being able to share her feelings and the freedom to be quiet when she just needed to listen. Although she was older and had been educated with Caucasians for several years, she still felt inferior in the presence of "majority culture people." Therefore, Alita promised to try an adult children of alcoholics group sometime later, which she eventually did a while after terminating her individual counseling.

Meanwhile, behavioral methods were introduced in the third and fourth sessions to teach Alita meditation and relaxation. Several tapes were used between sessions in conjunction with these interventions. One 10-minute relaxation exercise and a 30-minute guided imagery exercise were prescribed for her use each evening. She was fascinated with subliminal messages and enjoyed developing her own affirmations. Deep breathing exercises were prescribed for whenever she became aware of an overload of negative feelings or panic. Her daily routines were mapped and plotted for the purpose of scheduling physical exercise. Walking exercise schedules were also developed with progressively longer distances (i.e., up to one mile two to three times a week) to aid with relaxation. Alita eventually expressed an interest in visualization to help her to relax and to sleep better.

When asked about how connected she was to traditional healing practices, Alita said she believed in them and would be interested in learning more about them. Although she had been exposed to traditional healing practices at a very young age, she had only vague memories of these.

In both the talking circle and in individual counseling, Alita was supported in exploring the beliefs and cultural traditions associated with her grief. Her participation in the talking circle had calmed some of her conflicts about Indian medicine, religion, and spirituality, and had helped her to feel good about being a Native American Indian again. Furthermore, the group provided her with some guidance on how to live. Several women in the talking circle invited Alita to participate in a "sweat" or inipi (prayers and singing in a sweat lodge). She accepted their invitation as an opportunity to explore cultural healing approaches as well as to meet people who practiced and believed in these approaches.

Follow-up on Alita revealed that she did quit drinking entirely. Ten years after treatment she is working in a federal department and is self-supporting. Although Alita has experienced some stressful setbacks, she continues to feel positive about the outcome of her counseling and now knows that it is important to seek help before circumstances are out of control.

## DISCUSSION

The treatment plan for Alita required effective counselor attending and listening skills (Carkhuff & Anthony, 1979; Egan, 1986). It is imperative for counselors to convey respect to the client, to listen openly to his or her concerns, to be attuned to strengths, and to insure that intervention is tailored to his or her needs. It is also important for the counselor to embrace human differences rather than to rely on stereotypes or assumptions. The practitioner's ability to accept client variability in adaptation, acculturation, and adherence to dominant Native American Indian cultural values will have a significant impact on how open, trusting, and invested in the intervention the client will be. Furthermore, the counselor's ease with applying these relational characteristics is likely to promote the client's involvement in counseling beyond the initial session as well as lower premature termination rates.

Alita's counselor was a Native American Indian woman who understood and accepted traditional Native American Indian values. This enabled Alita to be authentic and to feel empowered in the helping relationship. In addition, the counselor's characteristics seemed to help Alita to feel confident in her ability to take charge of her healing. For example, Alita expressed concern about being accepted in her cultural community after being "removed" for so many years. When her concern was framed as a strength, she was able to explore what had been missed and, ultimately, to reclaim her identity. However, being a Native American Indian does not guarantee that one will understand a client from one's own tribe or another. Intratribal differences are not as simplistic as the division between speakers of the language and nonspeakers. Intratribal differences can involve conflict over "Who or what is traditional?", "What degree of Indian blood is required for tribal membership?", and "How do you prove you're an Indian?" Intertribal relationships involve even more complexity.

As previously stated in the introduction, the Native American Indian population only comprises a small percentage of the population of the U.S. Yet, it constitutes almost half of the cultural, racial, and ethnic diversity within the total population of the U.S. With hundreds of Native American Indian nations maintaining their individual beliefs, languages, names, and traditions, there are few general statements that apply to this highly diverse population. There is considerable diversity between and among tribal entities. To universalize these groups would be misleading and harmful to Native American Indian students as well as to others.

## Critical Cultural Considerations

Once differences between cultures are recognized and respected, the client can decide whether or not to pursue counseling. Alita's decision to do so was enhanced by:

1. the provision of information about the treatment process;
2. freedom to express comfort or discomfort with the treatment strategies;
3. having her self-confidence nurtured as she began to take control of her own "healing";
4. encouragement to explore her identity as a Native American Indian person in a non-Indian culture; and
5. the practitioner's openness to integrating Indian and traditional intervention strategies in the interest of the client's total well-being.

The first three conditions are germane to most counseling situations. The last two require attention to specific cultural differences. Another consideration would be to take the intervention out of the office. After all, harmony with nature is valued by Native American Indians. Alita and the counselor often went for walks during sessions which seemed to help build rapport and trust.

Webster's defines "psyche" to mean "the soul" (Mish, 1993). Unfortunately, in counseling and psychotherapy, spiritual matters are often misunderstood. For many Native American Indian cultures, spirituality is a way of living that is not to be confused with religion or superstition. In this respect, native people may embrace discussions about visions and dreams. It is not considered extraordinary to speak of spirits, nor is it evidence of a mental disorder, per se.

The healing of Native American Indians requires their trust and confidence in the treatment process and may be facilitated by simple strategies regardless of the race, ethnicity, or culture of the counselor. As previously suggested, these conditions may be achieved through embracing the world view of the client, educating the client about the treatment process, mobilizing hope, and by respecting the client's freedom to choose whether or not to pursue treatment. In Alita's case the first few sessions focused on providing information about the process, appropriate alternatives, and whatever other relevant information was sought. Although traditionalists may argue that this is not "real" therapy, it is important to remember that the best intentions of therapy are lost when such sharing with the client does not take place.

This case also illustrates that it can be important for the counselor to explore values and beliefs that have fostered conflict for a client who has become estranged from his or her culture. Often out of needs for security and acceptance a client may distort or fail to recognize the positive impact of cultural values or traditions on his or her life which may eventually influence problems in daily living. However, as for Alita, when the strengths of Native American Indian cultural values and traditions are recognized, negative connotations of being "Indian" are often discarded. It can also be beneficial for the counselor to discuss the benefits of cultural values and traditions with the client within historical and political contexts. For example, culture can be emphasized as a strength that has withstood efforts to annihilate the Native American Indian.

Counselors for Native American Indians must be aware of barriers to culturally and socially competent care for this population. These include linguistics, inadequate knowledge of the culture, and diagnostic labeling. Various languages and dialects, belief systems, and values may sanction behaviors that may seem unusual or abnormal to counselors from other cultural backgrounds. Attention to these issues requires replacement of negative attitudes and perceptions of Native American Indians and other pluralistic populations with affirmative ones. Culturally competent research efforts that include the input of Native American Indians could prove useful toward achieving this end.

Self-awareness on the part of the practitioner is absolutely essential to cross-cultural intervention. The counselor's attitudes, beliefs, and values have a significant impact on the outcome of intervention. Trimble (1981) cautions that many assumptions are related to the counselor's inability to go beyond his or her own focus, linear thinking, cultural encapsulation, and so forth. False acceptance of differences or the denial of conflicting beliefs about other groups can seriously compromise effectiveness. This is especially important in view of the imbalance of power that has typically existed in helping relationships.

The traditional practice of psychotherapy is rooted in dominant culture perspectives. In view of the history of majority culture dominance over indigenous populations it is understandable that Native American Indians, regardless of tribal affiliation and upbringing, need assurance early in the process that the therapeutic process is safe. In this regard, the beauty of the culture is that "being Indian" is an internal concept that is rarely compromised. In no way is this more evident than in its expression.

## The Expression of Emotion

One of the unique traits of many Native American Indians is how they express feelings. As Alita displayed, expression of the depth of a feeling can be limited to simply naming or recognizing it as well as subtle displays of such. It is more important to the client that feelings are identified or recognized than whether they are outwardly expressed. To recognize the significance of naming feelings rather than misperceiving this as a form of defensiveness would be respectful of the diversity between the Native American Indian and dominant culture of the U.S. Such recognition is also respectful of the reality that Native American Indian clients have a valid cultural legacy that influences their behavior. This is associated with whether or not help is sought.

## Supporting the Psychosocial Development of Native American Indian Students

Would Alita have come to the counseling center at all without the direction of a supportive community of Native women or a Native American Indian counselor? Clearly, the availability of these supports made a pivotal difference.

What happens, then, to those Native American Indian students who are without such supports? Or, what happens to those who seek help but leave feeling disillusioned, misunderstood, or hopeless as a result of incompetent intervention? They usually return to wherever they were prior to enrolling in college. For some, this is the reservation (land set aside for Indians as a result of treaties and federal policy). Others seek employment away from the reservation since job opportunities on most of these are very limited. Others may seek employment in a small town or an urban area. Those in the latter groups who find suitable employment may soon give it up to go home to be with family when a loved one is ill or dies.

Therefore, some students never overcome financial instability and hardship. There is a great deal of seeking and disappointment, an ebb and flow that always seems to be explained by a common meaning. In the Native American Indian world view, these patterns are not good or bad or right or wrong. Instead, they simply exist and are outcomes of ineffective mechanisms to address much of the stress associated with cultural and social problems that Native American Indian students encounter at colleges and universities. Because the natural healing mechanisms that were once available to Native people are no longer as accessible as in the past, this population must look to other interventions for help with some of the difficulties they encounter. This includes counseling and psychotherapy.

How can the fields of college counseling and college mental health become more helpful to this population? First, more deliberate efforts must be made to interest Native American Indian students in the helping professions. Secondly, academic programs and training sites for college counseling and college mental health must make a conscientious effort to recruit qualified Native American Indian students. It seems that reverse discrimination cases have influenced many graduate programs to be hesitant about implementing the affirmative action policies that could facilitate this. There seems to be a fear of doing too much for one group and not enough for others.

Then there are quotas and gatekeeping requirements that focus on recruiting high achievers with high standardized test scores. Academic and training programs and professional licensing requirements appear to give far too little consideration to the indigenous person who has successfully persevered through cultural, language, societal, and even academic barriers. Thus, there are far too few Native American Indian mental health professionals to serve the Native American Indian student population. Another persistent barrier to effective service delivery to this population is how it is perceived in relation to alcohol.

## Perceptions of Native American Indians and Alcohol: Considerations for Intervention

It would have been easy to assume that Alita exhibited alcohol dependency. Several factors were considered before developing a treatment plan that did not directly address this issue. First, there is an assumption that alcoholism is prevalent and out of control among Native American Indians. However, even though there seem to be no common patterns among tribes, there are high rates of use and abstinence, depending on the region and tribe, despite a higher average of drinking behavior for Native American Indians than for many other groups, even during recovery (Institute of Medicine, 1990). It is obvious that a "packaged judgment" about Alita's drinking would have compromised her healing process. Thus, it is important to approach the alcohol intake of a Native American Indian client cautiously and patiently.

## A Professional and Personal Perspective

As a Native American Indian woman counselor of Muskogee/Yuchi heritage, it was important for me to provide Alita with culturally competent care. Alita's response to our work was particularly rewarding after she had a basic understanding of counseling.

Even though I have generally loved my work with college students, I have been lonely as a Native American Indian woman trainee and professional. There have been times when I have wished I could have shared my thoughts and concerns with other Native American Indian professionals. Yet, I hesitate to encourage another to begin such a difficult journey unless he or she truly understands the sacrifices that are required to meet the challenges inherent to this field. Nevertheless, the gratification comes when a client like Alita is supported through a critical phase of life and clearly exhibits that the intervention has made a positive difference. This makes it all worthwhile and inspires me to continue.

**Summary**

The case study of a Native American Indian college student was used to highlight difficulties that are commonly experienced by this population. The importance of a holistic, integrative approach to intervention (e.g., relational, cognitive-behavioral, psychoeducational, Native healing) that is free from an emphasis on diagnosis and pathology was emphasized. Alita was given information about depression, alcoholism, and meditation. Her efforts to engage in a physical exercise program were supported, and she became more aware of her emotions and how she coped with stressful events. Finally, Alita participated in cultural strengthening, which involved her participation in the talking circle and sweats, cultural forums for attending to spiritual needs. Through these forums she found support for her spiritual needs as well as her Indian identity.

Alita's fears about her drinking were addressed effectively with appropriate referrals to support groups (e.g., AA, Al-Anon) in her community. A premature diagnosis of alcoholism might have inhibited her progress. Instead, deferring the diagnosis for a while allowed other aspects of the intervention to take effect until Alita could make healthier choices about her drinking.

In conclusion, Alita displayed identity confusion and a lack of self-confidence in relation to personal, bicultural, and academic issues. These guided the development and implementation of her treatment plan.

**DEFINITIONS**

**CREEK/YUCHI** (Yoo-chee):   Native American Indian tribes primarily found in the Southeastern United States before their removal to present day Oklahoma.
**INIPEE** (e-nee-pee) or sweat:   Prayer and singing in a sweat lodge.
**LAKOTA**:   Native term for language and people called "Sioux"; the largest division of Oceti Sakowin or "Seven Fireplaces." Around 1,000 AD "Seven Fireplaces" migrated to present day Minnesota from the southeast. In the 18th century

they moved to the northern plains where they reside today (Davis, 1994).
**MUSKOGEE:** The chief tribe in the southeast. Its Indian alliance is known as the Creek Confederacy because of its tendency to settle near running creeks. Most Muskogee people were located in present day Alabama and Georgia. According to their legends they migrated to the southeastern U.S. from the northwest. The Muskogee people relocated to Oklahoma in the mid-1800s. Today tribal membership is approximately 26,000 and growing.
**POW WOW:** Native American Indian intertribal social gathering where various dances are performed.
**TALKING CIRCLE:** A group usually composed of Native American Indians gathered to respectfully share, listen, and support one another.
**WASICU** (wah-see-choo): Lakota/Dakota word for "White man."

## REFERENCES

Carkhuff, R., & Anthony, A. (1979). *The skills of helping.* Amherst, MA: Human Resource Development Press.

Carter, D., & Wilson, R. (1997). *The 1996–97 report of minorities in higher education.* Washington, D.C.: American Council on Education.

Davis, M. B. (1994). *Native America in the twentieth century: An encyclopedia.* New York: Garlara Publishing, Inc.

Egan, G. (1986). *The skilled helper: A systematic approach to effective helping* (3rd ed.). Monterey, CA: Brooks/Cole.

Gritts, J. (1997). Personal communication. American Indian College Fund, Denver.

Hodgkinson, H., Outtz, J., & Obarakpor, A. (1990). *The demographics of American Indians: One percent of the people; fifty percent of the diversity.* Washington, D.C.: Institute for Educational Leadership.

Institute of Medicine (1990). *Broadening the base of treatment for alcohol problems.* Washington, DC: National Academy Press.

Leitch, B. A. (1979) *A concise dictionary of Indian tribes of North America.* Algonac, MI: Reference Publications, Inc.

Mish, F. (Ed.). (1993). *Merriam Webster's collegiate dictionary* (10th ed.). Springfield, MA: Merriam Webster, Inc.

Thin Elk, G. & Thomas, R. (April, 1966). Personal communication.

Trimble, J. E. (1981). Values differentials and their importance in counseling American Indians. In P. Pedersen, J. Draguns, W. Lonner, & J. Trimble (Eds.), *Counseling across cultures* (2nd ed.), (203–226). Honolulu: University Press of Hawaii.

CHAPTER 3

# THERAPEUTIC CONSIDERATIONS FOR AFRICAN AMERICAN STUDENTS AT PREDOMINANTLY WHITE INSTITUTIONS

Irving M. Allen

### INTRODUCTION

African American students seek counseling services for the same kinds of problems as other students. These may include transient adjustment difficulties (e.g., homesickness, relationship problems, roommate conflict, and so on), or more significant threats to maturation such as eating disorders, major depression, and substance abuse. Regardless of the presenting problem, concerns pertinent to the African American student's racial identity are likely to surface in the therapeutic relationship. Therefore, it is incumbent upon college mental health workers to be aware that race interacts with normal psychological development in complex ways that are relevant to the delivery of ethical and competent mental health services.

Many African American youth strive for success and a sense of well-being despite the failure of this society to overcome racism and ancillary forms of oppression. Unfortunately, college campuses are microcosms of the larger society and cannot reliably offer these students supportive milieus or "safe havens" from the profoundly ambivalent stance of this society toward them. In the current academic setting, a cornerstone of this ambivalence is the belief that African Americans cannot perform at comparable intellectual levels to Caucasians. Jacqueline Fleming (1984) has noted that "research on Black students in White schools indicates that they face an unaccepting environment that provides inadequate support. As a consequence, [some develop identity problems that sap their intellectual energies]" (p. xiii). Andrew

Hacker supports this view in *Two Nations* (1992): "Even after official welcomes and overtures expressing good will, [Black students] soon sense that they are seen as an alien presence at what still remain 'White' institutions" (p. 148).

Edwards and Polite (1992) suggest that the ability to understand this reality in an appropriate context is essential to success. They contend that successful students understand that problems are caused by the perverse reactions of others to the Black race rather than race alone. Claiming this perspective is by no means an uncomplicated task since most African American students at predominantly White universities are challenged in their efforts to develop or maintain healthy self-esteem due to stereotypes, prejudice, and numerous microaggressions as described by Chin, De La Cancela, and Jenkins elsewhere (1993).

College mental health workers and administrators are aware that even the most successful students, from every ethnocultural group, are often relatively immature and frequently require skilled and empathic guidance as they move into adulthood. In addition, African American youth face the complexity and ambiguity of maturing in a variably hostile society which has traditionally excluded their forebears from all levels of formal education. Furthermore, they have probably witnessed current political struggles over public education and integration of schools. Hence, African American youth are in particular need of competent professional support to help them resolve the obstacles, prejudices, and inequities that Edwards and Polite have noted in their profiles of successful African American adults.

*Testimony* (1995), an anthology of experiences of African American college students, edited by Natasha Tarpley, confirms the alienation many experience at predominantly White institutions. In Tarpley's account of a particularly troubling incident from her own college experience, she states, "I learned from it a painful lesson, one that so many Black students on campuses across the country are also learning: that my education, my family, my person, my life even, do not carry the same weight or have the same value as other students, White students, on this campus" (p. 1).

## CASE VIGNETTES

What follows are two case vignettes of African American students who sought mental health services on predominantly White campuses. The students to be discussed are not intended to be understood as "typical" in any way, given the diversity of the African American student population. Instead, each vignette demonstrates a complex interplay between racial identity concerns, universal maturational tasks, and the unique internal dynamics of both of the students discussed. In addition, the usefulness of the Black Identity Scale for evaluating and treating African American youth will become evident. It is hoped that the vignettes and the ensuing discussion will raise the consciousness of therapists to the reality that race does, indeed, matter, as Cornel West (1993) has so aptly emphasized elsewhere.

## MAYA

Maya was a 20-year-old junior who was hospitalized for several days after threatening to take an overdose of nonprescription sleeping pills. She was released from the hospital after rejecting her suicidal plans and agreeing to outpatient treatment. Mental status showed a depressed but somewhat defiant African American woman whose mental functions were intact. She showed no evidence of a thought disorder, minimized the significance of her suicidal threats, and believed that others had "overreacted" to her. Maya emphasized that she had only come in compliance with the hospital's directive to seek psychotherapy. She did not know anyone in her immediate or extended family who had been depressed, and believed that her parents would not approve of her participation in psychotherapy. Maya was difficult to engage, gave short answers to open-ended questions, and was clearly wary about revealing too much. She did not associate readily and only reluctantly agreed to my suggestion that we meet once weekly.

Within three weeks, Maya had returned to her prior level of high academic functioning. She was an A student in a prelaw program, and was moderately active in extracurricular activities. The reason for her suicidal threats remained unclear. She provided few details about her personal life on campus until the sixth session when she almost casually revealed concern about her roommate whom she described as very "moody" and not "functioning well." This turned out to be an understatement, as Maya further stated that her roommate's family had several seriously depressed members and the roommate herself had been hospitalized once for depression early in adolescence.

Furthermore, the roommate had been in therapy intermittently ever since. Maya had known her since their sophomore year in an exclusive private secondary day school. More recently, Maya had become her roommate's caretaker. She insured that the young woman arose for class in the morning, did her laundry for her, accompanied her to the dining hall, and often helped mediate the roommate's interpersonal conflicts.

Their friendship circle was primarily Caucasian American except for Maya and an Asian American woman. The young women in the circle, all aspiring actresses, artists, and writers, thought of themselves as highly sophisticated. As Maya spoke more about her roommate, the precipitant for her depressive episode became clear.

Several weeks earlier, Maya had become attracted to a young man in the group, and he seemed to reciprocate. However, just as they were beginning to date more seriously, Maya discovered that her roommate had become interested in him. Two days before her threat of suicide, Maya learned that they had slept together. As she expressed her feelings about this incident in therapy with increasingly genuine affect, she became more engaged in the process.

Soon after, race surfaced in the dialogue for the first time. During our first session, Maya had denied that race was a problem for her and she expressed the intention "not to be confined by race in any way." Subsequently, she seemed surprised to hear herself express anger toward her roommate as a White woman, for betraying her trust. Prior to this acknowledgment, however, she questioned her racial feelings by asking, "You don't think I'm upset because they're (i.e., her roommate and the young man) White, do you?"

Throughout Maya's school life before college, she had often been the only African American in her classes. She recalled that the sixth through eighth grades had been particularly difficult for her personally and socially. Maya was often excluded from parties at her classmates' homes. Although there were times when she angrily confronted her closest friends, she finally decided that her anger "wasn't mature." With this decision, Maya resolved to "rise above" racial problems.

Her parents seemed to reinforce this stance by telling her about their far more segregated school experiences which, at times, seemed to minimize her own problems. Maya established no close relationships with African American peers although her parents tried to arrange this through social activities outside of school. She always had one or two very close White women friends. Although Maya seldom dated, she had strongly hoped that the young man in her college group might become her first "real" experience. Even though she assumed the role of caretaker with her closest high school friends, Maya assumed this role more intensely with her college roommate.

After three months of therapy, Maya admitted that she had been overinvolved with someone who had betrayed her trust. Moreover, she had discovered that her inclination for caretaking was associated with early adolescent experiences of exclusion because of her race. From her perspective, caretaking was one method of establishing intimacy with White women. Through caretaking, Maya attempted to sublimate her feelings of disappointment, but also adopted a relational style which ultimately proved to be maladaptive. For example, her denial of racial issues was an immature response which precluded her from seeking more reciprocal relationships. Because of her academic achievements, Maya's personality seemed to serve her well until she encountered the complexities of college life without the parental support and structure that had been immediately available to her while she lived at home.

When Maya became interested in exploring the possibility of a real relationship with the young man mentioned previously, she took an important step toward moving beyond vicarious involvements through the lives of other women. At the same time, she suffered a significant disappointment which she initially attributed to her own failings. To add insult to injury, she had done "so much" for the person by whom she felt betrayed. Also of significance was the fact that Maya's relational style bore no resemblance to that of anyone else in her family. Furthermore, all her siblings seemed to be functioning well. Maya had always interpreted her parents' message about racism to be that she had the ability to overcome any obstacles. She could not recall ever talking with them in any detail about her social life, since from an early age on she considered them to be critical of her having only White friends.

## AHMED

Ahmed was a 21-one-year-old self-referred senior who had become irritable during the two months preceding his initial interview. The mental status examination revealed that he was fully oriented, quite poised, articulate, and immediately capable of a positive rapport. Although Ahmed seemed sad at times, he readily displayed an appropriate sense of humor.

In the first session, Ahmed referred to his light skin color by stating that he had been ridiculed and ostracized as a "White boy" by some other African American students at his urban high school. He had come from a large West Coast city where he had been raised by his mother and a maternal aunt. There had been occasional economic hardship, but he emphasized that he had never "gone hungry" because both mother and aunt usually had steady jobs.

When Ahmed was very young his parents had separated. Since then, his father had been only marginally involved in his life, and a chronic source of disappointment to him. At times, his father had tried to be close to him and his younger brother, only to disappear for months thereafter. During these absences, his father would break promises for visits or gifts, and would contribute little child support to his mother. In the second therapy session, Ahmed attributed his recent irritability to feelings about his father.

During early adolescence, Ahmed had become deeply concerned about possibly repeating his father's life history. He knew that his father, like himself, had shown strong academic potential. His father had attended two years of college on full scholarship during the late 1950s. He had then dropped out of college for reasons that were unclear to Ahmed. Since then, his father had never established a career, had become a chronic alcoholic, and often told Ahmed of his own deep self-dissatisfaction with life. As a consequence, Ahmed became obsessed with fears of failing and of disappointing the family. He developed an excessive concern about grades, despite his high achievement. In addition, he had no tolerance for any grade variation from course to course, so anything less than an A triggered a fear of starting a long downhill slide as his father had experienced many years earlier.

Ahmed had become irritable during the prior two months because he had begun to feel ambivalent about the possibility of chemistry as a career while in the process of applying to graduate schools. Due to his perfectionistic standards, he had begun to doubt that he could compete successfully with other graduate students. For the first time, Ahmed revealed that his primary interest had been liberal arts at the beginning of his freshman year. He had switched to a science because of the belief that there was too much subjectivity in the grading of liberal arts courses. Ahmed recalled one experience during a freshman writing course when his style was repeatedly criticized by a particular instructor who was certain that his prior education had been inadequate despite the fact that he had been the recipient of a prestigious city-wide essay contest. The instructor told him that he was determined to make sure that African American students had to meet the same "standards" required for "everyone else."

Since Ahmed was performing very well in other courses which required writing skills, he concluded that this instructor was prejudiced and was unable to acknowledge his real abilities. He recalled several other examples of problems with professors' racial attitudes. Remarkably, he managed all of these experiences in relatively adaptive ways, even though he never sought input from other adults who had always been encouraging and supportive of his academic endeavors.

As Ahmed reviewed his college career in therapy, he thought that he had "been driven" away from his initial academic interests by racial concerns. This perception, coupled with his internal fear of failing, had influenced him to become more and more self-preoccupied and mildly dysthymic as he approached graduation. His mood improved significantly during eight therapy sessions as he began to recognize how ingrained and powerful his fear of repeating his father's history had been, and how this fear influenced a sense of shame that prevented him from considering alternatives to his overly independent style of decision making during college that had only proved to yield dissatisfying results.

As the end of Ahmed's last semester neared, he appeared more sympathetic to his father. During the last two sessions he explained that his father had left college because of a financial crisis in his family. Thereafter, he tried to provide economic support for his younger siblings, but subsequently enlisted in the military. Ultimately he went to Vietnam where he engaged in considerable combat. His father never returned to college. In addition, Ahmed revealed that his father's family viewed his failings as simply "typical of Black males." Interestingly, even though Ahmed had known these things about his father's life story, he had never linked his father's family problems or war experiences with subsequent difficulties in his life.

After the eleventh session, Ahmed decided to devote all of his time and attention to pregraduation social activities, since he was to graduate in a few days. He met with his therapist a year later and revealed that he decided to work for at least two years, thereby deferring acceptances to graduate studies in chemistry until that time. Ahmed felt good, worked full time as a research technician, and had found considerable fulfillment as a volunteer in an inner-city boys club.

## MAYA AND AHMED: DIFFERENCES AND COMMONALITIES

Maya and Ahmed presented with distinct diagnostic differences. Maya's diagnosis appeared to be Major Depressive Disorder with possible personality problems. Ahmed presented with what appeared to be Adjustment Disorder with Depressed Mood. Maya was resistant to therapy and had been "ordered" by the hospital staff to come for treatment, while Ahmed was self-referred and very self-curious. Despite these important differences, both students responded well to brief treatment.

Racial identity concerns were important for Maya and Ahmed even though these concerns were expressed in very different ways. Maya initially denied any racial concerns. Ahmed spoke of race more immediately as he described his alienation from African American peers in high school. He readily associated to the history of his father's failings and his own concerns about failure like "other Black men." In contrast, Maya became aware of her racial identity issues only after she began to talk about her roommate's problems. She had no awareness that her preadolescent experiences as an African American girl in a predominantly White school were relevant to how she related to peers or how she responded to her roommate's seductive behavior with the young man she was interested in. When Maya finally began to acknowledge these experiences, she improved quickly. Subsequently, serious concern about her well-being lessened as it became more apparent that she had experienced a complex adjustment reaction.

Openness to the significance of both students' racial identity awareness enhanced their therapeutic processes. The evaluations of Maya and Ahmed included the usual components of a thorough diagnostic examination. In addition, attention to their levels of Black identity development (Cross, 1978; Cross, Parham, & Helms, 1991; Helms, 1990; Tatum, 1992) was central to understanding both students' presenting problems and relevant background information. Both students' perceptions of themselves as African Americans were deeply relevant to their relational styles, self-images, and defensive structures. As such, these perceptions were deeply relevant to their therapeutic processes and outcomes.

Clearly Maya and Ahmed were in different stages of Black identity development. Maya was in the Pre-Encounter Stage, a level at which she had been "stuck" since the social rejections she had experienced as a preteen. The Pre-Encounter Stage involves absorbing the values of the dominant culture, including the view that White is better than Black, and a quest to assimilate and to be accepted by Caucasians while minimizing the significance of race and ethnicity in one's life. Students at the Pre-Encounter Stage experience more anxiety, memory impairment, paranoia, alcohol consumption, and global psychological distress than those in more advanced stages of Black identity development (Carter, 1991).

Maya's view of herself as an African American woman was deeply unflattering, and she felt completely dependent on her White peers and dominant culture values to feel lovable, worthwhile, and attractive. Her caretaking role with White women was, ironically, a traditional gender role for Black women dating back to slavery and the Jim Crow era. When her roommate slept with the young man she was interested in, Maya muted her anger at the roommate and deplored her own Blackness, which in her view rendered her unattractive and unable to compete for adult male attention. This experience moved her to the Encounter Stage, in that it was the catalyst that forced her to recognize the impact of racism on her life.

In contrast, Ahmed had already experienced and recognized his own Encounter Stage interactions (e.g., the experience with the writing instructor). He subsequently moved into the Immersion/Emersion Stage as reflected by his primary affiliation with an African American peer group in social and extracurricular activities. Yet, an important facet of his senior year adjustment problem seemed to be related to unresolved Pre-Encounter issues which he associated with his father. The core of this problem was his perception that all Black men are failures. Even though Ahmed's fear of failing as an African American man had motivated him to become a high achiever, it did not have the same effect on his decision-making capacity as he encountered increasingly complex choices of adult life.

When Ahmed returned for a follow-up visit one year later and spoke of his work with inner-city boys, this was evidence that he had entered the Internalization/Commitment Stage, characterized by security in one's Blackness, the development of a personal identity that includes active interest in and pursuit of activities that are of benefit to the greater African American community. One at this stage of Black identity development is also able to see other African Americans more objectively, both as individuals and as members of a group.

## Implications for College Mental Health Services

Many therapists seem to deny the importance of racial, ethnic, and cultural themes in psychotherapy, as elaborated on by Comas-Díaz and Jacobsen (1991) elsewhere. Furthermore, Jones (1985) suggests that Caucasian therapists' resistance to racial, ethnic, and cultural themes in psychotherapy with African Americans is related to the power of these themes to evoke more complicated countertransferences than those for White patients, since social images of African Americans make them easier targets for therapists' projections. For these reasons, it is important to emphasize here that appropriate application of the Black Identity Scale and culturally competent intervention with African American students requires acceptance of the reality that their efforts to adapt to college life are interdependent with perceptions of race in the U.S. as well as their identity development on the basis of race.

African American and other therapists of color are also challenged by African American clients. It is common for some therapists to feel a strong urge to take care of or to even "fix" the concerns of these clients. Even though this urge is often understandable within the contexts of a therapist's life experiences and the intensity of a student's discomfort, an overly protective response can undermine a therapeutic approach which seeks to promote positive growth and development. Yet, to ignore themes pertaining to race, ethnicity, and culture is more detrimental to the client than an overly protective response.

My experiences in supervision, consultation, and conferences are consistent with what has been described by Comas-Díaz and Jacobsen (1991) and Jones (1985). I have often heard experienced therapists say, "I don't bring up race unless the patient does." I have also heard therapists challenge the relevance of race, citing a variety of rationales for this stance. A common perspective is that "people's problems are universal, so there is no need to discuss race." In addition, some therapists contend that "overemphasis on race interferes with 'real' therapy," and "that an emphasis on race prevents the client from taking appropriate responsibility for his or her life." I have also heard therapists admit to feelings of inadequacy about addressing race in the therapeutic process, without recognition of the reality that this admission reveals a problem for *them* that needs to be addressed.

A problem with placing the responsibility for introducing race, culture, and ethnicity on the client is that such content surfaces in many different ways, often in very obscure forms. As Maya and Ahmed have made apparent, this is because African American youth have varying levels of awareness of how racism has affected their experiences before and during college. Moreover, levels of therapist awareness of related issues vary enormously.

Therefore, to entrust such responsibility to therapists who do not take essential personal and professional development in these areas seriously is likely to result in an inability to understand clinically significant aspects of many African American clients' experiences. There would especially be an inability to help a client who avoids these issues. What is ultimately at risk for African American students whose therapists fail to address racial themes is repetition of the empathic failure and absence of effective service delivery that is so endemic to their everyday lives. Therefore, the therapeutic relationship becomes just another mechanism of disempowerment.

African American students cannot be expected to overcome therapists' resistances to these issues or to educate therapists on the "Black experience." Instead, therapists are responsible for acknowledging race as a legitimate dimension of adjustment to college life and the treatment process. If racial issues had not been recognized as potentially relevant to Maya's problems, she could have easily been considered more significantly disturbed than she actually was. Overdiagnosis of pathology in African Americans remains a problem which suggests that the standard practice of psychotherapy for nontraditional populations is problematic and regressive. This includes a lack of diversity in staffing.

The racial makeup of the staff is important to African American students. Nickerson, Helms, and Terrell (1994) found this population expressed higher levels of distrust toward college counseling services with no staff members of color. Boesch and Cimbolic (1994) surveyed 182 directors of college counseling services to investigate African Americans' utilization rates. While they found that these students generally did not underutilize available services, their utilization of facilities that had at least one African American therapist was more than double that of services that had none. These data suggest that administrators as well as clinicians should be familiar with the implications of African American students' racial identity awareness for staffing and socially competent service delivery to this population. Achieving the latter requires consideration of racial, ethnic, cultural, and economic realities that impinge on the client's current functioning.

College officials such as deans, instructors, and advisors often assume that African American therapists have the answers regarding African American students. This assumption is incorrect and tends to marginalize African Americans further, while it lets others "off the hook" in accepting responsibility for the entire student body. For example, a request for a consultation might involve this kind of tacit request: "I don't know what to do with this Black student and I don't want to make a mistake. . . . What should I do?"

Some White senior officials take extremely punitive, judgmental stances toward African American students who seek psychological validation or approval from mental health professionals. Others fail to take appropriate corrective or limit-setting action. Therapists have a complex role in these scenarios, since often the racial concerns of the administrator are neither expressed nor conscious. Therefore, judging how to "be helpful," while preserving the student's confidentiality, is by no means a simple task.

Toward this end, Bowser, Auletta, and Jones (1993) have identified the need for diversity and sensitivity training at all levels for college personnel. Mental health professionals could have a vital role in conducting training programs that facilitate the awareness of all levels of college personnel. The impact of campus police, cafeteria workers, secretaries, and others on the lives of students must not be underestimated; many of the most publicized negative incidents involving African American students have involved so-called "nonprofessional" personnel.

If such training is to be effective, the involvement of college mental health professionals as trainers must be supported by senior university officials (e.g., college presidents, deans, police chiefs, and so forth). Until diversity is addressed continuously and systematically, Black students will continue to feel unaccepted by predominantly White institutions, rebuffed by peers, and inhibited from taking part in anything but all-Black organizational activities. Moreover, this lack of acceptance will continue to influence signs of intellectual stagnation and academic frustration (Fleming, 1984).

## CONCLUSION

African American college students' access to predominantly White colleges and universities has increased dramatically during the past three decades. Yet, many still struggle against the ever-present legacy of oppression as they confront the daunting task of becoming resilient, healthy, and productive adults in college settings which remain ambivalent about including them.

Racial prejudice in the U.S., as reflected by the affirmative action debates, and ever-present questions about Blacks' intelligence, seriously complicate the development and maintenance of healthy self-esteem among African American youth. Furthermore, recent studies by Claude Steele (1995) have documented the stereotype vulnerability felt by many of the most able Black students influenced by internalization of negative expectations of their performance. This concept is particularly compelling, since it suggests the need to thoroughly investigate retention rates and performance determinants, and to identify and nurture those conditions that promote the academic and psychological well-being of this population. For college mental health practitioners, these conditions include:

1. an openness to acknowledging racial, ethnic, and cultural themes in interventions with college students;
2. ongoing participation in diversity and sensitivity training; and
3. participation in the provision of such training to other essential college personnel.

The overwhelming majority of African American students achieve adaptive resolution of racial identity issues prior to entering college. Therefore, the case histories of Maya and Ahmed illustrate only two examples of the "sorting out" and "working through" that is required of some members of this population for success at predominantly White colleges and universities. A critical aspect of these processes for some students involves coming to terms with societal and self-perceptions of what it means to be an African American and achieving whatever individual level of resolution indicated. College mental health practitioners could be immensely helpful to students who struggle with these issues. By being adequately prepared to address adjustment and developmental problems associated with race, highly complicated entanglements between racial issues and other psychological conflicts might be prevented. Finally, it is important to acknowledge here that the effectiveness of college mental health practitioners with African American students is interdependent with both the cooperation and cultural competence of other college personnel.

## REFERENCES

Boesch, R., & Cimbolic, P. (1994). Black students' use of college and university counseling centers. *Journal of college students development, 35,* 212–216.

Bowser, B. P., Auletta, G., & Jones, T. (1993). *Confronting diversity issues on campus.* Newbury Park, CA: Sage.

Carter, R. T. (1991). Racial identity attitudes and psychological functioning. *Journal of multicultural counseling and development, 19,* 105–114.

Chin, J. L., De La Cancela, V., & Jenkins, Y. M. (1993). *Diversity in psychotherapy: The politics of race, ethnicity, and gender.* Westport, CT: Praeger.

Comas-Díaz, L., & Jacobsen, F. M. (1991). Ethnocultural transference and countertransference in the therapeutic dyad. *American journal of orthopsychiatry, 61,* 392–402.

Cross, W. E., Jr. (1978). The Thomas and Cross models of psychological nigrescence: A review. *Journal of black psychology, 5,* 13–31.

Cross, W. E., Jr., Parham, T. A., & Helms, J. E. (1991). The stages of black identity development: Nigrescence models. In R. Jones (Ed.), *Black psychology* (3rd ed.) (pp. 319–338). Berkeley, CA: Cobbs & Henry.

Edwards, A., & Polite, C. (1993). *Children of the dream: The psychology of black success* (p. 6). New York: Anchor Books.

Fleming, J. (1984). *Blacks in college* (p. xiii). San Francisco: Jossey-Bass.

Hacker, A. (1992). *Two nations* (p.148). New York: Charles Scribner & Sons.

Helms, J. E. (1990) (Ed.). *Black and white racial identity: Theory, research, and practice.* Westport, CT: Greenwood Press.

Jones, E. E. (1985). Psychotherapy and counseling with black clients. In P. Pederson (Ed.), *Handbook of cross-cultural counseling and therapy* (pp. 173–179). Westport, CT: Greenwood Press.

Nickerson, K. J., Helms, J. E., & Terrell, F. (1994). Cultural mistrust, opinions about mental illness, and Black students' attitudes towards seeking psychological help from white counselors. *Journal of counseling psychology, 41,* 378–385.

Steele, C. (1995). Black students live down to expectations. *The New York Times,* August 31, (p. 25).

Tatum, B. D. (1992). Talking about race, learning about racism: The application of racial identity development theory in the classroom. *Harvard Educational Review, 62,* 1–24.

Tarpley, N. (Ed.). (1995). *Testimony* (p. 1). Boston: Beacon Press.

West, C. (1993). *Race matters.* Boston: Beacon Press.

CHAPTER 4

# DUAL TRAUMATIZATION
## A Sociocultural Perspective

M. Maureen Walker

### INTRODUCTION

Although there is a reputable body of research on the long-term effects of childhood sexual abuse, there has been little study of the complex psychological sequelae of dual traumatization that reinforces patterns of disconnection for African Americans and other survivors of color. That is, the immediate and long-term effects of sexual trauma are well documented. In contrast, the trauma of institutionalized devaluation is less well studied. Similarly, there is little inquiry into work function issues as they affect abuse survivors.

Sanford (1990) discussed career issues of survivors, focusing on women whose competence at work was a strength that sometimes deteriorated to become "work addiction." Elaborating on this line of inquiry, Brandi (1989) identified work function themes that seem to characterize the career paths of abuse survivors: underfunctioning, sidetracked, competent but reenacting, and work competent. Many authors (Jordan, 1992; Miller, 1986; Stiver, 1990) have stressed the importance of relatedness and the destructive impact of violations (Miller, 1988) on successful adjustments in any social arena. However, the impact of disconnections and violations that occur within a context of sociopolitical oppression has received scant research attention (Brandi & Walker, 1993).

For African American women, sexual trauma occurs in a sociocultural context that implicitly condones not only the devaluation of women, but of nondominant racial groups as well. In other words, the dominant culture may function as the agent of disconnection and violation. Whether the violations are perpetrated by an individual or the dominant culture, the sequelae of the trauma are remarkably similar: dissociation, disempowerment, and shame (Jordan, 1992). Thus, the sexual and racial violations create a dual traumatization, informed by both the individual-familial and the sociocultural history of the survivor. Specific relational themes and reenactment patterns are associated with such traumatization.

## Relational Themes and Reenactment Patterns for African American Women in Therapy

Preliminary professional discussions seem to indicate that African American women in graduate schools are less likely than their White counterparts to identify career dysfunction as an initial counseling concern (Brandi & Walker, 1993). This observation must be regarded with caution, however, because apparent trends in presentation may be partly a function of biased demographics. It is reasonable to assume that African American women graduate students have gained such access precisely because of their ability to negotiate successfully the professional arena. However, as in the case study that follows, work and academic concerns may eventually surface during the course of treatment.

It appears that the professional competence of some of these women may be somewhat fragmented, and may initially function as a protective shield against painful and intrusive life problems. Moreover, the sequelae of dual traumatization may have paradoxical effects to the extent that defensively organized behaviors have apparent adaptive value for the survivor, her therapist, and her work organization. In these instances, the strengths and competencies of the individual potentially become the source of further violation.

The complex nature of dual traumatization suggests the development of particular relational themes and patterns of reenactment that surface as work function concerns. Some of these concerns include the dichotomization of work and personal life functioning, fusion of work and personal life functioning, mismanaged emotionality, and problematic authority relationships (Brandi & Walker, 1993). These relational themes and reenactment patterns may also surface within the therapy relationship (Singer, 1965). The case of Tulani, which appears later in this chapter, illustrates the prominence of these themes within the context of a three-year therapy relationship.

Despite the prevailing tendency to artificially dichotomize love and work as separate theoretical domains, there is abundant clinical evidence that such distinctions are ill-conceived. Herman (1992) suggests that the task of counseling psychology is to explore the complex interactions between work and internal psychological processes rather than to perpetuate the illusion of compartmentalized functioning. In counseling relationships with sexual abuse survivors, exploring the interactions between professional functioning and internal psychological processes leads inevitably to issues of boundary regulation, as both treatment theme and relational process. Specifically, the reenactment patterns evident in Tulani's professional relationships were apparent in her vacillation between overly permeable to overly rigid boundaries.

## TULANI

Hailing me from across the crowded cafeteria, Tulani seemed to epitomize all of the qualities attributed to young women careerists: confident, capable, and self-directed. A woman of dark skin color with luminous eyes, Tulani introduced herself as a first-year law student and talked about her planned strategy to achieve academic excellence and, not coincidentally, to gain the respect and admiration of her peers, faculty, and the legal profession at large. My subsequent contact with Tulani came as a counseling referral. A number of her professors found her alternately "brittle and ingratiating" when attempting to give her mid-term feedback. Two of them suggested that she seek counseling.

When Tulani first appeared at my office, she had no particular goals other than to "[access] me as a resource for her career and academic goals" and to comply with her professors' suggestions. As we worked during the first few sessions to discover how I might be "resourceful" to her, she began to somewhat dispassionately disclose remarkable fragments of her childhood history.

### Relevant Background Information

Born in the Virgin Islands, Tulani and her sister lived with various relatives when their mother left to find work in the northeastern United States, and their father deserted the family to move to Canada. From the age of 7 until she was reunited with her mother at the age of 14, Tulani had lived with both her maternal and paternal grandparents as well as an assortment of aunts and cousins. Beginning when she was about 8 years old until she left the island, she was sexually molested by "a lot of older cousins, uncles, and neighbors who were always in the house." She explained that she had never told anyone, because it would have immediately been assumed that "Islanders beat their children for not respecting adults" and because it was her fault for "being too cute."

Tulani recounted another experience of sexual assault after she had joined her mother. While she was visiting a friend in his home, he pinned her to the floor, hurt her very badly, and she "had sex with him." Although she was very clear that she was unwilling to be sexual with him and had resisted his attack, at no point during the session did she describe the encounter as rape. When she told her mother what had occurred, her mother asked if she had used "protection." After the attack, Tulani continued to make herself sexually available to the man in the hope that she could salvage a good relationship out of it. Furthermore, her religious upbringing required that she marry the man who sexually "knew" her, or risk social and moral damnation.

When describing her career aspirations, Tulani remarked, "I want the earth to shake when I move." Among her peers, she was sometimes labeled as "brash" and "overambitious." Tulani reported more than a few occasions of conflict and misunderstanding, typically with a sense of having been betrayed by both her peers and her managers. She focused her academic striving and career posturing on one overriding goal: to become "special" to her faculty and work supervisors. This preoccupation became particularly exaggerated in the presence of other African American women, a group with whom she was unrelentingly, yet covertly competitive.

Tulani's need to secure her "special" status in multiracial settings resulted in her seeking out assignments in which she had no interest and requesting feedback for which she had little use. Whatever the outcome of the assignment, her satisfaction and confidence were exceedingly short-lived. Typically, she described a vague sense of foreboding following the successful completion of a task. At other times, however, the project would somehow get "derailed," with Tulani at a loss to explain the failure.

Accomplishment for Tulani became associated with a threat of impending doom. Imes and Clance (1984) have described this experience as the imposter phenomenon; however, the intrusion of sociocultural factors along with evidence of severe family dysfunction suggests a more complex etiology. As Tulani began to explore more of her story, she described her status as the "favorite and smartest niece" of a great uncle in whose care she was often left. This relationship, however, was marked by sexual abuse, with frequent episodes of fondling and digital penetration. It was within the context of this relationship that Tulani could experience some sense of connection and importance within the family; therefore, she would sometimes seek her uncle out to play their "secret game." Unable to risk the losses that her "specialness" afforded her, Tulani assumed responsibility for the sexual violations which continued for six years. In addition to reinforcing her guilt for his abusing behaviors, the uncle also frequently reminded Tulani of her vulnerability at the hands of her "older, fiercer cousins" were it not for his "protection."

The translation of these childhood experiences into workplace behaviors was evidenced by Tulani's tendency to develop relationships with exploitative supervisors to gain protection from her peers. Given the oppressive dynamics of a sociocultural context that implicitly devalues women as well as people of color, African American women become a trigger group for workplace reenactment.

Tulani observed that she often attempted to get relational needs met through work competence. Although this dynamic is typically viewed as a sequela to sexual victimization, it was useful during the course of Tulani's treatment to also frame this pattern as an attempt to redress social violations. As a member of two socially devalued groups (i.e., African Americans and women), Tulani had been rewarded throughout her life for "putting her best face forward." This pattern included appearing to be needless, extraordinarily competent, and self-sufficient. The admiration she was thus able to achieve came to function as a substitute for intimacy and nurturance. Unable to distinguish between external validation and emotional connectedness, Tulani initiated relationships from the vantage point of strength and competence.

This initial presentation, however, was often short-lived. During the course of the relationships, her supervisors typically came to view her as "inappropriately needy." One example of her inability to determine and regulate interpersonal boundaries occurred during a summer clerkship. Feeling challenged by the intellectual intensity of the legal environment, Tulani identified a Black male attorney early on to serve as her mentor. Although she never explicitly communicated her needs and intentions to him, she made herself available to take on extra work assignments under his direction, accepted his sometimes "harsh" criticisms, and attended social functions where he would be present. She also confided some of her career aspirations to him. When Tulani did not receive an offer from the firm, she was stunned to learn that he did not support her candidacy.

In a later feedback session with the attorney, she learned that the decision had not been based on the quality of her work, but on a "sense of unease about her work demeanor." When Tulani pressed for details, she discovered that the attorney had shared a note she had written to him, thanking him for his "tough love" and for providing a "strong shoulder for her to lean on." Tulani explained the note as her attempt to find a connection in what she termed "an overwhelmingly White world." She said, "I just thought maybe he could be like a strong big brother." Instead, her behaviors were interpreted as flirtatious and unprofessional.

The debatable validity of the supervisor's assessment is less the point than the meaning of the disconnections for Tulani. On a very fundamental level, there was a disconnection between her internal reality and her manifest behavior. Moreover, the interpersonal and sociocultural violations served to not only exacerbate the disconnection, but also to undermine the integrity of her internal world. While debriefing the summer experience, Tulani began to question whether she was, in fact, "promiscuous." This self-labeling served only to further her self-alienation and alienation from other relational possibilities. Given the premise that a woman's sense of self may be organized around her ability to make and maintain relationships (Miller, 1986), it was somewhat predictable that Tulani would interpret these relational disconnections as evidence of her personal unworthiness.

## Therapeutic Considerations

The therapy relationship itself presented opportunities to examine both the genesis and the impact of relational disconnections. Tulani presented in therapy not as a person in need, but as a woman seeking to marshal available resources to attain certain academic goals. However, as she was leaving the first session, she turned and asked if I would hug her. My initial reaction of surprise gave way to a sense of discomfort as I pondered an appropriate response to her request. Sociocultural factors and familial considerations were central to my response. For example, during that same session, Tulani suggested that telling "family business" to a stranger was not only countercultural, but also disloyal. She spoke of strong ties to her family church and indicated that personal problems were often addressed by having a talk with the minister. Because I was neither a family member nor a minister, I became the "stranger" who was inviting her into acts of betrayal. She seemed to need a visible or symbolic display of closeness to justify the "transgression" of violating family and cultural proscriptions.

Other hypotheses about this unexpected request surfaced, which seemed entirely consistent with observations about the impact of growing up in nonrelational circumstances. Stiver (1990) contends that such circumstances create persons who become adept at effecting the appearance of connection where none exists. Given the magnitude of the disconnections Tulani experienced in childhood, this hypothesis seemed worthy of exploration.

While interpretations about family of origin pathology, therapeutic framing, and boundary regulation were entirely relevant, these were inadequate to explain subtle political undertones of our exchange. Consideration of racial, ethnic, and power differentials affected the resolution of this relationship issue. First, significant ethnic and class differences belied our racial commonality. However, the fact that we were two Black women attempting to achieve relationship within the context of a White, patriarchal organization posed definitional challenges to the therapeutic process.

To the extent that Tulani constructed psychological therapy as a

"White" enterprise, my role as an African American therapist was somewhat suspect. In addition, to the extent that I represented membership of a socially devalued group, the therapy that I might offer was somewhat suspect to Tulani from the beginning. At this and various other points throughout our work together, the pressing question for Tulani was could I be trusted to be "real." A more pointed version of that question might be: What does "real" mean for two Black women within the context of this suspect enterprise and the larger organization?

Also not to be dismissed was the racial identity development themes that belied many of our interactions over a three-year period. Helms (1990) maintains that any theories seeking to explain human functioning must address racial socialization. Most of the stage models of ethnic identity development presuppose both numerical and political minority status for persons of color (Corbett, 1994). Because Tulani spent many of her formative years in a culture where she was in the racial numerical majority, the extant models of racial identity development may be inadequate to explain the richly nuanced texture of her socialization experience. Nevertheless, these models of racial identity development and their subsequent elaborations do provide a useful heuristic; Tulani's development along the proposed dimensions defied easy categorization.

Cross (1991) has identified Pre-Encounter, Encounter, and Immersion as the earliest stages of racial socialization. While the racial naiveté typically associated with Pre-Encounter adaptation does not adequately explain or describe Tulani's functioning, she did exhibit much of the ambivalence generated by the internalization of dominant culture values.

All at once, Tulani could be admiring and critical of the access other people of color gained in predominantly White institutions. On the one hand, success to Tulani meant being highly regarded by powerful White people. To that end, she was often combative and competitive for such access, not only with her peers, but also with university staff and faculty who were Black. She would, however, work to curry favor with these individuals in order to develop networking possibilities.

On the other hand, Tulani construed significant access to mean racial betrayal. A period during which I felt an unusual degree of impatience and vexation toward her illustrates the effects of such ambivalence. As she was wont to do, Tulani approached me on a campus walkway and smilingly demanded to know "why Black faculty and administrators were unconcerned about Black students." My carefully worded response was at best a thin disguise of resentment I felt about her indictment of my colleagues and me. In subsequent exploratory conversations, it became clear that her accusations were based more on her own ambivalence about career success than in any heightened social consciousness or a specific disappointment with me.

Recalling the disdain with which her family had spoken of "social climbers," Tulani discussed the dual threat of sociocultural dislocation and relational disconnections that could attend her entry into the world of corporate law. What might have been interpreted solely as an individual's dysfunction, possibly with hints of borderline pathology, was in large part one young woman's best effort to negotiate the complexities of sociocultural marginality.

It is important to note that whether in work, academic, or counseling contexts, Tulani's initial presentation of confidence and competence is one with which supervisors, teachers, and therapists might easily collude. In professional settings, eager work behaviors seemed to serve both her and the organization well. Consistent with her self-description as a "low maintenance kid," Tulani presented as one who could give much and require little. Furthermore, the fact that authority figures triggered her power-appeasing behaviors perhaps accounted for some early career advances.

In more personal contexts, the facade of needlessness could gain for Tulani the kind of welcoming that she craved. At least at the outset of the relationship, this demeanor could serve mutually soothing functions as neither party had to address potentially shame-inducing relational needs. Whenever Tulani interacted with the larger social environment, both parties initially appeared to be getting what they wanted; there was the appearance of connection. The eventual outcome, however, was one in which both parties felt betrayed, as the actual relational contract undermined opportunities for professional growth and personal intimacy.

## The Politics of Anger

It is noteworthy that the politics of anger suffused each of the problematic encounters Tulani explored in therapy. The psychological literature provides many useful insights about anger and trauma. Understanding the dual traumatization of African American survivors, however, requires a recognition of anger as a sociopolitical reality in the lives of African American women. It is widely held that victims of chronic abuse learn to manage the anger of their perpetrators to ensure their own survival (Brandi, 1989; Courtois, 1988; Herman, 1992).

In research presented by Brandi and Walker (1993), African American survivors seemed more likely than their White counterparts to discuss experiences in which their anger is viewed as problematic by others. Indeed, one woman reported having to reassure her previous therapist that her awareness and indignation about social injustice did not mean she was rageful or racially militant. According to Tulani, allowing supervisors and faculty to detect her genuine reactions to perceived violations could only result in additional conflict. As she put it, "The first thing I have to do when I'm around these White people is to make them feel comfortable with me." This situation is not unlike those in which the victim has to manage the anxiety and emotionality of the perpetrator. The perpetrator, as well as the abusive, unprotective society, attempts to silence the victim by questioning the appropriateness, or worse, the sanity of her response to violation. This silencing serves to not only protect current power arrangements, but also to disconnect the victim from her own voice.

## Moving Toward Relational Connection and Self-Differentiation

The issues of relational connection and self-differentiation were dramatically demonstrated in the final months of Tulani's law school career. Tulani was offered a position with a prestigious firm in a large West Coast urban area. Shortly before she was scheduled to leave, she announced her intention to take along her younger sister, a 17-year-old with a history of truancy and minor criminal violations. Tulani's professed intent was to "be a role model for her so she can get her life together." She garnered additional support for her decision from various religious preachments such as: "To whom much is given, much is expected."

Further discussion revealed that Tulani's mother had suggested that it was her moral duty to help her sister, inasmuch as Tulani's success had probably "caused her sister's failure." It was also her mother's contention that she "deserved a break after all the sacrifices she had made" for Tulani. Stunned by the impracticality of the decision and angered by the shame-induced manipulations of the mother, I launched what might be most benignly described as a logic attack. This countertransferential intervention was the result of failure to attend to critical sociocultural variables.

That there exists significant cultural precedence for kin sponsorship is a fact that was overlooked in my eagerness to countervail Tulani's decision. According to Brice-Baker (1994), African Caribbean American women are often expected to use their success to enhance the lifestyle and economic well-being of other family members. Failure to seriously consider this cultural mandate would hold far more serious consequences than failure to achieve as defined by individualistic norms of self-actualization. Indeed, the extent to which Tulani could provide for other family members might in itself have been a measure of her success.

Consistent with her family history and with sociocultural expectations, she experienced herself in the role of "Woman as Trailblazer." In this role, the work accomplishments of the woman enable the social evolution of the family. This role was not dissimilar from the one assumed by her mother decades earlier when she left her country to gain economic security, and thereby to uplift the social status of her family. To interpret the mother's demand only in terms of its narcissistic content was to preclude adequate consideration of the deprivational effects of this sociocultural expectation on the mother (Jenkins, 1995).

It is noteworthy that the viewpoints of traditional psychotherapies might function to support this countertransferential process. Had Tulani immediately rejected her mother's expectation, her behavior would have probably been interpreted as appropriate assertiveness. However, this interpretation affords an inadequate reckoning of the import of the sociocultural dislocation and the relational disconnections that such assertiveness might have created.

Learning to choicefully define family relations is a developmental task that poses formidable challenges to any therapeutic work. When the client and therapist differ on key sociocultural dimensions, the potential for misunderstanding and disconnection within the therapeutic process is increased. In this instance, differences in our ethnic backgrounds (i.e., African American and African American Virgin Islander) contributed to markedly dissimilar definitions of self and family. For Tulani, attempting to define self without regard for the perceptions of important family members was unthinkable. In fact, without accountability to family and the blessings of family, whatever the level of apparent toxicity, achievement itself had little meaning. To defy her mother's importunate proposal was to risk disconnection from her family and from herself. The threat of such disconnection was far more real and urgent than some abstract and alien notions of self-differentiation.

A more productive intervention involved exploring Tulani's expectations, hopes, and goals for her family, and to explore how the accomplishment of those goals would affect her own valuation within the family. This kind of framing as an intermediate step enabled Tulani to evaluate the feasibility of her assigned role in her sister's life, and to develop a counterproposal with a greater likelihood for success.

Another issue of collective historical significance might be viewed as survivor's guilt. In Tulani's family, achievement and dominant culture access were both lauded and criticized. On the one hand, family members were continually reminded of their own social and economic devaluation. Social degradation was equated with personal worthlessness. Furthermore, admiration was professed as well as disparagement of persons who managed to escape degraded social conditions. Lipsky (1982) suggests that these dynamics are the result of internalized oppression, as some group members attack, invalidate, and criticize each other. This condition was exacerbated in

Tulani's family by intergenerational attempts to prevent any one person from getting "the big head" (i.e., thinking too highly of one's own successes).

Throughout her life, Tulani gained special attention at home, school, and church by having good grades, reciting the longest Bible verses, and winning scholarships to the mission schools. Along with this praise, however, she was taught to feel at fault for her sister's failure to achieve similar accolades. She reported a quote by her mother: "Your sister was never able to get love from your father and other people because they were all looking at you." In Tulani's view, her success had come at the cost of her sister's failure as well as her own degradation. For all of her vaulting academic and career aspirations, actual achievement of her goals was an intensely conflictual experience.

One way that Tulani held onto a view of herself as a good person was by professing a rather stringent religiosity. Whatever the circumstances in her life, whether benign or devastating, Tulani responded by assigning religious meaning to it. For example, she was unable for 10 years to name her assault as rape, in spite of the continued sexual and emotional abuse. She interpreted the first attack as a sign that the man was meant to be her husband because he had "carnal knowledge" of her. Furthermore, it was her Christian duty to teach him "the ways of the righteous." Similarly, she believed that failure to attempt the reformation of her sister was "a sin and a shame."

Religious practices that promote such self-constructions are now being termed spiritual abuse (Beatie, 1992). This language helps to illuminate a crucial area of developmental vulnerability. It does not, however, account for the apparent adaptive value of spiritual rootedness for historically oppressed people. For many such people, religiosity may serve as a buffer against painful experiences. Additionally, it is often through religious teaching that oppressed people create hopeful interpretations of their lives in the face of sustained, collective degradation and destruction. Nevertheless, to the extent that such teaching is based on a standard of morality that is dehumanizing, it is toxic.

In Tulani's life, the fundamentalist religious interpretations had in themselves become oppressive. Therefore, the goals of therapeutic exploration necessarily included recognizing the value of religious faith as well as renegotiating the tension between resignation and acceptance. This task requires the therapist to actively engage the client, exploring the impact of religious beliefs on life decisions. Lewis (1993) defines this process as a psychospiritual intervention and contends that treatment of adult Black women necessarily includes this dimension. Although it is widely believed that psychologists tend to avoid this area of practice, neglect of religiosity and spirituality prevent the client from resolving crucial existential dilemmas.

## Implications for Therapists

Working with Tulani during a three-year period was nothing less than a panoramic experience. It not only provided insights into the effects of dual traumatization, but also into the complex relational processes through which many women of African ancestry create and interpret meaning. These meanings in turn inform and define the course and the conduct of the therapeutic process. Of particular importance are implications for the use and misuse of traditional psychological nomenclature. Because traditional nosologies are developed without regard for the sociocultural and political context of the person, they may be inadequate to illuminate the individual's experience, particularly when that experience may run counter to dominant culture realities.

The cultural blindness of traditional nosologies minimizes and invalidates the perceptions and constructions of persons of color in the United States. Failure to comprehend the complexities of experience results in disconnection and repeats microaggressions and violations of a dominating, race-based culture. Therefore, the therapist must attend to the psychological ramifications of an abusive society. While the process must encompass sociocultural factors as focus and context, the therapist and client must also attend to issues of more discrete psychological wounding. In other words, the therapist must work through whatever tendency there may be to become overwhelmed and distracted by ethnocultural differences.

Another manifestation of such abuse is the occasional lapse into exoticism, whereby the therapist overromanticizes the societal mandates of the client's native culture. In the case of Tulani, unquestioned allegiance to many of these norms might have resulted in severely intropunitive behavior. For example, the adaptive value of a belief in self-efficacy is overridden by exaggerated attribution of success or failure to personal agency. In the event of a successful endeavor, such attributions undermine the enabling relational contexts. In the event of a failure, these attributions can lead to internal disconnections, as the person mercilessly chastises herself for perceived deficiencies without accounting for the effects of systematic deprivation by a dominating society.

The generic admonition that the therapist must attend to his or her own process takes on crucial importance as well. Because therapists who are trained in the United States are inundated with the effects of race-based socialization, there is a high probability that they have internalized much of the shame that attends racial issues. This shame response may be activated within the therapeutic relationship and manifest in countertransferential interventions. Incorporating sociocultural perspectives into the practice of psychological therapy requires attention to differences that have social consequences and exploring how those consequences affect the construction of meaning and relationship to the life of the client.

## SUMMARY

Good psychological practice requires attention to the sociopolitical processes and sociocultural perspectives that inform identity formation and relational development. For women of African ancestry in the United States, the impact of psychological wounding is complicated by the usually cumulative and often traumatic effects of systematic devaluation by a dominating society. This multivalent experience is described as dual traumatization. The effects of dual traumatization are sinuously layered and evident in personal and professional arenas of life functioning. Aspects of personal and professional functioning cannot and should not be discretely compartmentalized. Defensively organized behaviors that were once adaptive are likely to eventually sabotage opportunities for optimal relational growth. Because multiracial settings in the U.S. are typically fraught with the effects of long-standing power imbalances, these settings can serve as potent targets for behavioral reenactment.

Traditional psychological nomenclature partially describes obvious consequences of dual traumatization. However, these classifications are inadequate to explain the more complex and nuanced phenomenology of the survivor's experience. This point is often illustrated via the regulation of boundaries between the client and significant persons in her relational context. Although inadequate boundary regulation is an often cited feature in many psychological problems, it is atypical for discussions of etiology to include the political and sociocultural contexts in which these adaptations are generated. Without this understanding, the client is likely to be overpathologized, as attributions tend to focus exclusively on characterological deficiencies.

As the case of Tulani illustrates, it is critically important that sociocultural perspectives include attention to the effects of class and ethnicity as well as gender and race. In this case, the client and therapist are same race women with different ethnic and class backgrounds. Too often, the therapist is inclined to gloss over these points of diversity in an effort to bond (Brice-Baker, 1994). Should this relational dynamic occur, it becomes in effect a reenactment of wounded relationships as both the client and the therapist join in the appearance of relationship rather than actual intimacy. Each source of diversity represents an opportunity for critical learning and relational growth.

Finally, psychotherapeutic practice which does not account for sociocultural diversity limits not only the client's growth, but also the therapist's opportunity for self-understanding. Traditional nosologies and interpretations may be used to support countertransferential processes, thereby undermining the prospect of mutual growth in relation.

## REFERENCES

Beatie, M. (1992). *Codependent no more.* Center City, NM: Hazelden Institute.

Brandi, E. (1989). Soothing: A guiding concept for the psychotherapy of trauma victims. Paper presented at annual meeting of the American Psychological Association, New Orleans.

Brandi, E., & Walker, M. (1993). Career adjustments of trauma survivors: Case study comparisons. *Workplace issues of women survivors.* Symposium conducted at Radcliffe Career Services, Cambridge, MA.

Brice-Baker, J. R. (1994). West Indian women of color: The Jamaican woman. In L. Comas-Díaz & B. Greene (Eds.), *Women of color.* (pp. 139–160) New York: Guilford.

Corbett, M. (1994). *Racial identity development and personality structure.* Annual cross-cultural roundtable in counseling and psychotherapy. Symposium conducted by Columbia University School of Continuing Education, New York, February.

Courtois, C. (1988). *Healing the incest wound.* New York: W. W. Norton.

Cross, W. E., Jr. (1991). *Shades of black: Diversity in African American identity.* Philadelphia: Temple University Press.

Helms, J. E. (Ed.). (1990). *Black and white racial identity: Theory, research, and practice.* Westport, CT: Praeger.

Herman, J. (1992). *Trauma and recovery.* Cambridge: Harvard University Press.

Imes, S. A., & Clance, P. R. (1984). Treatment of the imposter phenomenon in high-achieving women. In Claire Brody (Ed.), *Women therapists working with women.* New York: Springer.

Jenkins, Y. M. (1995). Personal communication.

Jordan, J. V. (1992). Challenges to connection: The traumatizing society. *Women learning from women.* Symposium conducted by Harvard Medical School and The Stone Center, Boston, April.

Lewis, S. (1993). Cognitive-behavioral approaches. In L. Comas-Díaz & B. Greene (Eds.), *Women of color* (pp. 223–238). New York: Guilford.

Lipsky, S. (1982). *Internalized oppression.* Unpublished manuscript.
Miller, J. B. (1986). *Toward a new psychology of women.* Boston: Beacon Press.
Miller, J. B. (1988). Connections, disconnections, and violations. *Works in progress, 33.* Wellesley, MA: Wellesley College Stone Center Working Papers Series.
Sanford, L. (1990). *Strong at the broken places.* New York: Avon Books.
Singer, E. (1965). *Key concepts in psychotherapy.* New York: Basic Books.
Stiver, I. P. (1990). Dysfunctional families and wounded relationships: Part I. *Works in progress, 41.* Wellesley, MA: Wellesley College Stone Center Working Papers Series.

CHAPTER 5

# ENGAGEMENT OF AN ASIAN AMERICAN WOMAN
## Cultural and Psychological Issues

Jenai Wu

This chapter integrates issues in women's psychology, particularly those related to mother-daughter relationships, the cultural influences in such relationships, and relevant factors that were considered for engaging a young Korean American woman in therapy. There is no attempt here to draw an idiopathic correlation between culture and the clinical issues presented. Such a correlation would not only be presumptuous but also offensive. Rather, in the spirit of this book, the fluidity of categories and characterizations between culture and psychodynamics are suggested. An integrative understanding of culture and psychology can enhance the mental health practitioner's understanding of a client. However, as the following case composite illustrates, neither culture nor psychology is a sufficient basis for definitive conclusions. Instead, both variables may influence perspectives that enrich one another.

Especially emphasized in this chapter are the culturally determined role of women and its effect on individual psychology and adaptation. Attention will also be paid to cultural differences in affective expression and management, as well as the effect of cultural differences on the therapeutic alliance.

The following case study, a composite, is drawn from several real-life clinical situations.

## TINA
### Initial Presentation

Tina was a 23-year-old Korean American woman, a second-year biology graduate student at an urban university. She was referred to therapy by the dean's office after she had been caught cheating on an exam. After she had been initially screened by the counseling center on campus, Tina was referred to a local mental health clinic where she was interviewed and assigned to work with me.

When Tina arrived for the first session, her unbound hair covered half of her face. Although her eyes were open, they appeared closed at times and half-closed at others. Her speech was difficult to hear, and a half-smile was fixed on her face for much of the initial hour. She desultorily mentioned a variety of problems in her life, but it was difficult to make sense of her complaints. Tina's sentences tended to trail off, her associations were disconnected, and her speech tended to obscure rather than offer a clear description of her situation. Several times during the hour I suppressed yawns. I did not mention her cheating, nor did she. The risk of forcing the issue did not seem worth the slow, patient work that would be involved in gaining her cooperation and investment in the work at hand.

In fragments, I gathered that Tina lived in a dorm with two other women; one was an Asian woman from China, and the other was Caucasian American. Tina spoke of both women with bitterness. Themes of envy and covetousness also become apparent. She particularly devalued the Asian roommate. For example, in the session after the Asian roommate slept through a class following an all-nighter, Tina critically examined her aspirations of being admitted to medical school and concluded "she doesn't have a chance."

Tina also spoke at length about Charles, a man she was dating who was eight years older than she. They had been involved off and on for two years. Although Charles had wooed and pursued Tina when they first met, rather disappointedly she found him to be ungiving and puzzling throughout most of their relationship. As Tina described their relationship, it became painfully obvious that the relationship was extremely one-sided. For example, she described her frequent and frantic efforts to get in touch with Charles, leaving him numerous messages at home, and trying to reach him at his office. Invariably, Charles would not respond to Tina's overtures and she spoke to him only if she succeeded in penetrating his rebuff by reaching him directly. In such instances, Tina would flay him with accusations concerning his lack of availability, his nonresponsiveness, and her confusion about his treatment of her.

The latter half of the relationship involved a pattern where Tina and Charles would meet after she had harangued him into agreeing to see her. They had not gone out for a while. Instead, in the past year or so they would meet at his apartment where stormy emotional evenings would end in sex. Tina would leave these episodes feeling terrible about herself, emotionally battered yet strangely comforted by the idea that at a minimum she still "had" him in some way. These episodes, which occurred once every month or two, usually led to brief episodes of binging and purging.

Even though Tina clearly displayed a love of biology that gained her respect, her school performance was spotty. One particularly supportive professor who liked her very much encouraged Tina to seek help. The same professor encouraged her to strive for fellowships and to submit research and internship proposals, while pointing her toward opportunities. Although Tina accepted each of these appreciatively, she never followed through. There were semesters when she performed poorly in classes, getting through most of the semester successfully, only to wreck her performance and grades at the end by not showing up for exams or doing inexplicably poorly on material that was expected to have come easily to her. Although generally reliable, Tina angered her professors by the occasional debacle of not showing up for an important field trip or other activities. Therefore, she had twice been threatened with losing her funding if she continued on this path.

## Initial Formulation

When I first met Tina, she struck me as a seriously depressed young woman. Her emotional turbulence, low self-esteem, and self-abusive tendencies (e.g., school performance problems; turbulent, dissatisfying love relationship) were deeply troubling, and seemed characteristic of women who had experienced serious deprivation or abuse very early in their development. Tina seemed unaware of the severity of her problems. In fact, the most difficult part of the therapy was influencing her to acknowledge her need for help. Instead, Tina wanted to flee after the first session and subsequent ones with the proviso that harder work and greater success at her studies would solve her problems more readily than therapy. She emphasized that she had to resolve her problems on her own.

My efforts to connect with Tina were difficult, given her tendencies for rapidly shifting emotions that ranged from the distancing and isolation of affect to punitive anger directed at herself and me. Then she would cast aspersions on the therapeutic process by referring to its "uselessness," by calling it a "sham," "nothing but talk," "no better than talking to a wall," or "not worth all that money." She would alternate between such aspersions by bitterly blaming herself for her troubles (e.g., "If I just did my work, I wouldn't be making such a mess of everything."). As Tina became increasingly aware of the magnitude of her self-hate and low self-esteem, she would alternate between viciously attacking herself and bitter, inconsolable sobs.

### Relevant Background Information

By the final session, I knew very little about Tina's personal background. She had insisted on talking about her current problems and how to address her immediate needs. Even though I suspected from the beginning that her problems might have been intimately related to her early background and family relationships, from the beginning she had given me "off-limits" signals whenever there was a hint of exploring this.

I have found that lack of detail about family relationships is not unusual for many Asian clients, since cultural values not only forbid discussion of family secrets outside the family, but moreover family secrets are left unspoken within the family itself. To complain about one's parents or to reveal that there are problems in the family would present an almost moral dilemma, given the priority that privacy is given to family matters in general. Therefore, Tina staved off questions about her personal background with vague generalizations, avoidance, and "freezing," an uncomfortable silence and constriction of affect that warned me to back off. Yet, over time I learned some relevant details about Tina and her family.

Her father had been separated from the family for several years due to immigration issues. Therefore, Tina grew up between ages 7 and 11 without her father at home. Her mother struggled at numerous menial jobs to support the family with two children. Meanwhile, there was little communication from her husband, so she relied on relatives to find out his intentions. When Tina met her father again, she felt as though she had never bonded with him. He was remote and noncommunicative, and she watched her mother's anxious futile attempts to reach him. Although he assumed an authoritarian stance with his wife and children, Tina perceived that her father made more attempts to relate to her younger brother.

Among the circumstances that disturbed the household most were her father's comings and goings without any attempt at communication. For example, he would leave the house or come home late from work, without saying where he was going or where he had been, but if there was no dinner when he came home, he would become angry. At times Tina and her brother witnessed their father beating their mother. Their mother would turn on them with harsh words when she had been ill-treated by her husband. Most painful of all, Tina recalled her perception of her mother's raw vulnerability and inability to protect herself.

### Therapeutic Engagement

From the beginning Tina was a client for whom the therapeutic "holding" seemed tenuous. My initial challenge was to establish a therapeutic connection with her. While I do not necessarily consider it my job to "hook" a client, I became invested in engaging Tina in therapy for several reasons. First, it was apparent through her obvious emotional pain, self-dissatisfaction, and academic difficulties, that she was in considerable distress. Second, I saw a woman who seemed to be functioning significantly below her potential and even seemed to sabotage possibilities for her life much of the time. Third, it appeared that Tina had no awareness of being stuck in a self-destructive pattern. With sufficient work, it appeared possible that she could redirect the course of her life.

My second challenge was to motivate Tina to get better. That is to say, although she would speak of feeling badly about getting into trouble and wished she was performing better, she seemed to be troubled by an attachment to pain and shame. Or as painful as failure and sabotaging herself were, there was something about these states that seemed so charged and meaningful to her that she anxiously gravitated around them, akin to the proverbial moth and flame. Therefore, to the extent that therapy might seriously threaten the status quo, I suspected that Tina was not sure she wanted to commit to it. Consequently, she vacillated between turbulent episodes of venting or distancing, and ambivalence about whether or not she wanted to pursue therapy.

My third challenge was to keep the therapeutic alliance open. At times our alliance felt fragile, especially when Tina suspected me of causing her to blame and to criticize herself. She assumed I had a negative opinion of her, and her sense of shame threatened to engulf us both in its unforgivingness. Although I explored Tina's view of me as critical and angry at her, she was not particularly convinced by my efforts.

My fourth challenge involved ensuring payment for therapy. Each visit was so fraught with turbulence and crisis, payment issues were obscured in confusion. How financial issues are managed in therapy often symbolizes internal dynamics of emotional neediness and efforts at external restitution. Therefore, since deprivation seemed so essential to Tina's subjective state, I was attuned to financial dynamics between us. This required me to respond sufficiently to her need to talk about whatever she liked, without allowing the therapy to succumb to insufficient boundaries concerning fees.

**The Psychotherapeutic Process**

Tina's ambivalence about the therapy was evident from the beginning. After she was referred, some five weeks passed before she called for an appointment. She arrived quite late for her first few appointments, and then had difficulty leaving when the hour was over. One out of two of the first ten appointments was missed for one reason or another. Even though Tina responded favorably to mild confrontation about her attendance, her agreement to change this did not reassure me. Somehow I felt that some vital part of her was missing in the interaction.

The tension mounted when Tina came in with stories that suggested self-sabotage. I began to feel helpless and under siege by the severity of her symptoms on the one hand, yet observed no substantial indication that she really wanted to work on her problems. Tina talked about stealing food from the cafeteria, skipping classes, and copying problem sets from classmates. Her affect was increasingly and openly dysphoric. She wept, pulled at her hair, rocked back and forth, and let loose a torrent of verbal self-abuse. Simultaneously, weekly accounts sent to me by the billing office revealed that she was not paying her bill to the clinic. When I broached this subject while questioning her investment in her therapy, she looked at me as if I'd said something inappropriate; indeed, I felt sheepish. Tina dismissed the subject with an explanation about insurance processing, and then skipped the next two appointments. When she returned for the next meeting, she talked a great deal about her frustration with therapy and was debating whether or not to return. As justification, Tina said she thought she could probably manage her problems on her own. Therefore, she thanked me for helping her so well and pensively enumerated how I had helped.

For the summer, Tina considered the possibility of going on a field internship with her favored professor. Yet, she feared spending so much time with the professor, since it could become evident beyond a doubt that she did not deserve his esteem.

Tina's final session was punctuated by painful tears and intense self-deprecation. It occurred to me that her control over negative self-appraisals and her tendency to externalize her problems were both important mechanisms for preventing her discomfort from becoming overwhelming. Once again I offered feedback that she was doing an admirable job of managing, despite all the stress she was feeling. Tina accepted this feedback with characteristic argument, enumerating the ways in which she was not doing a good job at all. It seemed important for her not to overtly accept praise.

Since Tina had terminated sessions for the time being with a plan to focus on her schoolwork, it was uncertain whether she would return. I was left feeling somewhat ineffectual, as if my help hadn't been worth much and as though I had done little for her. These feelings paralleled Tina's sense of worthlessness. It was somewhat surprising five months later when she left urgent phone messages for me everywhere. When I did reach Tina by phone, she could only sob; I arranged to see her immediately. Eventually she revealed that her boyfriend had terminated their relationship. His continued unavailability had been the source of ongoing anger and unhappiness for Tina. Her attempts to force an ultimatum had been unsuccessful. He had responded by telling her that he was no longer interested in her and was dating someone else, which left Tina feeling hurt and humiliated.

At this point in our work Tina revealed the relevant background information about her family that was offered earlier in this chapter. I wondered what would follow this openness and breakthrough. Her identification with her mother seemed to be the source of her low self-esteem and chronic self-sabotage. Tina's own insight into the need to protect and keep her mother company, in the context of her mother's alienation and suffering, was vital to her psychic growth. However, since Tina did not seem to value her own growth and progress, she seemed to have a rough road to travel. For her to feel better and improve might have represented a form of abandonment of her mother.

Therefore, I highlighted the conflict for her, which seemed to be a terrible dilemma between getting on with her life while feeling sorry for her mother and wanting to help her. Furthermore, I emphasized that the alienation and coldness she experienced from her boyfriend were all too familiar, based on what she had shared about her family. I also seized upon the opportunity to say that I could now understand why it was difficult for her to believe that she deserved good things.

Tina's vulnerability during this session left me feeling more connected to her than ever before. The most important progress in the therapy seemed to come next when Tina decided that she did, indeed, need help. She expressed the desire to make arrangements that would make therapy consistently available to her and wanted to start again after returning from the field trip with her favored professor.

## DISCUSSION

In many ways, Tina's personality and dynamics of her therapy do not significantly differ from those of any other client in and from similar circumstances. Severe depression, self-hate, and self-sabotage are by no means the exclusive domain of Asian clients; nor is ambivalence about therapy unique to this population. Furthermore, the intensity of Tina's pain, her rather desperate attempts to control intense feelings through action, and the nature of her defenses are not culture-specific. However, this case study does call attention to circumstances that are sometimes characteristic of Asian clients and their families.

As mentioned earlier, it is common for Asian clients to be reluctant about revealing details about family life. Obviously, such material has usefulness in the therapeutic context. Yet, shame and loyalty issues influence a cultural taboo against disclosure of intimate family secrets and any indication that all is not ideal within the family. Therefore, insufficient information may be provided to the practitioner to facilitate culturally competent treatment planning. This seemed to explain Tina's initial response to inquiries about her family. For this reason, her sudden disclosure under duress caused concern about how she would be affected by the likelihood of her wish to suppress feelings and to flee further treatment.

In view of the premium placed on the containment of turbulent emotions in many Asian cultures, Tina's parents' difficulty with expressing such emotions is not unusual. In their view, the therapeutic process could not be trusted or valued. Therefore, while Tina and her family seemed to suffer from strong and painful emotions, these were largely minimized or dismissed. Even if someone of Tina's generation has been acculturated to believe that therapy might be a good thing, needing one's parents to fund it may impose an additional barrier.

In cultures guided by Confucian philosophy, an Asian woman's cultural identity is defined by her family relationships. This involves her supportive and subordinate role with her husband as well as the roles of nurturer and caretaker for her husband and children. The male role is defined by authority and responsibility. Therefore, in many Asian families gender-based values are culturally fixed and ubiquitous, instilled early in life and reinforced perpetually thereafter. The birth of male children tends to be celebrated, while the birth of females may be denigrated. Whether the message is expressed subtly or blatantly, self-deprecation may become an integral part of an Asian woman's gender identity, the legacy of generations.

Tina struggled with her mother's precarious feeling of self-worth as well as her own. She pondered to what extent her own mistreatment was appropriate, since her mother had tolerated such. Therefore, Tina seemed to identify with her mother's efforts to develop self-esteem and a personal sense of effectiveness in their family over the years; this was accompanied by a pervasive sense of guilt at times. This does not necessarily suggest that Tina's domestic history is either a prototype for Asian American women of her generation or even prevalent for this group. Yet, her initial concerns, background history, and the status of women in Asian culture seem to bear a connection.

Conflict for Tina may have occurred as a function of her eschewal of the negative, powerless, and feminine role of her mother, and her aspiration to succeed. She may have feared abandoning her mother to unhappiness, while sabotaging her own goals (e.g., relationships with unavailable men, academic difficulties).

## CONCLUSION

The process of engaging Tina in therapy involved powerful cultural dynamics combined with powerful psychological issues. Such a complex blend is not specific to students of Asian ancestry but are most important in the early to middle phases of therapy. From a cultural perspective, engaging the Asian student may at times be challenged by minimization of the need for help, the suppression of intense emotion, family loyalty, and reliance on hard work and achievement as solutions to emotional difficulties.

From a psychological perspective, an important theme in Tina's clinical presentation was her poor self-esteem, which was manifested by punitive attacks on herself and self-sabotage. These dynamics may have been influenced in part by her identification with a "culturally negative" mother, as defined by Yuen and Depper (1986).

Overall, this case composite illustrates that culturally defined gender roles may affect psychodynamics in identifiable ways. Furthermore, this composite suggests that specific communication patterns and styles of affective expression, influenced by culture, have an impact on the therapist's ability to engage the client in the early stages of therapy and to maintain a connection thereafter.

## REFERENCE

Yuen, L. M., & Depper, D. S. (1986). Fear of failure in women. In E. Rothblum & E. Cole (Eds.). *Treating women's fears of failure* (pp. 21–40). New York: Haworth Press.

## SUGGESTED READING

Mace, D., & Mace, V. (1960). *Marriage east and west.* New York: Doubleday.
Person, E. S. (1982). Women working: Fears of failure, deviance, and success. *Journal of the American Academy of Psychoanalysis, 10,* 7–84.
Showalter, E. (1985). *The female malady: Women, madness and English culture, 1830–1980.* New York: Penguin Books.

CHAPTER 6

# CULTURE, SEXUALITY, AND SHAME
A Korean American Woman's Experience

Connie S. Chan

## BACKGROUND AND INTRODUCTION

As a Chinese American woman clinical psychologist, I sometimes get referrals from other mental health professionals looking for a clinician who is bilingual or bicultural. A potential therapist's knowledge of Asian cultures and sensitivity to the communication styles of Asian Americans are often essential components for Asian and Asian American students who consider entering psychotherapy. Since much of my research and writing are about psychological issues of Asian American women, particularly in the areas of sexuality and identity, I was not surprised when Kaya was referred to me by a psychologist who had read some of my articles.

## KAYA

The psychologist had sought out Asian American mental health professionals for this referral because she hoped that greater awareness and knowledge of cultural issues might help to establish greater rapport with this shy young woman. The clinician felt that the client's issues were strongly influenced by her familial and cultural background as well as her family's immigrant experience, and that my own experience as a bilingual/bicultural immigrant to this country would provide me with additional insight into this student's situation.

### Presenting Concern

I was given little initial information about Kaya's presenting concern or about her background. When I first interviewed Kaya, she described her concerns in this way: "I am having trouble sleeping and eating. I often have nightmares and wake up in a complete panic. Although I feel lonely and isolated, I find myself avoiding being around people, including friends." Kaya, a senior with excellent grades, had focused career interests, and no history of difficulties that would have brought her to the attention of any professors or college personnel. The following summary is based on our therapeutic work during a five-month period.

## Relevant Background Factors

An immigrant from Korea, Kaya had moved to Chicago with her family when she was 14 years old. While her parents pursued professional careers as engineers, Kaya and her younger sister worked hard at being successful in high school, achieving outstanding academic and extracurricular records. Kaya remembered always being busy and trying to be well prepared in her high school classes and activities. As a result, she appeared to others as being unflappable, poised, and successful. Although she did not feel she was popular or even well liked, Kaya believed that she was respected by most of the teachers and students. Also, she fondly recalled a few close friends who cared about her, and with whom she shared some fun times.

Kaya described her main strengths as her intellectual abilities and her motivation to work long and hard to be among the best of students at her school. She was also proud of her abilities to ignore her homesickness for Korean life and to take adjusting to a new culture and language in stride.

Upon her family's arrival in Chicago, Kaya had decided that because this was going to be her permanent home, she was going to make the best of it. She rarely let herself feel the longing to return or the pain of missing the friends or country left behind. Kaya had felt this urge to move on with her life so strongly that even when, at age 19, she was offered the chance to return to Korea for a summer visit with a college study group on full scholarship, she declined to go. Kaya recalled being sorely tempted and wanting to return to Korea very badly, but denied herself the trip with the rationale that she needed to stay and work to earn money for college. She confided, however, that the real reason was that it would have been too painful to sample a taste of her country, family, and friends once again, only to have to leave again after two months. To experience the loss and the readjustment all over again upon her return to the United States would have been too painful.

After graduating as salutatorian of her high school class and being awarded a full scholarship to an Ivy League college, Kaya found summer employment as a receptionist at a doctor's office where a friend of the family worked.

## The Therapeutic Process

In the course of her therapy, Kaya described what she experienced that summer to be the defining experience of her life, and the precipitant of her current difficulties. It was this incident that was the focus of treatment. Kaya felt that she would never progress until she could understand what happened, why she behaved as she did, and whether she should do anything to confront the perpetrator.

Kaya told me that several weeks into the summer, her former employer, a physician, a middle-aged Korean American man, began to express an interest in her. Initially, he inquired about her education, interests, friends, and family, and then asked her to join him for lunches outside of the office. Kaya was flattered by the attention and even looked forward to having lunch with Dr. K once or twice a week. His interest in her seemed to be of a fatherly nature, and she rather enjoyed talking with him about herself and her interests, matters her own father rarely spoke to her about.

After several weeks of lunches, Dr. K invited Kaya to attend a piano recital of a prominent Korean musician on a Friday evening; he explained that his wife would be out of town and he had two tickets. Kaya was pleased to be invited and accepted readily, telling her family of her plans. After work that Friday, Dr. K asked Kaya if she would like to have a drink with him in his office before going to the concert. Kaya declined an alcoholic drink, but did agree to have a soft drink while Dr. K had a glass of wine. Shortly after finishing her soft drink, Kaya began to feel dizzy. Afraid that she was going to pass out, Kaya lay down on the waiting room couch. The next thing she could remember, Dr. K was kissing her and lying on top of her; the room seemed to be spinning. Kaya described the scene as being very surreal to her. She felt as though she was floating in the room as Dr. K took off her clothes, kissed her, caressed her, and forced his fingers and then his penis inside her.

During the course of her therapy, Kaya was compelled to relive and remember this scene over and over, as if she were looking for something which might explain her behavior and Dr. K's as well. Not only did she not feel afraid while he was doing this to her, but Kaya felt some enjoyment and excitement along with physical pain. She then fell asleep and awoke two hours later, alone in the waiting room. Kaya found a note from Dr. K, expressing his hope that she would feel better and informing her that he had gone to the concert without her since she appeared to be ill. At first Kaya could not tell if what she remembered was a dream or if the kissing, caressing, and penetration had actually occurred. But she remembered the taste of his tongue in her mouth, the press of his body against hers on the couch, and felt the aching pain between her legs.

Kaya decided that Dr. K had forced himself on her while she was in a drugged state, probably from something he had put into her drink. She remembered feeling disgusted, dirty, and somehow excited, all at the same time. Kaya went home that evening and told her parents nothing about what had happened. Instead, she told them she had felt a little ill after work and slept on the office couch until she felt well enough to take the subway home. She denied ever attending the concert. Kaya remembered how calm she felt as she talked to her parents, and how she almost seemed to be outside of her body watching herself that night and the rest of the weekend.

The following Monday, Kaya felt anxious about how Dr. K would react to her when she came into the office. However, he acted as though nothing had happened. He inquired about her health and told her he was sorry that she had missed an excellent concert. Kaya felt bewildered and questioned her own sense of reality, but said nothing about the incident to anyone. That week, Dr. K took her to lunch as usual and behaved in his usual fatherly manner. During her final four weeks in the office before leaving for school, Dr. K's "normal" fatherly behavior continued.

Kaya felt as if she was an actress playing a role that required her to be calm on the outside even though she was filled with inner turmoil; this was a dissonant blend of guilt, confusion, disgust, and even desire. On her last day at work, Dr. K took her out to lunch again and told her that she had been a great asset to his office. He even invited her to return to work to him the next summer. Then he gave her a small gift of a wallet with $25, to "help with college expenses," and shook her hand goodbye.

Kaya went home that evening and cried quietly in her bed for most of the night. She continued to question her sense of reality and wondered if she had imagined the entire incident. She felt confused and ashamed; her chest was tight with pain. Kaya felt as if her entire childhood and sense of innocence had been taken from her and that she would never be able to trust anyone again. She never returned to Dr. K's office.

Kaya completed three more years of college before going to the counseling center and requesting a therapist. During our initial interview, I was the first person she told of the experience with Dr. K.

**A Retrospective Analysis of Treatment**

During the first few sessions, Kaya was eager, even compelled, to describe the events of that evening three years before and to search for explanations for her behavior and feelings. She wanted to determine to what extent she was responsible and to what extent Dr. K was responsible. It was as if she could place the various factors on a scale and assign numbers for blame.

When I tried to focus Kaya's attention on how the experience with Dr.

K affected her current relationships, she offered little information. By her own description, she had primarily kept to herself, studying and working constantly. Until recently, Kaya had been too busy to think about anything else. Because she spent more of her vacation time working at school than at home for family gatherings, she had become more distant from her family. Kaya had no close college friends, nor did she have a significant romantic relationship. When I pointed out to her that she had become more isolated at college than during high school, she shrugged and seemed resigned to this.

It gradually became clear to me that what brought Kaya into treatment was that she was nearing graduation and had just been accepted to the graduate program of her choice. She had achieved her goal at college, that is, entry to a career. All of her hard work had paid off, but the momentary "break in the action" provided a window into her inner turmoil which had previously been sealed off. A highly defended individual, Kaya held her emotions firmly in check with a busy work schedule. Cultural norms and expectations strongly reinforced her defense mechanisms.

For example, within Korean American culture it was perfectly acceptable to be quiet, to express little or no emotion, and to have acquaintances, but no intimate friends. Her family thought that her lack of openness about her life at college was common for "American" students, while her peers assumed that Kaya's self-containment and emotional restraint were part of her Korean upbringing. To some extent, both perspectives had merit, but Kaya's denial and guardedness began to break down just before she was about to move on to graduate school. It seemed to me that she was also experiencing symptoms of post-traumatic stress disorder, with her sense of splitting off from herself and sometimes feeling as though she was "above everything" watching herself interacting with others below. Consequently, she felt depressed, found it difficult to sleep, and felt a need to avoid contact with others.

During the five-month period that Kaya and I worked together, I allowed her to tell me her secret story again and again. I believed that the telling and retelling would give her a measure of relief. Furthermore, it would enable us to understand the meanings of silent periods in our work together and how her loss of trust had affected her relationships since she had worked for Dr. K.

After about five sessions focused on the assault and her responses to it, Kaya began to get in touch with her anger at Dr. K, particularly how enraged she was that he had taken advantage of her. With gentle prodding, I helped Kaya to see how she had been betrayed by a fatherly authority figure, someone from her own culture whom she had highly respected and trusted. She began to explore how her feelings for Dr. K and the anger she felt toward her father overlapped; although her father was caring, he had never demonstrated an interest in her. Initially, Dr. K seemed to be the type of father for whom she had longed. Yet, he had violated her trust and had abused her physically as well. As a dutiful Korean daughter, Kaya felt she had to respect both Dr. K and her father, never to tell anyone of her shame.

Kaya's intense sense of shame continued to surface in sessions, even though eventually she began to feel no responsibility for what Dr. K had done to her. Yet, if she had told anyone in her family about the assault, she would have "lost face"[1] thereby diminishing herself as a person forever. Meanwhile she still felt as if she had "lost face" and was only beginning to see how her self-esteem had suffered as a result.

With this in mind, I asked Kaya whether she felt as though she had lost face with me through relaying her experiences. She said she did not know since she was not sure that I could fully understand what losing face meant to her. I assured her that I understood the concept well, having been trained by my own family to act as honorably as possible and to avoid losing face and embarrassing the family at all costs. Kaya expressed relief that my cultural experiences enabled me to understand how much she feared losing face, as well as her reason for not revealing the incident to anyone else. When I told Kaya that my image of her had not been diminished in any way by her experience with Dr. K, she was somewhat taken aback. It was at these times that I understood my role as a therapist for Kaya and other Asian Americans to be a type of bridge between cultures.

There were times when I found myself speaking from a more acculturated "United States" perspective. As Kaya began to accept that she had really only lost face in her own eyes, I encouraged her to experiment with more Westernized cultural norms and to "try on" the perspective of a woman from the U.S. culture. This perspective would allow her to take on the role of the "wronged" victim, and would permit her to name the incident as a rape. It would also allow her to consider seeking legal or professional support to charge Dr. K with a crime. Although these "American" perspectives initially terrified her, Kaya understood the reasoning behind these and was able to consider what she might gain from them.

I was also careful to empathize with Kaya's Korean side; the part of her that wanted to simply put the incident behind her, to just ignore it in the hope that it would eventually disappear on its own. But I also believed that her dissociation and other symptoms of post-traumatic stress indicated that she could not do so completely, even if she were to frame it entirely within an Asian cultural perspective.

As treatment continued, Kaya demonstrated that she was a strong and courageous young woman who became more able to confront directly the rape, betrayal, and her defense of withdrawing from people to protect herself. In retrospect, she recognized that she had suppressed her emotions and her sexuality in a manner that seemed perfectly acceptable within Korean American culture. When I suggested that she might consider attending a support group for women who had been assaulted, Kaya's initial response was anger. She accused me of being culturally insensitive and questioned how I could possibly expect her to talk about what had happened to her in front of a group of strangers! I explained that a support group of women with experiences similar to her own might empathize with her experiences. Yet, at the same time I told Kaya I understood how scary the possibility of participating in a group must be for her, since her privacy was so important to her. However, the possibility that this group would consist of strangers she might not encounter again might make it a safe space for her.

Kaya did not agree with me; she could not imagine speaking about such personal matters in front of any group of people, even other women who had been through similar experiences. However, she did promise to consider the possibility of talking to a counselor who specialized in rape and assault trauma. Her willingness to do so demonstrated that I was on the right track and that Kaya trusted our relationship.

As I continued to push Kaya to confront the reality of the rape incident in whatever manner she could, she became increasingly agitated. She began to have nightmares and to feel more and more frightened in her daily life. Kaya accused me of making her feel unsafe. I agreed with her. I also told her that in the past her sense of safety had been based on suppressing her emotions and avoiding intimate contact with others. I observed with Kaya that now that she was considering letting go of those defenses, she was becoming vulnerable to feeling a variety of emotions, many of which might prove to be scary.

For a two-week period, as Kaya began to feel intense sadness associated with how distant she had become from her family, she agreed to attend therapy sessions twice a week to focus on her feelings about this. Knowing the importance of family relationships for Kaya and the losses she felt, I especially wanted to support her at that time. We focused on small steps she could take to become closer to her family. At the same time, Kaya decided she could not and would not ever tell them about the rape. Therefore, her secret would always stand between her and her family in some way.

In one session, we discussed Kaya's underlying feeling of shame. She revealed that she felt ashamed about having been raped and the loss of her virginity during that assault. She felt even more ashamed that she had felt a sense of desire for and even attraction to Dr. K, despite disgust and a personal sense of dirtiness. In view of the fact that Kaya had never been involved in discussions concerning her sexuality with family or friends, she was surprised when I asked her about her sexual desire, fantasies, and experiences. I acknowledged that I understood that within Asian cultures, sexuality and sexual expression were in a very private realm. Therefore, it was important to our work for her to determine whether her sessions could be included in that realm.

I also gave Kaya copies of two book chapters I had written concerning sexual expression and sexuality among Asian American women (Chan, 1995, 1996; Liu & Chan, 1996). In the next session, she was anxious to have an intellectual discussion focused on the theses of those chapters rather than how they applied to her personally. As tempting as it was to engage her in intellectual discourse, I had to remind myself to gently guide the session to focus on Kaya's sexuality and her feelings about sexual expression. Tearfully, she expressed her fear that she would never find sexual pleasure. I assured her that possibilities for this might be enhanced by her involvement in a trusting emotional relationship. Also, I reminded her that we were working to overcome barriers to relationships she had encountered through our therapeutic relationship. Kaya smiled and remarked, "Oh, is that what we are doing here?"

Near the end of our approximately 20 sessions, Kaya's symptoms of post-traumatic stress disorder abated, as she grappled with whether or not to confront Dr. K. She was both terrified and exhilarated at the prospect. I encouraged her to consider what she would hope to gain by confronting him. Kaya replied that she wanted to hurt him and to punish him for the suffering she had endured for three years. We agreed, somewhat sadly, that those years were already lost to her, and whether Dr. K would be punished or not would not change that. But I encouraged Kaya to consider taking legal action if she felt it would make her less fearful of Dr. K and others. She said she was not yet ready, and did not know if she would ever be.

At the end of the semester, Kaya's family came for her earlier than she had expected. Therefore, we terminated rather abruptly, two sessions ahead of schedule. I told her that even though her journey toward recovery had only begun, she had made a strong start. I also encouraged Kaya to continue therapy at graduate school, as it offered her an opportunity to make a meaningful connection with another person. In typical Asian style, Kaya gave me a quick verbal goodbye. However, rather unexpectedly she also gave me a card with a present, a candle. In her own words, she wrote that the candle represented "the light I now feel within my heart."

Six months later, I received a letter from Kaya. She was doing very well in graduate school. Although she still felt somewhat isolated, Kaya had made a few new friends and remained in touch with two of her college friends. She had consulted an attorney in Chicago whom she told of the rape. Although the attorney advised against pursuing the matter legally because of the time that had passed since the assault, Kaya said she was glad she had reported the incident to someone who understood the injustice she had suffered and offered useful guidance as to what to do. Just the telling of the story seemed to have afforded her, once again, some measure of relief.

**NOTE**

1. "Saving face" is a Confucian concept that combines honor, dignity, and persona, and provides a sense of fulfilling one's prescribed role in the family and in society. "Losing face" means that one has not met the prescribed public role and has shamed oneself and one's family.

**REFERENCES**

Chan, C. S. (1995). Issues of sexual identity in an ethnic minority: The case of Chinese-American lesbians, gay men, and bisexual people. In A. D'Augelli & C. Patterson (Eds.), *Lesbian, gay, and bisexual identities over the lifespan: Psychological perspectives* (pp. 87–100). New York: Oxford University Press.

Chan, C. S. (1996). Asian American women and adolescent girls: Sexuality and sexual expression. In J. Chrisler, C. Golden, & P. Rozee (Eds.), *Lectures on the psychology of women* (pp. 126–134). New York: McGraw-Hill.

Liu, P., & Chan, C. S. (1996). Lesbian, gay, and bisexual Asian Americans and their families. In J. Laird and R. J. Green (Eds.), *Lesbian and gays in couples and families: A handbook for therapists* (pp. 137–152). San Francisco: Jossey-Bass.

CHAPTER 7

# CULTURE SHOCK AND CROSS-CULTURAL THERAPY WITH A JAPANESE STUDENT

Suzanne H. Vogel

## INTRODUCTION

When encountering an international student in social or psychological distress, college personnel often seek out a therapist from the student's country or someone familiar with that country. As someone in the second category, I have had the privilege of consulting with many Japanese students in the Boston area, where Japanese therapists have been rare to nonexistent. Although I am unmistakably middle-class Caucasian American, since 1958 I have lived in Tokyo at various times, originally doing sociological research on Japanese family life, and more recently consulting with social workers and psychiatrists in Japanese hospitals and counseling offices. I speak Japanese quite imperfectly but rather fluently.

## CULTURE SHOCK AS A TYPICAL EXPERIENCE OF INTERNATIONAL STUDENTS

Although I have found that knowledge of Japanese society certainly does help me to understand some of the problems Japanese students encounter in the U.S., I have also found that my work with this population has helped me to understand students from other countries. What is more important than knowledge of any one country is a general awareness of the meaning of cultural differences and the impact of culture shock on most international students. This sensitivity to the nature of the cross-cultural experience of students is what is most essential for all helping professionals in college settings, particularly as we intervene in the lives of an increasing number of international students. Before discussing the specific case of one

Japanese student, let's take a look at how international student populations commonly experience culture shock.

It was Oberg (1960), an anthropologist, who first described the experience of culture shock as an "anxiety resulting from losing one's sense of 'when to do what and how'" (pp. 177–182). Without adequate familiarity with a country's everyday language and social cues, newcomers often do not know how to interpret what they see and hear and, hence, are unsure how to respond. Even those who have studied English, U.S. history, and social customs are often literally shocked and puzzled to discover that they do not understand fully many of the everyday interactions that routinely occur in this country. Not only does this discovery influence anxiety or even panic, but it also often influences a general loss of self-confidence, a feeling of helplessness, and a generalized distrust of the new environment. The newcomer may find it hard to understand such free-floating anxiety as well as difficult to explain it to others. The anxiety dissipates very slowly because true mastery of the new culture comes about only gradually, after months or years, if at all. With such constant insecurity, the international student remains vulnerable to specific "shocks," that is, unanticipated events that may destabilize him or her more than might be expected.

It is my strong impression that international students typically underreport their experiences of culture shock to helping professionals. Their pride may inhibit them from admitting how often they feel insecure, or they may not be fully cognizant of their own feelings since the anxiety that is associated with this condition becomes a constant in their lives while in the U.S. Therefore, counselors and therapists who work with international students need to keep some important considerations in mind. First, it is important for helping professionals to be attuned to signs of anxiety associated with culture shock. It is also important to recognize that many academic, social, psychological, or even physical problems presented by these populations may be related to ongoing stress associated with adapting to a new or different culture.

Second, although helping professionals cannot be expected to know about the country of each student they engage, it is vitally important for them to recognize that many things might be unknown to them about other countries. Therefore, many of their assumptions may not hold true. In reality, many of the things U.S. citizens think of as universal are actually only specific to U.S. culture. For example, it is often assumed that all the peoples of the world value independence and individualism in the ways that these are valued in the U.S. However, even a preliminary investigation of this issue will indicate that these values are associated almost exclusively with Western civilization and most clearly with the Caucasian U.S. middle class. A counselor or therapist then needs to listen carefully and patiently to gain a sense of the student's cultural assumptions and his or her experience of U.S. value systems.

Obviously knowing the experiences of one international student does not teach us about all students from other countries. However, to learn how one student experiences culture shock or to learn about specific cultural misunderstandings may enhance our sensitivity to the importance of understanding cultural factors in other cases. With this hope, I include the case of Keiko with an analysis of her particular experience at a university in the U.S.

## KEIKO

Keiko, a 22-year-old international student from Japan at a large university in the northeast, was brought to my office by Mrs. B, a family friend from New York. Mrs. B had received an urgent call from Keiko's parents after they had been unable to reach Keiko by telephone from Japan for three weeks. Mrs. B had immediately flown to the city where Keiko lived to search for her and had found her at a friend's apartment. She looked despondent and had been sleeping or watching television around the clock. Keiko had deserted her apartment about three weeks earlier. She explained to Mrs. B that her academic work had been poor, so much so that she had not been motivated to attend classes or to go to the library for most of the semester. Upon recognizing that she was not passing her courses, Keiko became panic-stricken at the prospect of talking to her parents and felt unable to tell them anything of her difficulties. As both panic and despondency overwhelmed her, she retreated to her friend's place where she could avoid her parents' phone calls as well as her professors' concerns.

Three and a half years earlier, Keiko had come to the U.S. from her middle-class home in Osaka. She had spent the first two years at a small women's junior college in the mountains of a southern state. There in a protective and supportive environment with only a few international students, she had done well academically and socially. Her teachers and classmates had found her quite appealing and responsive. They had also been glad to help her with her English and to orient her to "American ways." For her last two college years, however, Keiko decided to study at a university that had a strong program in business management. She had dreams of becoming an international businesswoman, and her parents expected her to complete a degree that would assure her a job upon her return to Japan.

Keiko's difficulties began almost immediately on arrival in the northeast. The dormitory room she had anticipated failed to materialize. The college gave her lists of apartments for rent and of students looking to share apartments. Having to find an apartment on her own and adjusting to roommates who turned out to be messy, irresponsible, and inconsiderate were nightmares Keiko could not have imagined. Japanese society, where family and school networks provide introductions and navigate one through life's transitions, never prepared her to negotiate on her own with landlords or roommates. She had heard scary stories of crime and drugs in U.S. cities, but had little knowledge of how to avoid or cope with such dangers.

Neither did she have much ability to assert her needs with her roommates. Keiko's social training had taught her to always be considerate and respectful of others, to never make demands or to show anger, and to defer to others' wishes. Both in Japan and in the southern junior college, this mindset had brought her friendly and mutually considerate relationships. Yet, in her new environment, it left her helpless to deal with selfish, inconsiderate roommates who expected each individual to be his or her own advocate.

Keiko's experience at the university also left her feeling confused, helpless, and inadequate. While orientation programs and various kinds of advisors were plentiful, she did not know how to use them effectively. Neither did she know whom to rely on for advocacy or support. No one offered these services or to introduce her to the appropriate resources. Neither did anyone try to get to know her well enough to advise her adequately on course selection. Keiko's contacts with both the International Students' Office and her academic advisor were brief and routine. She didn't know how to ask for what would have made her feel more comfortable because she didn't know what she needed! All she knew was that she felt quite alone and lost. Keiko thought that she was personally inadequate somehow, since she couldn't adjust and be happy in this "free and independent" society.

To make matters worse, Keiko had little interest in business courses. Instead she had enjoyed the language and literature courses, taken previously, much more. Keiko found it harder and harder to visualize herself as a businesswoman. Furthermore, she found required class discussions considerably stressful. Japanese schools, which represent a vertical society that views learning as a passive taking in of what is given from above, had required her to listen and retain information. However, schools in her country had not encouraged her to be assertive or to express her opinions.

Keiko attempted to tell her parents about her struggles during her visit home after the first year in the northeast. However, their response was not reassuring. As she had expected, they could not approve of her change of majors. Instead, they wanted her to finish her degree as quickly as possible as an outcome of the time and money spent on her education in the U.S.

Keiko's parents did not demand that she excel, as they recognized the difficulties of studying in a foreign language. Instead they only wanted her to do her best and to finish soon. Anything else would look like failure. Then if she wanted to study something else afterward, they would be willing to consider that choice. Keiko's parents had been aware of the messy roommates and supported her move to her own apartment. However, they did not comprehend her loneliness or other social difficulties. To them, life in the U.S. seemed free and enjoyable. Besides, even if this wasn't so, they thought it was preferable for her to concentrate on her studies.

After returning to school, Keiko continued to feel discouraged about her academic work. She would become paralyzed with anxiety during telephone calls from home and was unable to tell her parents of the increasing likelihood that she would graduate late or possibly not at all. Then as she became less able to study and to attend class, Keiko became increasingly panic-stricken and unable to tell her parents the truth. Mrs. B found her in this state.

## Diagnosis and Treatment

Diagnostically, Keiko's symptoms were consistent with that of dysthymia. She was tearful and despondent, sleeping too much, unable to concentrate on her studies, blaming herself for not studying harder, and feeling guilty because she had insisted on coming to the U.S. against her parents' advice. Her guilty feeling was exacerbated by the fact that her father had just been diagnosed with cancer. However, Keiko was not suicidal and her cognitive functioning was intact. Her ability to relate was good except in conversations with her parents and temporary social withdrawal. She was able to tell me as well as Mrs. B what she had been doing, not doing, and why.

My treatment goals for Keiko were as follows:

1. to initially offer empathy and emotional support, and
2. to enhance her understanding of the very real difficulties she had been confronting as she tried to adjust to a large university in a foreign country where social norms are quite different from those she absorbed as a child.

If Keiko could appreciate the enormity of these difficulties, two more goals could possibly be attained:

3. she might become more accepting of herself, and
4. she might become more comfortable with therapy and able to use it well.

Subsequent goals were:

5. to help her reopen communications with her parents, and
6. to develop more realistic academic goals and a plan for achieving them.

With her mother in route to the U.S., it was important to address the fifth goal as soon as possible. Subsequent to discussing her usual mode of communication with her parents and some understanding of the current impasse, a joint interview with her mother seemed as though it could prove useful.

It is important to acknowledge here that I did not immediately ask Keiko about goals for herself or for therapy. After all, she had not requested a consultation but had been brought in by a third party. Furthermore, Keiko probably would have thought that my asking her was strange, since her predicament was apparent and I was the "expert" whom she and Mrs. B thought of as knowing how to extricate her from a complicated predicament. This expectation can be explained by the fact that in hierarchical societies, the expectation is that knowledge or advice comes from above, which can be embraced or rejected by the person in need. However, the minds and hearts of subordinates in Japan are no more empty of opinions or wishes than Western minds are; the Japanese are simply less accustomed to asserting their own views. Therefore, as my discussion with Keiko proceeded, my discomfort with my "expert" role lessened as I was able to learn more about her thoughts and preferences. As all of this became clearer, our ability to collaborate on treatment goals and plans for the future was enhanced.

Keiko was seen twice the first week, initially by herself and then with her mother. She and her mother came again the second week, after the two had talked several times. By that time they were able to agree on how to prevent another breakdown in communication. The third week Keiko and I focused on the nature of her academic problems and how she wanted to handle them. Thereafter, we kept in touch once a month for the next three months. Keiko used these sessions primarily to make the most pressing academic decisions and to report on how well she was meeting the goals of speaking honestly with her parents and of doing her academic work.

Meanwhile, she withdrew from the university for a semester and returned the next summer. After successfully completing the summer term, Keiko returned to Japan to be with her sick father and to make more long-term decisions concerning whether to return to the U.S. the following year to finish requirements for her business degree, whether to change her major, or to stay in Japan and work.

While Keiko responded to empathy and gained in self-understanding and self-acceptance, she did not become interested in further self-exploration. What was crucial to her improvement was the intervention in her social situation, particularly help with confronting her mother and her academic problems. When she was able to deal with these issues realistically, her depression disappeared and her functioning returned to normal. Although I remained available to Keiko, she used me primarily as a check-in resource to keep herself on track.

## Crucial Cultural Factors in Keiko's Situation

In the case of Keiko, one immediately wonders why she had so much trouble speaking directly to her parents about her difficulties. Were they abusive, cruel, or dictatorial? Or was she particularly passive, withdrawn, or easily frightened? To the contrary, her parents, who were very caring and supportive people, had always had a good relationship with their daughter, who, under most circumstances, was outgoing and active. Some understanding of the Japanese family helps one to see that family relationships have a different "feel" to them from those of the dominant U.S. culture. Rather than encouraging individuality or self-expression, Japanese families cultivate group harmony, deference to the needs of the family, and achievement along expected academic and occupational channels. Parents guide their children in their social and educational development, and children look to their parents for leadership. Even though the strongest relationships are vertical ones (e.g., parent-child, teacher-student), the basic values in Japanese society are still caretaking, nurturing, and reciprocal dependency.

Keiko's parents were doing their best to give her supportive guidance. Even though they agreed to let her study in the U.S., they expected her to study conscientiously, to graduate within a reasonable time period, and to return home to a responsible job or marriage. Changing majors in the middle of one's academic program is almost impossible in Japan. Instead, the emphasis is on completing the selected program in order to become a responsible citizen, rather than on exploring one's individuality and making new and better choices for oneself. Keiko's parents could accept her academic difficulties in the U.S., but could not comprehend what could prevent her from finishing her courses and getting a degree.

For similar reasons, Keiko felt it impossible to tell her parents about her predicament because this would seriously upset their expectations and family harmony. Maintaining family harmony was particularly important now in view of her father's illness. In Japanese society, fulfilling parental expectations and "going with the flow" are encouraged at both school and home. Since strongly asserting one's feelings is discouraged, confrontation is to be avoided at all costs.

Many college helping professionals have encountered international students, particularly Asians, who are stuck in an impossible bind because of their inability to tell their parents of an impending failure, or even a wish to change a major. With the encouragement of a counselor, many are able to speak to their parents. Others are more reluctant, and some become suicidal. I have found that often the best way to lessen this paralysis is through an intermediary such as a therapist or other college personnel. Intermediaries have a respected traditional role in Japan in that they allow individuals to save face, to avoid confrontation, and to preserve social harmony. Japanese students seem to prefer being "saved" almost against their will by an outside force, rather than having to assume responsibility, and the guilt that often accompanies this, for provoking a confrontation. Again, self-assertion is not respected. It has been my experience that Japanese students have felt enormous relief once their parents were informed.

Just as Keiko had not been able to confront her parents or professors, she had not sought therapy on her own. In part, this seemed to have been influenced by a stigma among the Japanese against seeking professional help even though the use of counseling and mental health services is growing rapidly in Japan. Once Keiko was brought to my office by a family friend, she did not seem embarrassed to be there and had no apparent difficulty with telling me about her difficulties. For some Japanese, the foreignness of a non-Japanese therapist seems to diminish the stigma. Perhaps awareness that counseling and mental health intervention are more accepted in this country influences recognition that there is no need to feel the shame that would ordinarily be felt in the presence of another Japanese person. However, there are many Japanese who are more reluctant to see a non-Japanese therapist as they fear not being understood linguistically or culturally.

Keiko's case history indicates that she also had trouble with assertiveness and confrontation in relationships with her roommates and in the classroom. This expectation constitutes another aspect of culture shock that is commonly experienced by Japanese students in the U.S. In Japanese schools and colleges, students are expected to listen to learn. They may make formal presentations, but verbal expressions of their own ideas is not generally expected. Modesty and deference are valued rather than assertiveness. U.S. classes that require open discussion are almost always difficult for Japanese students. Not only are they disadvantaged by being required to speak in a foreign language, but also by their previous education, which taught them restraint and disapproval of outspokenness.

For similar reasons, Japanese students are often shocked by the behavior of other students in U.S. dormitories or apartments. Whereas their expectation is one of politeness and mutual consideration in social interaction, they are often dismayed to find U.S. students rude, selfish, unconcerned for others, noisy, messy, and so on. They are also so surprised and intimidated by others' aggression that they have no idea how to cope in such situations. Therefore, they usually withdraw silently. Japanese students have no model of this society's concepts of constructive assertiveness or negotiation. In those occasional situations where they attempt to imitate U.S. assertiveness, they often tend to overdo it.

Perhaps an even more important way of viewing culture shock is to recognize that U.S. college staff, including counselors and advisors, often assume that everyone values independence, individuality, and self-determination as highly as Euro-Americans do. This belief often serves as a barrier to seeing how deeply many international students need protection and guidance, preferably from someone who takes an almost parental interest in them. Note that Keiko did well at the small southern women's junior college where both faculty and students took an interest in her and were always nearby to answer questions or to explain things. I doubt that she was demanding or that they considered her particularly dependent. However, there was an easily accessible supportive network around her.

In contrast, at the large city university, there were many advisors and counselors available, but Keiko did not know how to use them. Sometimes international students find a host family or a particular advisor who assumes this role with them. However, I strongly believe that universities need to have a system whereby they insure that each international student has someone who takes an overall interest in their welfare.

## Cultural Contexts for Treatment

Even Japanese students who come for treatment often have no idea of what psychotherapy really is. What they usually expect is advice-giving or what is more often thought of in the U.S. as counseling. They have little notion of the possible value of ventilation and no concept of "working through." They see the patient/client-therapist relationship in vertical terms; that is, they look up to the therapist as a doctor or a wise problem-solver. Hence, they usually want to be given advice, or at least an explanation of how a patient or client and a therapist might work together. Often when the immediate problem is solved or symptoms disappear, they see no further need for self-exploration. If Japanese students are helped to realign their relationship to their group, they usually feel satisfied.

With Keiko, this was clearly the case. The most important work I did with her was to help her reestablish communication with her parents and to decide how to handle her academic dilemma. When these tasks were accomplished, she could move on without further distress and did not want to continue frequent sessions. After exploring the presenting problem, I did ask her about various aspects of her background, current situation, and so forth, in order to look for underlying problems and to allow her to bring up other concerns she might have had. However, there seemed to be no others. Perhaps this was influenced by the fact that Keiko was a fairly healthy young woman without severe symptoms and she was not seeking self-reflection. The introspection of psychodynamic psychotherapy has little value outside of individualistic societies.

There was one somewhat problematic area that we only touched on briefly, namely Keiko's rather unrealistic motivation for coming to the U.S. to study. Her dream of being an international businesswoman sounded as though it was primarily based on glamorous images rather than on a realistic assessment of her strengths or interests, or on a realistic understanding of what such work would entail.

Very often Japanese students' motivations for coming to the U.S. are complex and more clinically central than U.S. therapists might expect. The choice to study in the U.S. often represents an attempt to save face in response to not passing the entrance exam to one of the high-ranking Japanese universities. Thus, such students, more often male, come to the U.S. with a preexisting sense of inadequacy and with questionable motivation. Women students are more likely to come to escape a confining gender role or simply to have fun in a "free" environment for a few years before getting married. Those in the latter group are often quickly disillusioned by the hard work of studying in a foreign language and by the discovery that "freedom" is often accompanied by loneliness and the burden of being totally responsible for oneself. This seemed to resonate with Keiko's experience. Although reality testing her career plans was a task we started, she was left to complete this within the context of her family and country. Japanese women are just beginning to learn to make their own decisions.

At the beginning of our relationship, Keiko needed much emotional support and empathy that influenced greater self-acceptance. Japanese students do not respond well to a neutral or objective stance. Therefore, I was quite assertive in expressing my understanding of and concern for her distress. But more importantly, I was emphatic in informing her that much of her experience involved culture shock, a commonly experienced condition among international students. Of course, Keiko would have trouble with class participation; of course, she felt lonely and lost in a city and at a university where she knew no one and had no one to guide her; of course, noisy and aggressive roommates were hard for her to deal with, particularly in view of her upbringing, and so forth. In other words, I made a deliberate effort to normalize rather than to pathologize her feelings and to offer her some way of understanding her experiences. Although I did not impose therapy on her, I did keep in touch with Keiko just to maintain a connection and out of concern for her well-being.

## CONCLUSION

My therapeutic relationship with Keiko was cross-cultural and cross-racial. However, I had the advantage of knowing how to speak Japanese, although imperfectly, and of considerable familiarity with Japanese society. Nevertheless, I do not believe that speaking the language is of prime importance for Japanese students in the U.S. Rather, the linguistic problem is more of a problem for helping professionals. Japanese students are accustomed to struggling with English and are able to communicate. It is more often the U.S. therapist who finds this population difficult to understand and who may become impatient in response to the time and effort required to achieve effective communication.

Knowledge of the Japanese culture is more useful than speaking the student's native language. However, the U.S. therapist who is not a Japan specialist should not hesitate to work with students from this population. What is needed to work effectively with Japanese students is the same as is needed for others; that is, a genuine desire to understand the student's problem, symptoms, personality, social situation, and so on, in the context of his or her cultural background. International students may require a little extra patience and effort, but they also teach us new perspectives on diversity, broaden our capacities for relationship and connection, and offer us new and deeper insights into ourselves.

## REFERENCE

Oberg, K. (1960). Cultural shock: Adjustment to new cultural environments. *Practical Anthropology, 7*, 177–182.

CHAPTER 8

# DIVERSITY AMONG LATINAS
Implications for
College Mental Health

Margarita Alvarez

**INTRODUCTION**

In the field of mental health there are presently emphases on the centrality of human diversity to psychosocial development and functioning, and the need for culturally competent mental health services. These emphases are important from an ethical perspective in view of current demographic shifts in the U.S. Moreover, from a college mental health perspective, these emphases have considerable relevance, since diversity influences the world views and daily experiences of students as well as the paths their lives take beyond the college years. Less is known, however, about how practitioners process and manage diversity effectively.

The literature has paid considerable attention to race, ethnicity, gender, and social class (Aponte, Rivers, & Wohl, 1995; Comas-Díaz & Griffith, 1988; De La Cancela, Jenkins, & Chin, 1993; Garcia Coll, Cook-Nobles, & Surrey, 1995; Jablensky et al., 1994; Miller, 1986). Yet, migration and immigration are also key dimensions of diversity that have a significant impact on some students' lives (Alvarez, 1995). Given the complexities of immigration and migration trends throughout the world community (Cole, Espín, & Rothblum, 1992; Kraut, 1994), it is no longer likely that the work of practitioners will be limited to students from backgrounds that are similar to their own. Therefore, practitioners are now challenged more than ever before to confront their own biases concerning difference if they are to embrace effectively the needs of their clients.

This chapter focuses on diversity and shifting identifications in women of Latin American ancestry who are pursuing a higher education in the

United States. Vignettes from case composites will be used to highlight key social and cultural variables that shape the identities and psychological needs of these women. It is hoped that this perspective will facilitate a departure from stereotyped perceptions of Latin American women, embedded in universalism, toward ethnoculturally specific frameworks. It is also hoped that this more progressive focus will enhance the ability of college mental health professionals to respond more effectively to the needs of this diverse client population. Although the case material that follows highlights the diversity within this particular population, it is further hoped that readers' appreciation of the commonality of human experience will be enhanced.

## CASE VIGNETTES

### MIRIAM:
### ON CROSSING GEOGRAPHICAL AND PSYCHOCULTURAL BORDERS

Miriam was a 19-year-old Mexican American Catholic woman at a predominantly White women's college in the northeast. She was a sophomore majoring in women's studies. The youngest of three sisters, she was the first of her family to attend college. Miriam's oldest sister, a 27-year-old hotel receptionist, was living with her parents with her 8-year-old son. She separated from her husband because of physical abuse. Their second sister, age 23, was single and also lived at home. A high school graduate, she worked as a teacher's aide at the kindergarten level. She also had aspirations of attending college to become a nurse but repeatedly postponed this decision. Their mother, a bookkeeper, was fully supportive of Miriam's academic ambitions, although her preference for her daughter was to attend a college in the U.S. that was closer to home.

Unlike the other members of her family, Miriam was born in the United States. Her parents immigrated to this country while they were in their twenties with their first two daughters who were 8 and 5 years of age at the time. Miriam's father's family of origin and other relatives lived in the western part of Mexico in a city that borders on the United States. She had almost no contact with them. Her mother's family of origin lived in the same border city. Miriam grew up feeling close to her maternal grandmother, with whom she spent a great deal of time when she went home. Her maternal grandfather died before she was born. After his death, his widow, children, and extended family immigrated to the U.S. Miriam lost her father at the age of 7. Her mother had not remarried.

Growing up in a border city made Miriam aware of feeling "divided" inside. The border and river that separated Mexico and the U.S. served as daily reminders of her conflicted loyalties to Mexico and the U.S., since she never felt as though she genuinely belonged to either.

## Initial Concerns

Miriam's initial concern was that she felt sad most of the time, as if she had a "bleeding wound" in her soul. She could not explain this. Miriam had never talked to anyone about this before, since she disliked being a "burden" to others and would have perceived this as such. Even though she had never been in therapy and felt considerable anxiety about the possibility, her curiosity about the therapist, a Latina at the college counseling center, encouraged her to report for a first appointment. It should be noted that although Miriam was fluent in Spanish, her primary language was English. Therefore, all of her sessions were conducted in English. The themes that surfaced captured Miriam's developmental struggles. Particularly evident was her emerging awareness of how complex the conflict was that she experienced between her love relationship and family loyalties. Conflict was also experienced with maintaining her ethnocultural identity.

## Negotiating Loyalties to Significant Others and Ethnocultural Identity

As the therapeutic process unfolded, other relevant background data surfaced. Miriam had a passive dependent relationship with her Mexican boyfriend of seven years in which she tolerated his verbal and psychological abuse. He attended a small college two hours away from the more prestigious one that Miriam attended. The problems in their relationship seemed to worsen after they started college. At the time of her initial visit, Miriam and her boyfriend were spending most of their weekends together. Meanwhile, the fear of losing him prevented her from establishing and maintaining relationships with other students. Yet, Miriam's academic functioning continued to be outstanding.

Miriam's idealization of her boyfriend seemed to be connected to an idealized father figure and an unresolved grief reaction. Her mother and older sisters had negative memories of the father, since he had physically abused them. Miriam often felt torn between her love for him and the wish to be accepted and understood by her mother, whom she secretly blamed for her father's death. Her relationship with her mother was conflicted in other areas as well.

While Miriam was appreciative of her mother's efforts to send her to college, she also felt guilty about having the educational opportunities no one else had in her family. In addition, she felt obligated to stay near her mother to take care of her emotionally. To make matters worse, she felt a sense of loss and anxiety in relation to growing apart from her family, her community, and her changing identity. Miriam no longer felt assured of who she was and was afraid of the person she was becoming. The family's pressure for her to stay the same was reflected in her sisters' perception that she had become a "snob" while away at college. These difficulties were further complicated by grief and broader social issues. For example, her father's untimely death and the oppression suffered by her ancestors were injustices that seemed to underlie her loyalty conflicts.

### Negotiating Dual Social Identities, Migration, and Social Injustice

The framing of Miriam's difficulties within sociopolitical contexts allowed her to express her rage about the injustices her family suffered in the U.S. Furthermore, she became aware of her own deepening sense of disloyalty in relation to embracing a culture that, in her view, had oppressed her ancestors and robbed them of their cultural identity and pride. This influenced Miriam to experience a painful sense of uprootedness and a strong desire to belong. For example, even though she loved both Mexico and the United States, Miriam felt as if she did not belong to either country; a similar sense of disconnection was experienced in relation to her family.

All of this influenced Miriam's determination to find her "sense of personhood" as an alternative to being defined by her ancestors' country of origin, skin color, gender, and socioeconomic status. She negotiated this challenge by identifying herself as a U.S. citizen without betraying emotional connections and loyalties to her ancestors. However, this was not easy in a country so obsessed with race, skin color, and social stratification.

Miriam was quite aware of how race and ethnicity connected with her identity struggles. Initially, she described a sense of disbelief, rage, and pain after being called a Chicana soon after arriving at college. This was followed by anger, a sense of unworthiness, and shame about her ethnicity even though she had always felt proud of her heritage prior to this incident. That day Miriam became painfully aware of her "place" as she gradually disconnected from the general student population.

Miriam's gender role expectations were also filled with conflict. Perhaps most painful was her dual identity as an oppressed woman of Mexican ancestry and as a U.S. citizen with the privilege of access to a prestigious academic institution.

## ANA:
## IDENTITY CONFLICT MANIFESTED THROUGH CAREER CHOICE

Ana, a 23-year-old senior at a large university in the northeast, was a Chilean Jew from a wealthy family. Ana did not spend many of her early years in Chile, since her family moved to several Latin American countries because of political unrest and military terrorism. During her adolescence, Ana moved to Israel but returned to Chile to finish high school after democracy had been restored.

Although Ana's family valued education, achievement, and success, they valued men even more highly. She was the youngest and only female of four siblings. Although Ana's ethnic identification was primarily Jewish, her gender identity was influenced by traditional views of women prescribed by the Catholic Church. The Church continued to be powerful in shaping sociopolitical struggles in her country. It was very likely that her gender identity may have been influenced by her mother who had been raised as a devout Catholic and educated in boarding schools. However, Ana's mother converted to Judaism shortly before her marriage.

### Initial Concern

Ana presented with conflict about her career choice. At one level she wanted to become an educator, which was congruent with her family's expectation. Furthermore, her mother was also an educator. Yet, Ana secretly dreamed of becoming a journalist but felt inhibited from choosing this field due to difficulties with written English. She also felt embarrassed about her accent. Since Ana was White, people tended to be surprised by her accent and her Latin American background. Her therapy sessions were conducted in Spanish.

### The Bind of Shifting and Conflicting Identities

As the therapy unfolded, Ana's identity conflicts became apparent on several levels. From a developmental perspective, Ana believed that her identity and sense of belonging were strongly rooted in her family's expectations of her. She worried about potential family losses if she decided to pursue a career other than education. While her consideration of other career possibilities felt exciting, Ana felt disloyal to her family's expectations. At one level, she felt comfortable with familiar traditional Latin American gender roles. Yet, she also wanted to fulfill her vocational dreams, which challenged her perceptions of her competence and raised uncertainties about whether she could become successful in a less familiar career.

Ana expressed pride in being Jewish, which allowed her to have a special bond with her father. Since she believed that her mother blocked her from direct access to her father, religion helped her to connect with him without her mother's intrusion. In fact, religion became an important context for understanding some of Ana's conflicts with her mother. One of these conflicts involved their views about sexuality and womanhood.

While the roles for women in most Latin American countries have been highly influenced by a patriarchal cultural system and the Catholic Church, Ana's Jewish identity allowed her options that had not been available to her mother as a young woman prior to converting from Catholicism to Judaism. Like her mother, she embraced religion. During adolescence she went to Israel to study Judaism because of her desire to become a rabbi, which was influenced by her ties to her father. Unfortunately, she was excluded from this possibility because her mother was not Jewish by birth.

Ana's identity and family conflicts were exacerbated by her struggle to decide on a career. This was an emotionally charged endeavor for several reasons. First, by challenging her family's expectation of her to be less successful than her brothers, she felt disloyal and fearful of compromising her "place" in the family. Furthermore, if Ana was to choose not to become an educator, she would risk the loss of an important source of identification with her mother. Finally, her potential career choice would determine whether she would return home to attend graduate school or stay in the U.S. Choosing the latter would possibly require Ana to become a permanent resident of the U.S.

Although she seemed to long for permanence and autonomy, Ana also feared the potential loss of her transitional status. The lack of a permanent home during childhood and adolescence and exposure to two sets of religious beliefs simultaneously may have contributed significantly to her confusion and indecisiveness. Perhaps with the choice of a career and a professional identity, Ana could more easily differentiate from her family. Metaphorically speaking, however, it seemed that Ana feared losing her place at home if she found her niche in life through her differentness.

**Culture and Treatment: Parallel Dilemmas and Conflicts**

The transference which was influenced by several aspects of Ana's background may have also been facilitated by my own background as her therapist. For example, my identity conflicts as a South American non-Jewish woman were similar to Ana's, after leaving my country to study in the U.S. Perhaps I was too closely identified or empathic with Ana's dilemmas, thereby increasing her level of anxiety. Furthermore, my theoretical orientation as a relational therapist (Jordan, 1991; Miller, 1986; Miller & Stiver,

1994) might have been annoying to Ana, since she came from a culture and socioeconomic class where traditional psychoanalytic psychotherapy was both familiar and comforting to her. However, my approach was based on an integration of the relational theory of women's development and social constructionist theory. Ana had been in psychoanalytic psychotherapy in her country of origin and in Israel. Therefore, she experienced my tendency to avoid psychoanalytic interpretations as an inability to fully understand and help her.

## The Cross-Cultural Encounter Between Therapist and Client

This case illustrates that certain assumptions about diversity and what constitutes a positive match in the therapeutic relationship may not always be true. While Ana had specifically requested a Spanish-speaking South American-born woman therapist, there proved to be several cultural and acculturation differences between her and me. The first was national identity. Jenkins, De La Cancela, and Chin (1993) contend that world views and personal values are associated with national identity, as influenced by sociopolitical and historical experiences. Furthermore, in Latin America, identity and character are also influenced by the culture and folklore of the particular geographical region of the country in which one grows up.

Thus, there are diverse and distinct interpersonal styles of relating within one country. The contrast becomes even greater when a Spanish-speaking therapist and client come from different countries with markedly different accents, interpersonal styles, world views, and awareness of social and political issues. For example, Ana came from a conservative region in Chile, but had lived in several Latin American countries and Israel. In contrast, I am from a Caribbean region of Colombia, and have endured several migrations and cross-cultural experiences in the U.S.

As mentioned previously, another important difference between Ana and me were our stances on therapy. Ana felt more comfortable with a conservative psychoanalytic approach, while my approach integrated principles of the relational theory of women's development and social constructionist theory.

I was particularly interested in learning about the underlying familial and sociocultural contexts for her experiences. Therefore, my conversations with Ana examined the roles of family dynamics and belief systems, intergenerational patterns, and family losses and conflicts in shaping her relational and developmental dilemmas. At a broader level, the influences of sociopolitical forces and religion on Ana's identity were explored as well. It was particularly important for me to understand what meaning she attributed to her life stories.

In a study of how immigrant women use narratives to define identity, Espín (1994) emphasized how life stories are told in accordance with standards of intelligibility specific to their culture and society. She concurred with Ochberg's (1992) perspective that "the tales people tell each other and themselves of who they are and might yet become are individual variations on the narrative templates our culture deems intelligible" (p. 21). Mair (1988) also emphasized that "we are the stories by which we live and . . . locations where the stories of our place and time become partially tellable" (p. 127).

**The Intervention**

Ana considered my approach "too Americanized" and responded with hostility. Therefore, impasses occurred at several points in the therapy. At the core of these was her belief that others, like her mother, did not take her needs seriously. Although she yearned for her mother's acceptance, Ana was convinced that her mother was more interested in meeting her brothers' needs. She frequently complained of not getting enough of what she wanted in therapy. She preferred more interpretation, less reframing and clarification, to be seen more frequently during the week, a lower fee, and so on. Therefore, I began to feel inadequate, incompetent, and angry.

Shortly after I returned from vacation, after a year of working with Ana, she decided to terminate because of the plan for professional coverage arrangement I had left in place. Even though the arrangement had previously been discussed with her and she had not objected to it, later she believed I wanted to "get rid of" her. Ana's fear of abandonment was connected to an earlier experience when her parents went on vacation and left her in the care of an aunt.

My efforts to influence Ana to stay in therapy were met with ambivalence. She would either reject them or would say that she had been told these things before. Clinical interpretations addressed her longings to feel connected to the therapist. Yet, her fear of abandonment lingered, seemingly influenced by longings to be understood by her mother and the rejection she had suffered. Similarly, Anna had difficulty with letting go of her previous treatment and her culture, since these provided her with a sense of familiarity and comfort. I wondered whether her identification with me, a Spanish-speaking Latin American-born therapist, influenced her to fear the possibility of becoming "too Americanized," distant from her roots, and disloyal to her family. However, the more I encouraged Ana to explore other ways to understand the impasses, the more she felt that her needs were not being met through our work. Therefore, her desire to terminate was respected.

In retrospect, I have wondered whether the transference paralleled Ana's first major separation from her mother, which occurred when she moved to Israel. Did her mother then desperately try to influence her to stay at home? I also wonder whether Ana eventually resolved her conflict and overcame her struggles concerning loss to the extent that she experiences more contentment in her life.

## Other Considerations

With abrupt terminations, therapists are often left with questions about what went wrong and how this might have been prevented. Thus, I wondered whether Ana would have felt more comfortable telling her story in a psychoanalytic frame, given the prominence of this intervention in her culture and because her previous analysts were Jewish. Furthermore, I questioned whether it would have proved useful to determine how she constructed the difference in our religious affiliations. I am inclined to believe that in view of Ana's negative transference, the possibility of effecting significant change through our work was unlikely. Perhaps our time together did serve a vital supportive function that Ana will recognize sometime in the near future. Unfortunately, I may never know.

## SONIA'S CHOICE: INVISIBILITY VS. MISREPRESENTATION

Sonia, age 35, came from the Dominican Republic as an international student to complete a doctoral degree in political science. She was the oldest of three with a 33-year-old brother who was an attorney, and a 30-year-old sister, a psychologist. Her family was quite conservative and politically prominent in her country. Sonia came self-referred, following the suggestion of a friend who knew the therapist. Although she was perfectly fluent in English and had lived in the U.S. for about four years at the time of the referral, Sonia wanted to work with a Spanish-speaking woman of Latin American ancestry. In therapy sessions, Sonia tended to switch back and forth from Spanish to English. This seemed to reflect her true bilingual nature, comfort with both languages, and emotional connection to Spanish.

### Initial Concern

Sonia sought therapy because of anxiety attacks and difficulties with sleeping and concentration. She also felt depressed and unclear about what might be precipitating her symptoms. Several background factors and some unfolding events in Sonia's life appeared to influence her mental status.

In Sonia's family, direct emotional expression was considered a weakness and associated with shame. Communication was usually superficial and about daily events. This seemed to underlie her difficulty with revealing her symptoms during the initial stage of psychotherapy. Also, Sonia had considerable difficulty with connecting external events to her emotions and conflicts. She felt anxious about having her vulnerabilities explored and ashamed of allowing anyone to be privy to her sadness, a feeling which represented a loss of control.

### Background of the Problem

In therapy, Sonia recounted many of her early traumas related to political unrest, threats to her family's safety, and family tragedies. While threats to the family and other traumas were discussed openly, Sonia had never before shared her feelings about these events. At a very early age she had learned to keep her emotions and needs inside to the point that they became inaccessible. This protected her from her mother as well as from emotional connections to loved ones. Miller (1988) elaborates on how women use such protective strategies.

### The Process of Identity Consolidation

At the core of Sonia's anxiety was terror related to her eventual return to the Dominican Republic after graduation and the inevitable disclosure of her newly found identity to her family. In addition, this feeling was also associated with an impending sense of psychological death, should she have to give up her newly found identity. After all, it had provided her with a frame of reference for understanding a series of events and experiences that had previously been incomprehensible to her. Upon graduation her visitor's exchange visa would expire, leaving her with no alternative but to return home. As Sonia began to feel comfortable with identifying her emotions and experiences without feeling shame, her internal self began to surface.

Central to her identity struggle was an emerging clarification of her identity. Sonia's internalized homophobia and terror of becoming emotionally exiled by her family and friends made it difficult for her to fully embrace this identity. She also felt embarrassed for not living up to what she perceived to be the therapist's standards for what is proper for Latin American women. Idealization was apparent in Sonia's assumption that the therapist "had made it" in the U.S. At the same time, Sonia's homophobia and idealization of the therapist caused her to fear the loss of our relationship. After these fears were addressed and Sonia was assured that there was no threat of losing the relationship, much of the work focused on gains and losses associated with her new identity.

The U.S. was the place where Sonia had learned to defend her rights as a woman and to have a voice as a lesbian. Therefore, it had become home. Returning to the Dominican Republic meant having to be the person she was prior to coming to the U.S. Sonia joked about having come out in English. However, as she pondered how she might tell friends and relatives back home that she was a lesbian, she found this extremely difficult, since the Spanish for this aspect of identity is derogatory and vulgar. She also knew that her family would disown and abandon her if she came out to them. Therefore, Sonia perceived herself to have two choices: invisibility or misrepresentation. In the final analysis, she chose to misrepresent her identity due to the belief that there was no other alternative.

Espín (1994) argues that migration provides lesbian women the space and permission to cross identity boundaries which transform their sexuality and gender roles. Therefore, she contends that the coming out process is yet another means of crossing behavioral, emotional, and lifestyle boundaries. Espín has also found that Latina lesbians tend to be conflicted about loyalty to their families and cultural traditions, while finding these same traditions frustrating and restrictive of their lesbian identities. However, she overlooks what a woman like Sonia experiences when there is no perceived choice but to return to the place that confined and oppressed her identity.

While the coming out process in the U.S. continues to be complex at the societal level, there are organized groups, institutions, and informal mechanisms that validate, support, and protect the rights of lesbian and gay people. In contrast, Latin American culture, strongly influenced by the Catholic Church, is known for homophobic attitudes and the undermining of women's rights. Latin American culture is also far less progressive in acknowledging the existential, legal, and social rights of these populations.

A complicating factor for Sonia was the visibility and political prominence of her family. Not only would her coming out have clashed with her family's belief system, but it would have also threatened their political prestige and ties with the Catholic Church. Therefore, Sonia's coming out would have been considered a subversive act, a betrayal, and a sin. She believed that all of this left her with no option but to keep her lesbian identity invisible to her family to protect their image and belief system as well as her own ties with them. In her view, to have approached this in any other way might have led to tragic consequences.

## Embracing Difference and Shared Realities

Spanish and Catholicism shaped my own and Sonia's cultural identities as Latin American women. There were also parallels in our migration to the U.S. and subsequent identity transformations. Furthermore, both of us anticipated loss, fear, and anxieties in relation to the possibility of returning to our homelands. Nevertheless, our commonalities did not negate the cultural differences between us.

It is evident from this case study that competent practice with college students requires therapists to attend to multiple levels of identity. For Sonia, this included the influences of family, ethnicity, culture, social class, sexuality, and circumstances associated with her migration. In addition, this case emphasizes how goal attainment is nurtured most effectively within an open and progressive therapeutic environment where new and consolidated identifications can be acknowledged.

## DISCUSSION

In the U.S., women of Latin American ancestry are often targets of social bias which influences misperceptions of their diversity. For example, Latinas have primarily been portrayed as Puerto Rican, Cuban, and Mexican women in search of services from public resources. Other women of Latin American ancestry have consistently been excluded. The case studies that have been presented suggest a much broader range of diversity among Latinas based on national origin, racial and religious identity, fluency in either Spanish or English, and socioeconomic status.

Inadequate appreciation of the influence of ethnocultural variables, family dynamics, and Latinas' identity, pose significant obstacles to effective therapeutic work. As the previous cases have highlighted, all three women had conflicts regarding their newly emerging identities. Their new identifications were lived with fear and pain, since their connections to themselves and significant relationships back home were threatened. Ana and Sonia immigrated to the U.S., while Miriam migrated from the west to the east to pursue educational opportunities. In the Latin culture, the prescribed custom for women to leave home is marriage. In fact, leaving home to pursue a career is sometimes viewed by those who do so as a betrayal to maternal loyalties.

All three women experienced conflict regarding what place they should call home. The conflict seemed to become more complicated after they decided to separate from their culture of origin. The notion that one has to separate from one's roots to become independent and successful is strongly upheld in Anglo-Saxon tradition. However, the opposite is true for collective societies where interdependence rather than independence is valued; interdependence and success are measured by the extent to which one maintains a connection to one's family, history, and culture.

The evolution of different identities that is fostered by migration, acculturation, and education influences how one establishes roots away from home. Miriam was at a stage of identity development where she had not differentiated from her country of origin or her family despite her move to the U.S. She kept connections with her family alive through identifying with her father, the relationship with her boyfriend, and by limiting her involvement with the college community. Miriam seemed to know that her emerging professional identity would inevitably influence her to establish new roots.

Ana, on the other hand, while apparently more experienced at living away from her family and country, still had difficulty with claiming her right to success and establishing roots away from home. Sonia, the oldest and closest to achieving her educational goal, had established a sense of stability in the U.S. through her lesbian identity. For her, it was difficult to claim her family and country openly because of this sexual orientation.

Access to educational opportunities and different cultural experiences enhances women's growth and development. Even though an integration of several cultures (Szapocznik, Kurtines, & Fernandez, 1980) and identities (Polster, 1995) can challenge and enrich one's life, this process can also be slow and painful.

## Common Struggles of Latinas in the U.S.

1. CONFLICTING IDENTITIES AND DIVIDED LOYALTIES. Emotional conflict is often experienced by those who cross geographical, cultural, and educational boundaries that influence the emergence of new identities. Conflicting family loyalties may be experienced when these identities are at odds with family expectations. Also, shifts in gender roles and lifestyles, as determined by socioeconomic status, can add to family disloyalty. Furthermore, intergenerational differences and conflicts are magnified as a result of students' bicultural or multicultural identities.

2. DISTURBING EMOTIONS. Anxiety and depression are prevalent in Latinas who become distant from their cultural roots as a consequence of their experiences in the U.S. A common consequence of this is low self-esteem. Grappling with these issues while attempting to learn in a different culture and in a second language influences underlying feelings of shame, guilt, and inadequacy. While these feelings are common to many Latinas who seek therapy, they are more intense in women who are of the first generation of their families to pursue or complete a college education.

Latinas experience shame and guilt when unable to master subjects in English or to excel in academic settings where standards for success are markedly different from those to which they are accustomed. Furthermore, members of this population tend to experience difficulties with competition and competency (Gomez & Fassinger, 1994) in institutional settings that promote White, North American, middle-class standards of achievement. Studying alone, competition, and isolation are often new experiences for them. Feelings of inadequacy are usually accompanied by guilt because of the belief that one is depriving the family of necessary resources.

In Latin American countries, the mother-daughter bond is extremely strong and close. In contrast to expectations for young women in the U.S., daughters are not expected to leave home and become independent. The departure of a young woman to pursue an education is usually experienced as a relational loss that is intolerable for both mother and daughter. Many daughters experience a deep and unconscious sense of disloyalty for having the privilege of an education and other opportunities that have not been available to their mothers or other women relatives from previous generations. Breaking with traditions, role expectations, and relational patterns is often painful because of the sense of disconnection engendered by the novelty and unfamiliarity of these experiences.

3. VISIBILITY, SUCCESS, AND LOSS. Pride and an increased connection to one's family heritage may develop when a Latina's career choice and lifestyle in a different culture are syntonic with the values and experiences of her family of origin. However, when a Latina studies and develops far away from her family, it can become a monumental task for her to accommodate changing self-perceptions along with expectations of significant others. Also, conflicting values, belief systems, and lifestyles sometimes create relational fractures beyond repair.

To avoid this, many women, like Sonia, choose to keep their newly found identities and experiences secret from their families and others who are important to them to preserve their bonds with them. Success and visibility may generate a sense of disloyalty if the student is the first in her family to pursue a higher education. For example, upward mobility may be difficult to achieve if poverty and inaccessibility to resources continue to affect the lives of loved ones. Clearly, the internal sources of distress that have been discussed and negotiating the challenges of a newly budding identity can deepen ambivalence toward achievement.

### The Meanings of Separation

The growth process inevitably leads to autonomy and differentiation from one's family of origin. In traditional Latin American cultures, however, women tend to separate from their families of origin while in the process of establishing their own families through marriage. With the increasing availability of educational opportunities for women, Latinas are more frequently migrating to different parts of their countries or abroad to pursue higher education. However, their families may expect them to return home after completing their degrees.

Separation is often associated with loss and can be responded to with intense grief and mourning. In some instances, this is related to earlier separations and migrations, as was true for Miriam and Ana. It can also be related to the loss of a family's structure. In Latin American culture, the family provides predictable roles, functions, and expectations. Creating a new structure after leaving home often becomes a challenging and difficult task, especially when the college does not offer a similar structure via resources that facilitate a sense of belonging. If, as in Sonia's case, separation has led to an increased sense of belonging in a culture that is incompatible with the culture of origin, a return home to family can be costly at an emotional level and problematic.

It would be useful to evaluate how the immigration experiences of Latinas earlier in life impact on the anticipation of graduation and returning home (Alvarez, 1995).

## CULTURALLY COMPETENT SERVICE DELIVERY

How mental health practitioners position themselves on those dimensions of cross-cultural intervention that have been discussed in this chapter may be related to several factors. These include:

1. awareness of the influence of standard practice theoretical frameworks on concepts of psychological development, health and illness, relationships, identity, and other pertinent characteristics;
2. prior training focused on the impact of migration, displacement, familial, cultural, and social variables on mental status; and
3. familiarity with the pressures experienced by international students who are often required to adjust to divergent cultural expectations in the U.S. For example, unfamiliarity with a new city can influence a student to reside in an unsafe neighborhood or to become an easy target for discrimination and exploitation.

College mental health practitioners' self-understanding, clinical sophistication, degree of acculturation, and knowledgeability of sources of cultural identity and related biases must determine to what extent the aforementioned variables influence interventions. It is also essential for practitioners to commit to learning about others while being aware of how personal reactions, biases, and assumptions affect therapeutic process. An openness to mutual learning can transform and facilitate empowerment for both the client and practitioner.

## REFERENCES

Alvarez, M. (1995). The experience of migration: A relational approach to therapy. *Work in Progress, 71*. Wellesley, MA: Wellesley College Stone Center Working Paper Series.

Aponte, J. F., Rivers, R. Y., & Wohl, J. (Eds.). (1995). *Psychological interventions and cultural diversity.* Boston: Allyn and Bacon.

Cole, E., Epsín, D. M., and Rothblum, E. D. (Eds.). (1992). Refugee women and their mental health: Shattered societies, shattered lives. New York: Harrington Park Press.

Comas-Díaz, L., & Griffith, E. E. H. (Eds.). (1988). *Clinical guidelines in cross-cultural mental health.* New York: John Wiley & Sons.

De La Cancela, V., Jenkins, Y. M., & Chin, J. L. (1993). Diversity in psychotherapy: Examination of racial, ethnic, gender, and political issues. In J. L. Chin, V. De La Cancela, & Y. M. Jenkins, *Diversity in psychotherapy: The politics of race, ethnicity, and gender.* Westport, CT: Praeger.

Espín, O. M. (1994). Crossing borders and boundaries: The life narratives of immigrant lesbians. *Division 44 Newsletter, 10*, 18–27.

Garcia Coll, C., Cook-Nobles, R., & Surrey, J. L. (1995). Diversity at the core: Implications for relational theory. *Work in Progress, 75*. Wellesley, MA: Wellesley College Stone Center Working Paper Series.

Gomez, M. J., & Fassinger, R. E. (1994). An initial model of Latina achievement: Acculturation, biculturalism, and achieving styles. *Journal of Counseling Psychology, 41*, 205–215.

Jablensky, A., Marsella, A. J., Ekblad, S., Jansson, B., Levi, L., & Bornemann, T. (1994). Refugee mental health and well-being: Conclusions and recommendations. In A. J. Marsella, T. Bornemann, S. Ekblad, & J. Orley (Eds.), *Amidst peril and pain: The mental health and well-being of the world's refugees.* Washington, DC: American Psychological Association.

Jenkins, V. M., De La Cancela, V., & Chin, J. L. (1993). Historical overviews: Three sociopolitical perspectives. In J. L. Chin, V. De La Cancela, & Y. M. Jenkins, *Diversity in psychotherapy: The politics of race, ethnicity, and gender.* Westport, CT: Praeger.

Jordan, J. (1991). The meaning of mutuality. In J. Jordan, A. G. Kaplan, J. B. Miller, I. P. Stiver, & J. L. Surrey. *Women's growth in connection: Writings from the Stone Center.* New York: Guilford.

Kraut, A. (1994). Historical aspects of refugee and immigration movements. In A. J. Marsella, T. Bornemann, S. Ekblad, & J. Orley (Eds.), *Amidst peril and pain: The mental health and well-being of the world's refugees.* Washington, D.C.: American Psychological Association.

Mair, M. (1988). Psychology as storytelling. *International Journal of Personal Construct Psychology, 1,* 125–138.

Miller, J. B. (1986). *Toward a new psychology of women.* Boston: Beacon Press.

Miller, J. B. (1988). Connections, disconnections and violations. *Work in Progress, 33.* Wellesley, MA: Wellesley College Stone Center Working Paper Series.

Miller, J. B., & Stiver, I. P. (1991). Movement in therapy: Honoring the "strategies of disconnection." *Work in Progress, 65.* Wellesley, MA: Wellesley College Stone Center Working Paper Series.

Ochberg, R. L. (1992). Social insight and psychological liberation. In G. C. Rosenwald & R. L. Ochberg (Eds.), *Storied lives: The cultural politics of self-understanding.* New Haven: Yale University Press.

Polster, E. (1995). *A population of selves: A therapeutic exploration of personal diversity.* San Francisco: Jossey-Bass.

Szapocznik, J., Kurtines, W., & Fernandez, T. (1980). Bicultural involvement and adjustment in Hispanic-American youths. *International Journal of Intercultural Relations, 4,* 353–365.

CHAPTER 9

# THE BIRACIAL BIND
## An Identity Dilemma

Diane Hart-Webb

> . . . identity provides the anchor for individuality and continuity with others. (Hussein A. Bulhan, 1985, p. 124)

> . . . there is no feeling of being alive without a sense of ego identity. Deprivation of identity can lead to murder. (Erik Erikson, 1963b, p. 240)

As college populations become increasingly diverse, mixed race identity is acknowledged more freely now than ever before. Despite the reality that, in the United States, race is both a primary source of identity and a significant basis for the polarization and stratification of groups, internal conflict associated with mixed race identity and the ways in which this trait contextualizes experiences in college settings are often overlooked or ignored by helping professionals. Therefore, this chapter includes a case study of a biracial student (i.e., African American and Caucasian) who does not feel accepted by African Americans or Caucasians. As a consequence, he feels hurt, angry, and resentful, and has resolved to live by the laws of revenge.

A preliminary review of the literature on the centrality of identity issues for mixed race persons follows to provide a context for understanding some of the challenges this population faces.

### LITERATURE REVIEW

The central task of adolescence is to form a stable identity. Erikson (1959) describes this as a "sense of personal sameness and historical continuity." The literature on mixed race adolescents suggests that for *some* individuals within this population, mixed race identity complicates the development of a cohesive well-integrated self-concept. Therefore, for some, it may threaten the overall process of identity development. A few studies dispute this point of view by attributing such findings to differences in research design and sampling. For example, Kerwin, Ponterotto, Jackson, and Harris (1993) found that biracial children did not view themselves as marginal. However, because most of their subjects were preadolescents, it might be assumed that significant identity conflict had not yet surfaced in their lives. In addition, this population was from biracial neighborhoods where their identity was more often accepted.

At a preliminary level, the research suggests that avoidance of problems and the successful achievement of identity in this population is related to the availability of supportive families, cohesive social networks, and integrated schools and neighborhoods (Poussaint, 1984). However, much of this was not in place for Ryan.

## RYAN

The case study of Ryan poignantly illustrates how mixed race identity issues can both affect and complicate developmental conflicts. It also illustrates how racial identity provides a frame of reference or "language" for the client as he struggles to describe his presenting problem, the history of the problem, and to interpret traumatic life events.

### Background

Ryan was a 25-year-old single biracial man who presented, self-referred, at a university counseling center. This was his first encounter with therapy, which he pursued at the suggestion of his girlfriend following a fist fight with a fellow band musician. He attended night school at the university, with the hope of obtaining an undergraduate degree. Ryan was also working as a data entry operator at the university.

Ryan was born in a small town in the northeast. Until recently, he had never known his father, who had been "run out of town" when Ryan was only an infant. His mother was the younger of two Irish Catholic sisters who were sexually abused by their father, a very successful and high-profile business executive. His mother was considered the "family renegade," a title influenced by becoming pregnant out of wedlock by a Black man and other exploits. Ryan described his mother as "very strange" in that she was "hyper" in her emotionality and constantly repetitive. He believed she had betrayed her children. For example, she never told Ryan that he was part African American until his junior year in high school when peers called him "mulatto" along with other derogatory epithets.

Following Ryan's birth, his mother was involved in a series of other relationships. Her first husband was an ex-convict who had used a car bomb with intent to murder. At the time of Ryan's therapy, she was married to a former executive of a prominent company, a man who divorced his wife to marry her.

As a result of his mother's liaisons, Ryan had three siblings, all by different fathers. The oldest was Jerome, a 23-year-old landscaper, who was part Native American. Ryan's sister, Megan, age 20, was attending a state university in the northeast, while their youngest brother, Michael, age 18, attended another college despite his drug addiction.

Ryan disclosed that he was repeatedly molested by his first stepfather between the ages of 6 and 9. Even though he believed his mother was not aware of this, he also believed that this same stepfather, an alcoholic, abused various foster children his mother brought into the home. Ryan was beaten frequently by his first two stepfathers with minor provocation. The only positive relationship that he could remember was with a boy he considered to be his friend when he was in the eighth grade. This friend was White and someone Ryan could talk to "about anything." Upon completion of eighth grade, apparently they went to different schools.

At age 16, Ryan began to abuse drugs "from pot to acid and everything in between." Apparently, this problem was never noticed by any of the adults in his life. By age 22, Ryan decided he had had enough of the drug scene and stopped using without any professional support. At that point, his academic problems were noticed and he was sent to a private school for gifted learning-disabled students. While the school was helpful, his school performance suffered because the help came so late in his academic career.

Ryan continued to have problems with writing, numerical calculations, and with sequencing and organizing his ideas on paper. Fortunately, his full-scale IQ of 118 helped him to get a scholarship to a state university. After one year, however, he dropped out and hitchhiked to Boston, motivated by the hope that a "diverse population would be kind" to him. There he immediately joined Greenpeace, the environmental action group, because this organization provided him with a place to sleep. Ryan then worked on one job after another, saved some money, and rented an apartment with several people he referred to as "losers."

After arriving in Boston, Ryan had two serious relationships with women. It was the first relationship that made him feel as though he might "fit in" somewhere. His girlfriend had been impressed with his independence, and he by her stable way of life. She graduated from college and moved on to New York City. While he wanted to marry her, he recognized that their relationship was going to end because he was Black, and her father, a rabbi, would never approve of him. At the time of the initial interview he was involved with another young woman who helped him to find a better job. It was also she who prompted Ryan to seek therapy.

Because Ryan had endured his parents' divorce, sexual and physical abuse, several stepfathers, biracial concerns, and substance abuse, he assumed he had to be "superman," or capable of tackling just about any situation effectively.

**The Intervention**

Ryan arrived 15 minutes late for our first session, dressed in tattered jeans and an old sweatshirt. His swarthy good looks could easily be taken for either African American or Caucasian. Although his speech evidenced that he was bright, he presented with agitation, restlessness, excessive use of profanity, and provocative body language. He complained about the injustice in the workplace and his own problems there resulting from being "an underdog and Black." However, when asked to tell me about his workplace late in the session, he dissociated from his Black identity. Ryan spoke about how "those Black people at work are seen as lazy by [the] boss, but I see them as relaxed." "I don't know why," he continued, "we Whites are always shoving our values on others."

In a labile tone, he also spoke angrily about people who were "dreamers." When asked about whom he was referring, he said, "fellow musicians, and intellectual-do-nothings" like most of the university community. Yet he admitted to a fear of doing nothing, which he compensated for by struggling to be a "superman." This proved to be a recurring theme in his life.

Ryan's need to be a superman resonated with Conflict #5 in Gibbs and Moskowitz-Sweet's (1991) framework which involves ambivalence toward achievement and upward mobility. Ryan seemed unable to identify fully with Whites. Therefore, he assumed that to achieve he would need to compensate for the stereotyped image of the lazy, or perhaps passive Black male worker. Ryan's awareness of prejudice and discrimination seemed to deflate his ambitions and to sabotage his achievement.

In the second session, I told Ryan there was a no smoking policy. This seemed to provoke intense hostility and rage, particularly toward authority and society-at-large. In another tirade filled with profanity, he complained that the world is divided into two groups: the Judeo-Christians and the Gypsies. The former are the repressive power-based dictators of the world, and the latter are free-spirited victims of the powerful. Ryan identified with the Gypsies because of his spirited values. Yet, he also identified with the Judeo-Christians, who "hold the goodies." In Ryan's view, the "goodies" were material success and a perceived sense of power and control over the environment.

The theme of powerlessness versus powerfulness was most evident in this session and seemed to represent Ryan's biracial identity. This theme persisted as he railed on about "feeling out of sync with the world" and "like two people." His shifts in identification between two races and two opposing value systems also seemed to be indicative of this.

The first conflict in Gibbs and Moskowitz-Sweet's framework, that of basic identity, also seems to be relevant to this case. The fundamental concern here is, "Who am I?" which is accompanied by considerable anxiety. Ryan was aware that he was only partially a member of White society. Furthermore, he could not fully identify as Black either, because of internalized feelings of hatred and shame about this aspect of his identity. Although Ryan described himself as a free-spirited Gypsy, he clearly disliked being cast in the role of victim. He required a lot of energy to cope effectively and to maintain his ego integrity. For instance, at times evidence of his rage was apparent despite the fact that he was well defended.

Not only was Ryan's initial transference influenced by his anger and feeling that he was "out of sync" with the world, but also by the visibility of the therapist's Caucasian identity. He also perceived the therapist to be a member of the "Judeo-Christian power structure."

The following dialogue occurred in the second session:

R: I bet you live in Lincoln or maybe Sudbury (i.e., predominantly White middle-upper class suburbs of Boston).

T: Is it important for you to see me living in Lincoln or Sudbury?

R: No, I was just wondering where you live, maybe Newton (i.e., another White middle-class suburb)?

T: What do those towns mean to you?

R: Oh, you don't have to be so evasive. I'm not going to call you or follow you home.

T: I really wasn't thinking of myself. I just find it interesting to know what you're feeling about where I live.

R: (Silence)

T: I'm wondering if you may be seeing me as a Judeo-Christian and those towns may signify that to you?

R: Maybe.

T: I'm also wondering if my being a White therapist is comfortable for you. Certainly we can talk about any feelings you may have around this issue.

R: Well, what the hell do you know about being out of sync; being in two worlds, but having no home?

T: You're quite right. I don't know that experience. I suspect I can learn much about that from you, but I do know a little about human pain, and I gather this has been a struggle for you for a while.

R: Don't be so sure. As long as I hang in I'll be fine.

T: Perseverance is a strength of yours. You wouldn't have gotten this far, nor would you have come in, if you weren't so tenacious.

Ryan missed the next session, but did call to cancel, stating he had a severe cold. At our next session, I mentioned that I was glad he was feeling better. He was markedly better dressed and seemed slightly less angry as he asked me if I really thought he was persevering, since this was a positive trait he claimed. I told him that I always tried to be honest with him and I only said what I meant and this was an example.

He talked in this session about feeling that "his life is a reversal." He continued, "I have some schematic organization problem, there's something in my physiology. I'm left-handed, I have severe disgraphia, I'm biracial and I have grey spots in my sexuality. I guess I'm sort of bisexual. These identities confuse me. Like I said, I've got two sides." Once again, his efforts at ego integrity seemed to fail him.

Gibbs and Moskowitz-Sweet's framework seems to explain this as the conflict between impulse management and sexuality. This conflict finds expression in several ways: sexual orientation issues, confused gender identity, sexual activity patterns, and general impulse management. Often those who experience this conflict feel driven to behave sexually in accordance with misperceived cultural expectations, rather than their own personal needs or desires. Here sexual orientation seems to be generated by sex role identification conflicts between adolescents and their parents, particularly when ambivalent or negative feelings toward the same-sex parent of color exist.

Ryan then reflected on previous sexual encounters and his desire for a relationship with a woman based on unconditional love. With a shift in tone and increased profanity, he continued by speaking in sexually graphic terms about how many women, especially in liberal settings like the university, find him mysterious and a "way out of their middle-class White snobbish upbringing," yet "they would never bring me home to Daddy." Ryan made angry derogatory remarks about women, which seemed to express confused feelings about them in general. The rage he felt about having to live with this much anxiety seemed to be projected onto other women, notably White women like his mother. As stated earlier, his mother could not bring Ryan's Black father "home to Daddy." It was his mother's family who "ran him [his father] out of town."

Ryan's fear of repeating his father's experience became clear in a subsequent session. He explained that his girlfriend was pregnant with his baby and planned to have an abortion. Ryan expected that she would leave him, as other women in his life had done, once the abortion was performed. Although he wanted to marry her to make it right for their child, in reality, he could hardly take care of himself. Furthermore, he considered the reality that their baby would be an "Oreo,"[1] and he could not be around to protect it from the pain of that experience.

I asked Ryan who had protected him; he spoke of his special friend at age 14. In exploring the meaning of that relationship, I learned that Ryan was able to be "just Ryan" with this friend while no one else really accepted him because he was "mixed" at a predominantly White school. Yet, this friend was always there. After they finished eighth grade, Ryan and his friend went their separate ways. Since then he had primarily been concerned with survival.

In revisiting the question of who had protected him, it became apparent that one aspect of Ryan's ego was painfully struggling against identifying with a father who left him. Paradoxically another part of Ryan seemed to succumb to his perception of this identification.

I praised Ryan for his survival skills and decided to treat him as a trauma survivor. Therefore, the treatment process moved slowly, focused on survivorship rather than victimization. In this initial phase of treatment, I also thought it was important to create an atmosphere of containment, since his anger was spilling out with the slightest provocation or frustration. In addition, I hoped that the continuity of sessions would offer some predictability for Ryan. The initial phase of treatment was structured in alignment with his treatment goals which included attaining a degree, a decent job, and three meals a day. My hopes for our work were:

1. for Ryan to look at it as a time and place where he could be accepted for being "just Ryan," and
2. eventual internalization of the introjects experienced in the process.

During the next two sessions, I tried to help Ryan to stay focused on his goals. A notable shift came when he arrived at one of these sessions wanting to sort out what caused much of his "self-destructive behavior." In relation to this, not only was he concerned with his own background and how society affects biracial individuals, but Ryan was also concerned about to what extent he was responsible for this trait. He said he recognized that his self-pity provoked either passivity, as evidenced by his extreme procrastination, or anger which he projected onto the world. He also said that he allowed his problems to build up in order to justify his anger and self-pity. I acknowledged how important and positive it was that he understood and accepted some of the responsibility for his behavior.

This proved to be an important focus, since Ryan had procrastinated in submitting his application to the university, in accordance with one of his immediate goals. I assigned him the task of writing two pages of the application process per week with the hope that these small increments toward goal completion would transfer to a greater sense of achievement and responsibility.

By then he spoke with profanity less often and he thanked me more often at the end of sessions. At the end of one particular session he told me how comforting he found my voice, and that he carried that comfort with him during the week. My voice had become his temporary transitional object.

A test for what seemed to be at least a tentative positive therapeutic alliance took place in the eighth session, when Ryan brought in a lengthy letter of intent to the university he hoped to attend. He read the letter and asked my opinion. The application letter was inflammatory, offensive, and disconnected. When pressed for my opinion, I was aware of the possibility of getting trapped in a manipulative situation, but proceeded to take a risk anyhow. I was careful not to arouse a feeling of rejection, so I acknowledged some positive aspects of the letter (e.g., his commitment to authenticity, completion of this monumental task). Then I followed up on the past session when he had talked about allowing problems to build up to justify anger and self-pity. I asked if he was going to do this now. Immediately he became defensive, but I pursued this. It was my impression that Ryan would have difficulty with taking on the perspective of another, so, using the metaphor of a basketball game, I asked him to pretend he was an admissions counselor and to react to the letter. I suggested that he keep his goals firmly in mind while examining the letter. At the same time I said that he might need to send the letter just as he wrote it, but emphasized "that the ball is in his court" and that he had equal time in this game.

Ryan had felt powerless in situations where he had perceived the demands and expectations of others as uncomfortable and controlling. He also interpreted such expectations as coming from either a Black culture or a White culture, and felt connected to neither. As a consequence, he had often reacted, rather than responded more proactively. The metaphor of a basketball game offered him the opportunity to shift his thinking to being an active participant in this admissions process. The idea of active participation versus passive reaction also introduced the idea of personal responsibility in the college admission process for Ryan. My hope was that he would inevitably recognize his own sense of power in this process.

He seemed to like and to use the game metaphor effectively, so I pursued it and asked whether or not it might be a good idea to stop carrying the past on his back into the game. In response, the following exchange took place:

> R: The past is me.
> T: Partly, but remember you came here with some aspirations. Those are a part of you too. They are not the past—they are the present and the future.
> R: But I believe in the gospel of vengeance.
> T: I think you need to decide something very honestly. Are you more interested in revenge, which seems to be a purpose that is connected to your past, or in reaching your aspirations?
> R: If I don't give them a fight, I'm selling out.

Surprisingly, he shook my hand, thanked me, and told me that he had a lot to think about as he left.

Ryan's fear of "selling out" seemed to result from conflicting loyalties. He abhorred the values of White society. Yet his goal, admission to a university which epitomized the White power struggle, suggested that he also bought into those values.

Another turning point for Ryan came at the ninth session which was two weeks later. He entered with a big smile and began to share his second attempt at an admissions letter. Even though it was honest, this version was more tempered and focused on why he wanted a degree. He told me that he did not feel like he was selling out with this letter, because its contents were focused on why he wanted a degree. Rather reflectively, he added, "I didn't think of how much of myself I am really destroying by living a life of revenge."

Ryan then revealed that the first university he had attended would not send a copy of his transcript because of an outstanding balance on his bill. Initially in response to this, he had felt brutalized again, he explained. However, he made an effort to stay focused on problem solving, and finally called his mother and stepfather to request a small loan. Ryan played our "what if game" before he called. In a straightforward but undemanding manner, he told his mother about his difficulties. Although she initially hesitated, before their conversation ended she had offered to refinance his loan. I complimented Ryan on taking this risk, which I framed as a leap of personal faith. His ability to tolerate the ambivalence of a possible giving-yet-rejecting mother was remarkable in view of all he had been through.

Since Ryan had come to Boston, a place where he thought he could have dreams, he had been trying to differentiate enough from his past to form a more positive and unique image of himself. Toward this end, he had progressed from exercising rebellious and rejecting behavior to a greater degree of independence. He also felt less angry and "very psyched" that he was able to focus on gaining acceptance to the university.

As we waited to hear of the status of his application, Ryan's insurance benefits were terminated because of a change in his work hours. For the next three weeks I continued to see him on a limited basis. During that time he asked me to write down what I had observed as changes in him, as he needed to look at and study my observations. I began to do so with his input. Ryan then told me that a drunk acquaintance had called him a "Celtic-nigger," and he was able to walk away, rather than "trying to take his face off." He felt this was a real indicator of some shifts in his thinking. While the incident made Ryan angry, which he expressed, he was aware that it did not represent the "lifetime of hurts" he had experienced. At that point he told me that he felt ready to look at the "lifetime of hurts," since he did not want the rest of his life to be a "wasteland."

The following lines from a T. S. Eliot poem seemed to be meaningful and appropriate to share with Ryan at that point:

> We shall not cease from exploration
> And the end of all our exploring
> Will be to arrive where we started
> And to know the place for the first time.

I told Ryan that my hope for him was that he would begin to integrate the different parts of his identity and to know himself as whole for the first time. Sometime later, I learned that Ryan had received word of his acceptance to the university.

### NOTE

1. "Oreo" is colloquial slang that derives from the well-known cookie of that name. It refers to someone who is Black on the outside, but perceived to have White values on the inside.

# REFERENCES

Bulhan, H. (1985). *Franz Fanon and the psychology of oppression* (p. 124). New York: Plenum.

Eliot, T. S. (1993). Little Gidding, from Four Quartets. *Norton anthology of English literature, 6 (2)* (p. 2170). New York: W. W. Norton.

Erikson, E. H. (1959). Growth and crises of the healthy personality. In G. S. Klein (Ed.), *Psychological Issues*. New York: International University Press.

Erikson, E. H. (1963a). *Childhood and society* (p. 40). New York: W. W. Norton.

Erikson, E. H. (1963b). *Identity and the life cycle*. New York: W. W. Norton.

Gibbs, J. T., & Moskowitz-Sweet, G. (1991). Clinical and cultural issues in the treatment of biracial and bicultural adolescents. *The Journal of Contemporary Human Services*, December, 579–591.

Kerwin, C., Ponterotto, J. G., Jackson, B. L., & Harris, A. (1993). Racial identity in biracial children: A qualitative investigation. *Journal of Counseling Psychology, 40 (2)*, 221–231.

Poussaint, A. F. (1984). Study of interracial children presents positive picture. *Bulletin/Interracial Books for Children, 15*, 9–10.

CHAPTER 10

# COLLEGE ENROLLMENT AND ACADEMIC SUCCESS AMONG PUERTO RICAN WOMEN

Brunilda De Leon, Michelle Stefanisko, and Belinda Lopez Corteza

## INTRODUCTION

Deviating from the case study format of previous chapters, this chapter will identify and discuss personal, psychological, social, and cultural factors that influence college enrollment and academic success among Puerto Rican women. Both qualitative and quantitative data are used as bases for this discussion. Excerpts from interviews with several Puerto Rican women students are used also to explain their perceptions of these factors. Perceptions of the following are highlighted:

1. determinants of academic success;
2. the relationship between the participants' personal qualities, sociocultural variables (e.g., family, social networks, friends, school, church, and other community institutions); and
3. ethnicity, gender, and socioeconomic status as sociopolitical issues.

Profiles of the participants are outlined to suggest guidelines for informing culturally competent counseling, mental health, and other supportive services for this student population.

## THE PROBLEM

Despite increasingly competitive job markets, downsizing, and other challenges to occupational success, a college education continues to be one of the most effective pathways to socioeconomic mobility and the mainstream of U.S. society. Educational and occupational attainment are intimately related and have a tremendous influence on one's quality of life and prospects for the future. Yet, the figures that reflect educational and career attainment of women of color, particularly Puerto Rican women, are alarming. Despite the presumption that conditions are improving for people of color, colleges and universities are failing to enroll and retain students of color at a rate consistent with increases in the total population.

Hispanics (i.e., Spanish-speaking populations) are the fastest-growing and second-largest ethnic minority group in the United States (Banks, 1991; National Council of La Raza, 1992). According to the U.S. Bureau of Census report for 1990, Hispanics will become the largest pluralistic population in the U.S. around the turn of the century. Yet, Hispanics are likely to retain the distinction of having the lowest level of educational attainment and the largest percentage of families living in poverty.

The total population of Puerto Ricans is estimated to be six million, about half of whom live in Puerto Rico and the remainder in the United States (Banks, 1991; Fitzpatrick, 1987; U.S. Bureau of the Census, 1990). This population division has origins in Puerto Rico's long and complex relationship with the United States.

## Relevant History and Demographic Information

In 1898, as a result of the Hispanic-American war, Spain ceded Puerto Rico to the United States. Citizenship was given to Puerto Ricans in 1917. Although the citizens of the island elected their first governor in 1949, Puerto Rico remained a Commonwealth of the United States (Fitzpatrick, 1987). Therefore, unlike other Latin American groups in the United States, Puerto Ricans, as U.S. citizens, have easier access to their homeland and move continuously to and from the island.

Of the Latin American population, Puerto Ricans have the largest number of families living in poverty. Only 51.3% of all Hispanics 25 years or over have at least four years of high school compared to 80.5% of non-Hispanics (U.S. Bureau of the Census, 1990). Puerto Ricans and other Latinos continue to be among the most underrepresented groups in institutions of higher learning. Furthermore, the percentage of Puerto Ricans and other low-income populations enrolled in college has been steadily declining since 1976 (National Puerto Rican Coalition, 1991).

The plight of Hispanic women has been of longstanding concern to educators, mental health professionals, and policy makers (Amaro & Russo, 1987; Comas-Díaz, 1987, National Council of La Raza, 1992). In addition, the steadily increasing number of female-headed families, the large number of adolescent mothers, and the poor socioeconomic conditions of Latin women are considered problematic (Amaro, 1993; Amaro & Russo, 1987; Zambrana, 1982). Furthermore, Hispanic families are also at risk because of poor housing conditions, substandard health care and psychological problems (Amaro, 1993; Canino, 1982; Comas-Díaz, 1987; Espín, 1987).

Despite these dismal reports, the literature contains sufficient evidence that some Latinas have made progress and have achieved success in the educational, occupational, and sociopolitical arenas (Acosta-Belen, 1966; Amott & Matthaei, 1991; Baca-Zinn, 1980). Nevertheless, impoverished living conditions shape and determine the daily realities of the great majority. Low income levels and limited occupational, and career opportunities are, to a great extent, a result of limited educational attainment among this group. These conditions perpetuate poverty and, thus, the vulnerable position of Latinas in U.S. society.

## WHY THIS CHAPTER IS IMPORTANT

Currently, enough data exist to indicate that the underrepresentation of Latina students at colleges and universities is associated with socioeconomic status, poor learning environments, academic limitations, inadequate access to college-bound curricula, and other institutional barriers. However, the research on factors that have influenced the educational development and adjustment of Puerto Rican and other Latinas to college is very limited. Therefore, the interviews which are the basis for this chapter are particularly valuable in that they offer a first-hand account of some women's perceptions as well as a "feeling" for their current situations. Finally, some of the stressors that exceed the capacities of support networks are identified for this population.

## RELEVANT LITERATURE

The literature suggests that educational and occupational attainment results from complex interactions of family background, socioeconomic status, personal characteristics, previous academic and work experiences, academic performance, educational history, parental and teacher encouragement, and educational attainment (Arbonna, 1990; Bingham & Ward, 1994; Brooks, 1990). However, several theorists have related the educational success of women to additional variables.

There have been many efforts to develop theories that more accurately explain women's educational and career development. Hackett and Betz (1981) proposed that due to the socialization process, women have lower and weaker career-related self-efficacy expectations than men, have a more restricted range of career options, and underutilize their capabilities and talents. Betz and Fitzgerald (1987) and Fitzgerald and Crites (1980) also concluded that the career development of women is more complex than that for men for two reasons: (a) women are more likely to experience work and family role conflicts, and (b) women's career development differs from men's in terms of sequence and patterning. Forrest and Mikolaitis (1986) proposed that because existing theories have been developed from a male perspective, they fail to incorporate the female perspective, which recognizes and values connection and relationships as central to self-identity and personal growth.

The development and educational success of ethnic minority women involve another set of variables that aid with defining the experiences of Hispanic women. The growing interest in the mental health and psychological development of this population as mediated by culture, gender, ethnicity, race, and social class is increasingly recognized. Contemporary scholars and practitioners concerned with cultural sensitivity and social change are confronted with a difficult task; that is, challenging the notion that Hispanic culture is a liability to the personal educational development of this population. Although these researchers recognize that some cultural practices limit the development of Latinas, it has been asserted that others may need to be examined in the sociocultural and historical contexts from which they have evolved.

Positive aspects of cultural practices tend not to be recognized or appreciated. Therefore, De Leon (1993) identified the following as having positive effects on the educational and career development of young Puerto Rican women:

1. an orientation toward group work and collaboration;
2. a strong family orientation, with the family as the major source of support and pride;
3. a strong value for the extended family and social networks;
4. a strong religious orientation;
5. socialization to assume multiple roles; and
6. perceptions of individual success and accomplishments as success for the family and the group.

The literature also indicates that while Latinas are questioning oppressive elements of their culture, and are displaying more flexible gender role behaviors and attitudes, positive cultural institutions are important to their development (Amott & Mattaei, 1991; Comas-Díaz, 1987; De Leon, 1993;

Vasquez-Nuttall, Romero-Garcia, & De Leon, 1987). These include family, church, schools, friends, and community. At the same time, researchers and practitioners emphasize the need to identify and challenge those cultural patterns and institutions that are oppressive to Hispanic women.

## METHODS
### The Interviews

The approach to the interviews discussed in this chapter located the psychological development of Puerto Rican women as influenced by social and cultural factors. Furthermore, the interviews elicited their aspirations, concerns, interests, and newly acquired knowledge.

### Sample

Fifteen undergraduate Puerto Rican women, ages 18 to 22, enrolled at a large university in New England participated in the study. All participants were full-time students, single, and lived on campus. They also held campus jobs and received student financial assistance. Their distribution by year in college was as follows: six were first-year students, three were sophomores, four were juniors, and two were seniors. All participants completed high school in the United States, and only two reported that they had resided in this country for less than ten years. Eight of the participants reported that their parents do not have a college degree; the remaining seven women's parents have college degrees. Eight of the women have siblings in college. Nine reported family incomes between $30,000 and $50,000. Two reported family incomes of $9,000 or less, one between $10,000 and $19,000, and three between $20,000 and $29,000. In addition, three reported family incomes of $50,000 or more.

### Data Collection

Participants were interviewed individually and asked to complete four questionnaires:

1. the *Bem Sex Role Inventory (BSRI)*, an inventory which assesses gender role identity and psychological characteristics (Bem, 1974);
2. the *Self-Efficacy Scale (SES)*, an assessment of generalized expectations of self-efficacy that are not linked to specific situations or behaviors (Sherer et al., 1982);
3. the *Minority Status Survey (MSS)*, an assessment of the four stages of ethnic/racial identity development included in Cross's

Identity Development Model (1971);
4. *Family Environmental Scale (FES)*, an assessment of the social and environmental characteristics of families (Moos & Moos, 1974; Rueschenberg & Buriel, 1995).

## A Summary of Results

These data reveal influences of the following variables on the academic success and college enrollment of this sample: personal qualities, family, church, friends, community, life transitions, and sociopolitical awareness. For the purposes of this book, quantitative results of this study are summarized in this chapter.

### Bem Sex Role Inventory

The results of the Bem Sex Role Inventory indicate that the majority of the women described themselves as having nontraditional gender role identities.

### Self-Efficacy Scale

Most of the respondents obtained a high score on the General Self-Efficacy subscales scores. The result of the Social Self-Efficacy (SSE) subscale indicated that most of the participants scored above the mean. An examination of the gender role identity scale and the complete Self-Efficacy Scale indicates that women who were classified as low on both the femininity and masculinity scales of the BSRI also scored below the mean on both Self-Efficacy subscales (i.e., Global and Social), with both of them obtaining the only two significantly low scores on the GSE.

### Minority Identity Scale

The majority of the women reported being at the Encounter Stage, even though only three obtained a single Encounter Stage score. Instead, a common pattern for this group was a combination of more than one stage simultaneously. Eight of the respondents obtained scores at the Encounter and Internalization stages simultaneously, and one of them had a combination of Encounter, Immersion, and Internalization stages. Two respondents obtained scores at the Internalization stage, while one respondent was identified with a Pre-Encounter/Internalization stage profile.

### Family Environment Scale

The results of the FES indicate that the participants described their families as highest on Moral/Religious values, followed by a strong emphasis on Control and Cohesion, which preceded Conflict and Expressiveness. The majority also described their families as having a high Intellectual-Cultural

Orientation. Several participants also indicated that their families fostered independence. The subscales with the lowest scores were Active-Recreational Orientation and Organization.

## Personal Qualities that Facilitate Puerto Rican Women's Educational Experience

The results of the Bem Sex Role Inventory (BSRI), the Self-Efficacy Scale (SES), and the narratives provide insight into the qualities that have promoted the success of these young Puerto Rican women. First, according to the BSRI, the majority of these women scored high on instrumental (i.e., stereotypical masculine) qualities. There were four participants, who, in addition to being high on instrumental qualities, described themselves as being high on traditional feminine qualities. Thus, these four women can be described as having high levels of both masculine and feminine traits (i.e., androgynous). They were high on affection, compassion, sensitivity to others' needs, gentleness, and love for children. Interestingly, some of the instrumental qualities such as "strong personality," "independent," "assertiveness," "leadership abilities," and "defend my own beliefs" were important to women who scored highest on the masculinity scale of the BSRI, as well as those who scored highest on femininity.

Participants were also asked to talk about the personal qualities that facilitated their educational success and their transition to college life. Their narratives substantiated the results of the BSRI and the SES. In addition, the narratives highlighted other dimensions of personality that contribute substantially to academic and social success that were not measured by standardized tests. Some of the most frequently mentioned attributes were responsible, perseverant, highly motivated, determined, hardworking, ambitious to succeed, adaptable, and of strong personality:

> Personal qualities? Ambition . . . to succeed. I was very distressed and . . . was going to leave [college] and go to a different school. . . . I was failing. . . . I decided to just change my major and go . . . a different path which was better . . . to move forward and to keep going and to succeed no matter what kind of obstacles I find.
>
> I tend to be determined to accomplish something that I [start]. Even if . . . it is totally different, like what I am doing now.
>
> Hardworking, responsible, I just wanted to be independent. I just wanted to be successful. I'm smart. I didn't see myself as being

smart but my parents did. [A] desire to help people. Patience. That helps a lot. . . . I can understand . . . other people's feelings.

### Family Influence in Participants' Development and Decision to Attend College

The influence of the family in these women's social development, and most importantly in their decision to continue their higher education, is evident throughout their interviews. Parents emerged as the single most important influence in several areas. Fourteen of the fifteen participants identified their parents as the key people involved in their process of developing an interest and deciding to attend college. The college education of these young women was a major priority to their parents, regardless of whether or not they had attended college themselves.

For those parents who had not attended college, sending their daughters to college carried a special meaning:

> My parents never went to college so they were always telling me, "So you have to go to college. I don't want to see you working in a factory or something like that."

> My parents always told me, "You know we didn't go to college and we would like you to go. It would be admirable for you to be successful. You know we didn't have the money, we didn't have the time or anything. It was hard for us. Nowadays it is easier."

For those women whose parents attended college, higher education was an expectation. This was not without appreciation and recognition of the difficulties encountered by Latinas in pursuing an education:

> I moved to the U.S. when I was nine, then I confronted the language barrier and I confronted discrimination. I was discriminated against because of my background [and] because I was Puerto Rican, in an all Anglo-Saxon community . . . we were the second Hispanic family in that community and there were no African Americans, so it was hard. . . . My teachers always put me down because I wasn't at the same level that the other kids were. . . . Nor were there . . . programs to help me with . . . English as a Second Language . . . That's why I think I've always wanted to keep going with my education, and to do better and to go to college. So I can prove people wrong.

Only one participant did not mention either of her parents as the person that she admired most. The other participants agreed that their parents believed in them and were their primary source of emotional support while at college. They also admired their parents for their "patience," "strength," "ability to adapt," "positive outlook on life," "good sense of humor," and "flexibility."

Participants also acknowledged that in addition to their parents, members of their extended families served as role models. Members of the extended family were frequently seen as sources of emotional support, nurturance, and transmitters of cultural values. These role models provided information, advice, and assistance in their assessment of academic and career options. Many of these role models were women who were described as "very determined," "strict," "clear about their goals," "strong," and "nontraditional." Teachers and counselors were particularly influential to those who were first-generation college students. The following responses were typical of those offered by most of the participants:

> My guidance counselor from high school . . . really spoke to me about it, she was the one who helped me decide to come to [this college]. In my senior year I was with the guidance counselor every other week talking about where I wanted to go and trying to get the letters of recommendation all set. She helped me through the procedure to get into college. So that was really helpful.
>
> What do I admire about my high school teacher? She was very strict and she always . . . knew what she wanted. And she was always encouraging people to go to school and to get good grades.

Having siblings and friends in college was also influential to these women's decisions to attend college, particularly first-generation students:

> I decided to attend college through my advisors, high school counselors, and following my brothers' and sisters' steps. They went to college. They didn't finish appropriately, but they're trying to finish now . . . actually, it wasn't much as an encouragement, but I just followed their steps.
>
> Well, some of my friends, they [told me]: "Oh! Go for it! It's the best." And I would be like, "So is it hard?" They know it's hard, but in the long run you know it's great. So they were always encouraging me.

Women whose parents had a college degree were less likely to include teachers or counselors as individuals who had influenced their educational aspirations. At the same time, these women had a larger network of support and knowledge upon which they could rely. They could turn to parents, grandparents, and other relatives for support and knowledge. This added level of support provided an important lens for thinking critically about their goals and their circumstances. Others whose parents did not attend college did not usually have other close relatives they could rely on for such support and direction:

> Actually no, I think it was my grandmother. She wanted [her] grandchildren to go to college, something she didn't do . . . . She just told them [my parents] to tell us that we have to go to college. One thing she told me once, that if she . . . had my age now she wouldn't be . . . a housewife. She would go out and have an education.

> My friend _____, who is graduating this year with an associate degree in nursing. She has a really high GPA. With a 3-year-old son, so that just takes a lot out of people and I admire her for that.

### Influence of Other Sociocultural Factors

The participants in this study identified several life events as influential to their process of becoming college students. They also acknowledged the importance of their affiliation with a church, the experience of work, and their involvement in and concern for their community. These young women attributed their opportunity to obtain a college education as well as their success to membership in these institutions.

Churches are central to community life in Hispanic communities and provide a range of support for their members. Interestingly, all but one of the young women in the sample indicated that they were members of a church. The commitment to the church was present in high school and continued through college; this commitment was strongest in those whose parents had not gone to college. The majority attended Pentecostal churches which were fundamentalist in orientation:

> Influential people? Yeah, and my pastor would always preach in front you know . . . to me. He would always tell the youth, "really think about going to college," like he would be just like my par-

ents. "We didn't have the opportunity you guys have and now you know, take advantage of it."

They [people from church] try to help me, if there's any problem I think my parents and the people from church, like the pastor or something, they'll try to help me in any way that they can . . . they try to say positive things.

The individuals and experiences these students encountered provide insights into the complexities of their cultural and ethnic backgrounds. When describing the critical events that encouraged them to pursue a college education, for example, they also discussed many of the barriers that prevent Latinas from pursuing a higher education. Furthermore, they described the difficult and harsh realities of the majority of young people in Latino communities and how this recognition had increased their motivation to succeed.

The social circumstances in the Puerto Rican community are a reference point for these young women. They recognize the lack of educational opportunities, the lack of adequately paying jobs, the debilitating influences of crime and drugs, and the continuing struggles of parents and others to succeed. The participants in this study valued work. The entry-level positions that are available to them provide a perspective and an experience that influences them to continue their education:

Well, it was mostly because the community, well, the place where I live is . . . mostly Hispanic people, Puerto Rican people, and . . . not people that have many opportunities and once I had an opportunity to go to college . . . I didn't take it seriously, but once I went to work and I was getting paid the minimum and I was doing . . . hard work and it was terrible conditions . . . I just realized that wasn't what I wanted, plus I was working while I was going to school and I knew that's not what I wanted to do . . . Just . . . get a regular job and get paid the minimum and not be able to get the stuff that I wanted. And just grow as a person more than I have already grown.

I thought it was important for me to go to college so that I could get a better job than working at McDonald's, like I was in high school . . . , 40 hours a week, and I had my own apartment. . . . I realized that I didn't wanna live the rest of my life like that.

Not only were these young women aware of limited economic opportunities in their communities, but they recognized other significant barriers:

> I just wanted to be successful, . . . some of my friends, my young friends . . . would . . . get pregnant and not attend college and . . . would just finish high school and that was it for them. I wanted something else . . . something better.

> An incident that happened to me . . . in high school, tenth grade. . . . It was in town, I was in town waiting for the bus with my siblings and we were talking in Spanish and this man came and told us to go back to Puerto Rico, that we don't belong here, and it really helped me decide that it was really important to come to college.

## TRANSITIONS

The transitions these young women are undergoing take place at a time when the Puerto Rican culture is in the process of change. The changing role of women in the culture is a key element in negotiating this process. Traditionally, Puerto Rican women have played a major role in private and informal areas of cultural life while the public and more visible aspects of the culture have been under the hegemonic influence of men. In public the influences of machismo have appeared to signal a culture dominated by men. However, this perception is only partially accurate; it overlooks the reality that Puerto Rican men are raised by Puerto Rican women whose strengths have shaped the basic character of Puerto Rican culture.

The young women who participated in this study are simultaneously initiating and undergoing a variety of changes on cultural and personal levels. In addition to their academic responsibilities, they are undergoing family, friendship, cultural, and cross-cultural transitions. This is especially challenging for those young women who are of the first generation of their families to attend college. Such transitions hardly ever occur without resistance.

### Family

Implicit in some of the responses of these young women are underlying concerns about potential changes in familial relationships:

> Things have changed with my family. . . . I was very attached to them but not as much as I used to. I'm more independent now so

like, that has changed a little bit. . . . I don't like them like, always telling me what to do, when to do it, and how to do it. Like, I just told them, I know how to do it. I know when to do it, and what I should do. I'm not a little girl. All that has changed.

Yes, it [the relationship] has changed with me and my father. I can sit there and . . . talk to him and reason more with him. Before he would not want to listen. . . . It would be his way and that's it! . . . Now when I have something to say he will stop and . . . listen to what I have to say. It's all changed in a positive regard ever since I came to college.

## Friends

These women see the most changes in their friendships. Their college experience has changed the ways they relate to and are perceived by friends from high school and the community:

I guess with friends . . . it has changed. I have friends from high school that . . . didn't want to go to college and now . . . we can't talk about anything. We talk but . . . it's different. . . .

No, I don't think it has . . . we're not as close now, but I guess I think they look at me differently, although the relationship hasn't changed.

## Cultural

One of the most significant findings of this study was awareness that the participants' college experiences have led to a series of life transitions characterized by periods of introspection and self-examination of values and attitudes in several important areas.

One of the transitions that currently challenges Puerto Rican women is the complexity of trying to integrate family roles and expectations with efforts to become more independent and self-reliant:

I hope that the changes are not too great because we've always been very tight, so when I complete college . . . they will still back me in the decisions that I make, and I will continue to back them in the stuff they have to do. I'm just hoping that we stay as tight as we are right now. I mean, there may be new dimensions, better dimensions to our relationships, but nothing too drastic.

> And the thing is that with her [mother], it's hard sometimes because I get conflicting messages, like she wants me to be independent, but she still wants me to be her little girl, so I don't know how to please her. And the thing is that since I went to college, I realized that if I was going to survive here I would have to cut myself off and she'd take that personally.

One of the participants expressed her concerns about the way her enrollment in college has changed her relationships with people in her church:

> You can tell that people are intimidated by just me being there.... And then knowing that you're in college ... they say things like, "Stop being like...." If I say a phrase or something, they say something like, "Was that English? Perfect English?".... So in many ways you can see the intimidation they might feel towards me.

### Emerging Sociopolitical Awareness

Another important theme for these women was awareness and concern about sociopolitical issues. Apparently, the college experience is providing them with opportunities to learn about social issues that affect their ethnic group as well as other racial and cultural groups on campus. The growing interest in social justice and multiculturalism is promoting a deeper exploration and questioning of sociopolitical issues. The women appear to be developing a new perspective that integrates issues that pertain to race, gender, and social class as they embrace social diversity and support other students of color through new friendships and social networks via participation in various student organizations. However, these experiences that transform their world views can also be stressful when shared with parents and others who are from their inner community circle:

> I remember the first two years I was in college, I used to go home and we [me and my mom] ended up in these long arguments. From religion to the White culture and discrimination to racism. Primarily because they haven't been exposed to different ways of racism. At that point I was just beginning to be exposed, or greatly exposed to the White culture.... They know just because I've changed, that my horizons and my "knowledge" [has] expanded.
> I'm a strong person yet understanding, you know ... this college is full of different people. Diverse. So ... being here you have to be very understanding of other people's points of view.

Women role models were frequently mentioned by participants. The following example is typical of the responses offered about the role of women in their lives:

> I recently heard _____ speak, and the way she spoke about Latinos and Latino education. . . . Because I've come from a very sexist background . . . and the fact that despite [my] surprise about how my aunts and my mother have survived as well as us . . . we don't fall into the typical female role, and therefore when I see other women . . . especially women of color, take on the initiative to be strong and be assertive, that is really, I don't care what, they can be a mechanic or whatever they do, I just find it to be very admirable.

The participants in this study are now exploring resources available to them on campus. Also, they now receive support from faculty, counselors, and advisors, and readily seek other sources of support. Many agreed that while their transition has not been all that difficult, trying periods of sadness, loneliness, and despair have been experienced. However, they reported that it has been helpful to meet Hispanic students as well as students from other reference groups from outside mainstream U.S. culture. Affiliation with a Hispanic students organization enabled many students to receive academic support, advice, and assistance in finding work-study and other financial aid. The opportunities for social interactions with other students, counselors, and staff this organization offered were considered the most important characteristic of that organization. Also of major importance to the women was the availability and genuine interest of counselors, faculty, and staff in their academic progress and personal well-being.

> I get support from the _____ program. That's basically where I get most of my support from. They help me out, I stay there just to do my work so I will be away from my friends and get my work done.

> I get support from where I work [a Latino program]. They are very encouraging, most of the time they are really lenient about how or when or how much time I have to spend there. There's flexibility and emotional support there.

Relative to additional support and services, the participants mentioned academic support, study skills programs, tutoring, time management workshops, and support groups as helpful in their adjustment to college life. Discussions concerning discrimination and women's issues also proved to be helpful.

## DISCUSSION

This chapter focused on personal characteristics, critical events, and influential individuals that have facilitated the college enrollment and academic success of Puerto Rican women. This particular study took place at a time when Puerto Rican culture is in the midst of significant social and cultural change. This includes more progressive endeavors for women than traditional gender roles have allowed.

In some respects, the women in this study are the bearers of cultural change. While they are learning about their cultural roots, they are also becoming more aware of career opportunities that are increasingly available to all women and taking advantage of many of these. The responses of the participants were analyzed to examine the psychological characteristics and sociocultural variables that have influenced their personal and academic development as well as their motivation to pursue a college education. In addition, this study examined their sources of emotional, financial, and academic support.

The majority of the participants in this study exhibited strong instrumental qualities (e.g., independence, assertiveness, leadership) that are usually associated with masculinity; these qualities have facilitated their enrollment and adaptation to college life. The participants also seemed to integrate traditional roles with new roles and displayed high levels of self-efficacy.

Culture proved to be salient to the career development of these women. In addition, family, church, friends, and school provided networks of support that guided and nurtured them as they learned new and different roles.

The majority (12) of the women in the study were found to be at the Encounter Stage of ethnic identity development, which implies initial awareness of racism and discrimination. Only one of the participants at this stage scored at a single stage of identity development. Most, however, identified themselves as simultaneously within two categories of identity development, with the Encounter and the Internalization stages specified most frequently. This finding suggests that these women are reflecting on their experiences while exploring matters concerning race and discrimination with members of other ethnic groups. One participant even placed herself at three different stages of identity development (i.e., Encounter, Immersion, and Internalization).

Ethnicity and membership in a disenfranchised group were of critical importance to these young women's motivation to pursue a college degree. Practically all of them expressed their awareness and concern about the plight of youth in their communities.

The participants described their families as strong in moral/religious values, control, cohesion, and even conflict. These findings suggest that their families can be supportive and protective as well as stifling of personal ambitions.

This sample also reflects the growing prominence of Pentecostal and other Protestant churches in Hispanic communities. These churches are community-oriented and have provided social support systems to many families. Participants reported that they attend services at least once a week and that their religious beliefs had not changed since they enrolled in college.

Another finding was that parents were the major source of financial and emotional support for the women while they attended college. Furthermore, parents were identified as the most influential sources of their daughters' development and success. The women expressed a great deal of admiration for their parents and emphasized their support, ability to care for their families, and perseverance in giving their children a better education than their own as strengths. Parents were also described as hard working, determined, flexible, and positive. Interestingly, these young women described themselves as possessing the qualities they admired in their parents.

In addition to parents, participants identified members of their extended families, such as aunts, grandparents, and cousins, as individuals who positively affected their lives. Friends, members of their churches, teachers, and guidance counselors were also significant. The latter group was most frequently mentioned by those whose parents did not have a college education.

Women role models were also frequently identified by participants as significant. Many had provided support, encouragement, and advice to participants during their junior high and high school years. Women role models continue to be important to the participants during the college years.

The participants reported several areas of change and sources of distress. Almost all of them reported that their relationships with friends from high school or the community had changed due to college experiences which set them apart from those friends who did not go on to college. Those women with more friends who did not attend college experienced more changes and expressed more concern about those changes.

## CONCLUSION

The women in this study revealed how their pursuit of higher education has changed their relationships with parents, members of their extended family, church, friends, and others from their inner social circles. Although most reported positive and close relationships with their parents and perceived them to be the major source of encouragement and emotional support, they had begun to examine positive and negative traits of their families as well as other aspects of Puerto Rican culture. These women viewed the college experience to be a "natural" phase of change in relationships between parents and children. Furthermore, the college experience was perceived to offer an opportunity to embrace diversity as they came into contact with different world views. Therefore, at the same time that these young women were becoming less attached to their families, they were building new friendships to others from the world community. Even members of their churches started to view them differently.

Finally, the findings of this study indicate that although these young Puerto Rican women have made a smooth transition to college life, they experienced some difficulties with integrating personal experiences, cultural values, and their current college situation. Nevertheless, they were determined to succeed in life. It is of particular importance for college helping professionals to know that with the continuing support of interested and culturally competent counselors and therapists, parents, their extended families, their communities, and their institutions of higher learning, perhaps many more young Puerto Rican women are likely to succeed.

## REFERENCES

Acosta-Beíen, E. (Ed.). (1966). *The Puerto Rican woman: Perspectives on culture, history, and society.* Westport, CT: Praeger.

Amaro, H. (1993). Women don't get AIDS, they just die from it. Paper presented at the American Psychological Association Convention, Toronto, Canada.

Amaro, H., & Russo, N. F. (1987). Hispanic women and mental health: An overview of contemporary issues in research and practice. *Psychology of women quarterly, 11*, 393–407.

Amott, T. L., & Matthaei, J. A. (1991). *Race, gender and work: A multicultural economic history of women in the United States.* Boston: South End Press.

Arbonna, C. (1990). Career counseling research and Hispanics: A review of the literature. *The Counseling Psychologist, 18, (2),* 300–323.

Baca-Zinn, M. (1980). Employment and education of Mexican American women.

The interplay of modernity and ethnicity in eight families. *Harvard Educational Review,* 50, 47–62.

Banks, J. A. (1991). *Teaching strategies for ethnic studies.* Boston: Allyn & Bacon.

Bem, S. L. (1974). The measurement of psychological androgyny. *Journal of Counseling and Clinical Psychology,* 43, 155–162.

Betz, N., & Fitzgerald, L. F. (1987). *The career psychology of women.* New York: Academic Press, Inc.

Bingham, R. P., & Ward, C. M. (1994). Career counseling with ethnic minority women. In B. Walsh & S. Osipow (Eds.), *Career counseling for women* (pp. 165–195). Hillsdale, NJ: Lawrence Erlbaum Associates.

Brooks, L. (1990). Recent developments and theory building. In D. Brown & L. Brooks (Eds.), *Career choice and development* (pp. 364–394). San Francisco: Jossey-Bass.

Canino, G. (1982). The Hispanic woman: Sociocultural influences on diagnoses and treatment. In R. Decerra, M. Karno, & J. Escobar (Eds.), *Mental health and Hispanic Americans* (pps. 117–138). New York: Grune & Stratton.

Comas-Díaz, L. (1987). Feminist therapy with mainland Puerto Rican women. *Psychology of women quarterly,* 11 (4), 451–474.

Cross, W. R., Jr. (1971). The Negro-to-Black conversion experience: Toward a psychology of Black liberation. *Black World,* 20, 13–27.

De Leon, B. (1993). Sex role identity among college students: A cross-cultural analysis. *Hispanic Journal of Behavioral Sciences,* 15 (4), 476–489.

Espín, O. M. (1987). Psychological impact of migration on Latinas: Implications for psychotherapeutic practice. *Psychology of women quarterly,* 11, 489–503.

Fitzgerald, L. F., & Crites, J. O. (1980). Toward a career psychology of women: What do we know? What do we need to know? *Journal of Counseling Psychology,* 27, 44–62.

Fitzpatrick, J. P. (1987). *Puerto Rican Americans: The meaning of migration to mainland.* Englewood Cliffs, NJ: Prentice-Hall.

Forrest, L., & Mikolaitis, N. (1986). The relational component of identity: An expansion of career development theory. *Career Development Quarterly,* 35, 76–88.

Hackett, G., & Betz, N. E. (1981). A self-efficacy approach to the career development of women. *Journal of Vocational Behavior,* 18, 326–339.

Moos, R. H., & Moos, B. S. (1974). *Family environmental scale manual.* Palo Alto, CA: Consulting Psychologists Press, Inc.

National Council of La Raza (1992). *State of Hispanic America: An overview* (Report No. 141). Washington, D.C.: National Council of La Raza. (ERIC Document Reproduction Service, No. ED 344 967.)

National Puerto Rican Coalition (1991). *A blue print for change: A Puerto Rican agenda for the 1990s* (Position Paper No. 120). Washington, D.C.: National

Puerto Rican Coalition. (ERIC Document Reproduction Service, No. ED 334 321.)

Rueschenberg, E. J., & Buriel, R. (1995). Mexican American family functioning and acculturation: A family system perspective. In A. M. Padilla (Ed.), *Hispanic psychology: Critical issues in theory and research* (pp. 15–25). Newbury Park, CA: Sage.

Sherer, M., Maddux, J. E., Mercandante, B., Prentice-Dunn, S., Jacobs, B., & Rogers, R. W. (1982). The self-efficacy scale: Construction and validation. *Psychological Reports, 51*, 663–671.

U.S. Bureau of the Census (1990). *Current Population Survey.* Washington, D.C.: U.S. Printing Office.

Vasquez-Nuttal, E., Romero-Garcia, I., & De Leon, B. (1987). Sex roles and perceptions of femininity and masculinity of Hispanic women: A review of the literature. *Psychology of women quarterly, 11 (4)*, 409–425.

Zambrana, R. E. (1982). Introduction. In R. E. Zambrana, *Work, family and health: Latina women in transition.* New York: Hispanic Research Center.

# GROUP SERVICES FOR STUDENTS OF COLOR

Doris J. Wright

## INTRODUCTION

Groups have long been recognized as an effective intervention for college counseling centers and campus mental health services. Groups for psychotherapy, academic skill building, and psychoeducation as well as a variety of outreach groups and workshops provide support to many students. In view of the increasing diversification of the student population and the presence of more pluralistic populations, college counseling centers are challenged now more than ever before to design and offer a variety of effective group services.

Many students of color (e.g., Native American Indians, African Americans, Asian Pacific Americans, and Latinas/os) use groups at some point during their college careers. Counselors and therapists seem to recognize that groups are a particularly valuable resource for students of color, as many contend with managing college life in socially oppressive environments. Yet, there appears to be no formal documentation of what percentage of this student population participates in groups or how it benefits from various group interventions.

Group counselors and therapists are challenged to design interventions that are culturally competent and sensitive to the needs of this population. This includes the capacity to embrace critical cultural dynamics in the change process. Unfortunately, even though the focus on embracing diversity in the helping professions has influenced more awareness and sensitivity concerning social and cultural issues, some group facilitators still lack competent training in these areas. Therefore, this chapter offers some examples of how groups offered by college counseling and mental health services support students of color at a large state university. In addition, it discusses relevant considerations for addressing the mental and social health needs of students of color.

Case analyses from three types of groups are offered. Each highlights a particular way in which culture and race contextualize group issues. Examples of how group leaders may effectively manage social and cultural issues in group processes are also offered. This is followed by implications for intervention and training. Finally, practical suggestions are made for developing and implementing effective multicultural group services for diverse student populations.

An understanding of the terminology that is used by professional group facilitators is important to exploring how groups support students of color. Therefore, working definitions of relevant terminology follow.

## Relevant Terminology

Ponterotto et al. (1995) defines "multicultural counseling" as "a process in which a trained professional from one cultural/ethnic/racial background interacts with a client of a different . . . background for the purpose of promoting . . . cognitive, emotional, psychological, and/or spiritual development" (p. 18). In applying this definition to group interventions, Merta (1995) defined "multicultural group work" as involving one of the following themes with members of one or more of the four major racial or ethnic minority groups (p. 569): (a) task/work; (b) guidance/psychoeducation; (c) interpersonal problem solving; and (d) psychotherapy (ASGW, 1990, p. 14). Multicultural group work also involves participants who have multiple world views and perceptions of reality which reflect both a unique spirit and a college group consciousness (Ivey, Ivey, & Simek-Morgan, 1993).

These definitions suggest that multicultural counseling recognizes the significance of culture, race, and ethnicity to group dynamics and the determination of appropriate group intervention strategies. The professional's understanding of how cultural issues affect group process is critical to the development of trust and cohesion among participants, as well as their psychosocial growth and development.

The advantages of culturally competent approaches to group work are evident in the following case studies.

## CASE STUDIES

Case studies for three specific types of groups for college students follow. Each case study highlights the group's process from a socially contextualized perspective. First, a psychoeducation group designed for women rape survivors is discussed. This is followed by a vignette from a mixed race psychotherapy group. Finally, the focus shifts to a vignette from a support group for African American women. The groups met in college counseling centers and were led or co-led by senior level professionals. Participants were required to complete a pregroup screening interview. Each of the groups met on an average of once per week for 90 minutes for at least one semester.

## GROUP VIGNETTES
### The Rape Recovery Group

The rape recovery group was a ten-session structured theme group designed to assist women in their recovery from either an attempted or completed sexual assault. Created from a structured rape group model developed by de las Fuentes and Wright (1991), this group was designed to help participants address a specific recovery issue each week. For example, during session two, participants learned to recognize their own post-rape trauma symptoms, while in session six, their relationships with family members were explored. Each session included a checking-in period, a structured exercise, and a checking-out or summary phase. The average time that had elapsed since the assaults was two years and nine months. The most recent assault occurred three months prior to the first group session, while the earliest assault occurred twelve years prior to the initial group session.

There were seven participants, ranging in age from 18 to 35; they were either self-referred or referred by mental health professionals. Three were women of color, one was biracial, and three were Caucasian.

Eva was a 20-year-old Japanese American sophomore who was assaulted by a Hispanic male stranger in her off-campus apartment. The youngest of two girls, Eva was born in Hawaii but her family moved to a mainland West Coast city when she was 2 years old. Eva's psychological response to the assault was like that of most survivors, in that it involved self-blame, distrust, fear, and anger. However, other more culturally based responses complicated her recovery. For example, Eva was afraid that her family's knowledge of her assault would bring them shame and dishonor. Therefore, she had not told them all of the details about her experience. Instead she told them that she had been beaten and her apartment robbed.

Rochelle, a 23-year-old Nigeria-born student, had attended college in the U.S. for more than five years. While attending a Catholic boarding school in France previously, she was raped by two male acquaintances following a church outing. She told her family and school officials that she was mugged because she feared expulsion from the school if officials knew about the rape. Rochelle did not reveal the names of her assailants to authorities. Her participation in the group was her first counseling experience.

Freda was a 25-year-old biracial African American senior who had been raped by a Caucasian man that she dated. Her overprotective mother cautioned her about dating "sleazy brothers." Freda had light-colored skin, hazel eyes, long brown hair, and "other White facial features." She had begun to date Caucasian and Hispanic men after several unsuccessful relationships with African American men.

Gloria was a 22-year-old junior majoring in languages. Of mixed ethnic heritage, she was an Israeli citizen with French Sudanese and Caucasian U.S. background. Gloria had studied in the U.S. for three years. She had been assaulted by her boyfriend during a visit to Israel several months earlier. Gloria blamed herself for the assault. She told no one, fearing the loss of her student visa. At the insistence of one of her college professors, Gloria sought counseling.

## The Process

During one of the earliest sessions, Eva expressed her discomfort about telling her family the intimate details of the rape. In the following vignette, other participants and the group therapist respond to her disclosure:

> EVA: No, I haven't told them exactly what happened to me. I do not want to hurt them or bring dishonor or shame to them. If my neighbors and friends knew about the rape, they would look differently at my family. I just couldn't do that to them. So, instead, I told them that I was robbed and beat up. That's horrible, too, and yet that seems easier to say than to tell them what really occurred.
>
> DR. WHALEY: Eva, you seemed convinced that what you told your family was in their best interest. You're worried that their knowledge of the rape will change their status . . . in the community. I can understand your concern . . . Eva, and yet, I wonder. What is in your best interest? Is there any way you can honor your family while taking care of yourself?
>
> EVA: (shrugs) I don't know how to do both. It seems to me that my family's concerns are [more important]. Without them I don't exist, you know. I don't know if I could continue if I didn't have their support.
>
> ROCHELLE: Eva, I feel the same way about my family. I think that's why I, too, kept some details from them about my own rape. I didn't want my family's name to be hurt by my tragedy. I suffered

enough. I don't want them to go through what I felt. I guess I was worried that they might reject me if they knew all the details. I couldn't bear that either.

DR. WHALEY: And, just what do you mean, Rochelle? Are there things you can or want to share with us now? . . . We'd be glad to listen. . . .

ROCHELLE: Well (pause), I didn't want to have sex with either guy who raped me. I said no to them that night. But, I had slept with one of the assailants before; we had dated briefly. Because my family is very traditionally Catholic, my parents would have been quite upset to know that I was no longer a virgin. I just couldn't tell them the truth. I really hated lying to them, but . . . was afraid they would turn away from me, and I so desperately needed them during that time. I don't know if I will ever tell them.

DR. WHALEY: I appreciate your telling us about this. You took an important risk here with us and I'm glad you did. How do you think other group members feel about you now? I'd invite you to select a person to ask, if you want to.

ROCHELLE: Freda, what do you think?

FREDA: (emphatically) I like you now just as much as I did before you shared that information. It doesn't change how I see you. You were raped by those two guys! End of story! I can understand how you felt, though. I, too, was reluctant to tell my mother that the man who raped me was White. I felt ashamed, embarrassed, and stupid, as if I had done something terribly wrong by sleeping with a White man in the first place. I realize my situation is not exactly the same as yours, Eva, but I think we both have to deal with some old cultural family messages that still affect us now. I feel stupid for having bought into those rape myths about African American men. I now see how racist and biased those beliefs are. Just like maybe you were told that "good Catholic girls" don't have sex until they marry," I believed the myth that Black men were only out to have sex. I bought into the myth about White men being safe. Thus, I avoided dating Black men like the plague. And look what happened. I falsely believed that White men were safe and I ended up getting raped by one! Somehow part of my healing and yours has to be for us to let go of those beliefs that contributed to our hurts. While I'm in this group I have to give myself permission to challenge these sexual myths so that I don't put myself at risk like that ever again.

GLORIA: I guess we all were reluctant to tell our families everything about our rapes. I was reluctant to discuss the intimate details with my family. They are back in Jerusalem. When I lived there, we were treated differently because my mother is French/Sudanese and my father is one-half American Caucasian. I'm biracial. My family and I were socially ostracized when I was young and my parents were threatened once by Israeli militants. So, you can see I was terrified that my family would suffer additional harassment if they discovered that I was raped by an Israeli citizen. Mostly, I feared U.S. immigration officials would rescind my student visa, forcing me to return home before I finished my college education. This issue of race has always affected me and now it sort of complicates my recovery. I didn't even report the rape to Israeli officials for fear of reprisal. Recovering from this rape means I am going to have to deal with these racial and cultural myths because they complicate my efforts to recover.

Dr. Whaley: I hear some themes in common here. Each of you is concerned about your family's loss of face and respect if they really knew all the details surrounding your rapes. Preserving your families' integrity is very important for each of you because you need their support as you attempt to manage your own pain. Yet there has to be a way for each of you to act in your best interest and still receive that much needed family support. How that happens is going to vary from woman to woman. Perhaps none of you has the answer to that all-important question now, but I invite each of you to use this group to explore some possible solutions. I believe that is something this group can help you to achieve.

Rochelle, Freda, Gloria, and Eva: (almost in unison) I'll try. (Other participants nod in agreement.)

## Discussion

For all these women, the ability to challenge troublesome self-attributions and feelings is essential to their recovery. The fear of bringing dishonor to one's family demands an examination of the family's beliefs and values. It also requires one to find constructive ways of managing such perceptions and feelings. Therefore, an effective group counselor or therapist must maintain a stance of gentle support while conveying sensitivity to various cultural issues and dynamics.

Cultural competence is also critical for professionals who lead groups such as this one, given the diversity that may exist between participants. For instance, if Eva's feelings of dishonor are minimized, then an important part of her recovery would be disowned. If either the group or its counselor colluded with or ignored such feelings, then Eva would be stuck with unproductive, potentially harmful feelings which, if left unchecked, could continue to compromise her self-esteem and limit her recovery. For these reasons, it was important for the therapist not to ignore racial and cultural issues. Instead, grief, sadness, and other related feelings were contextualized within a cultural framework.

As for Eva, it was important for other group participants to learn that familial and cultural values play essential roles in their own rape recovery processes. Since it was important for Eva to reconnect with her family as well as to reaffirm her family's cultural values and beliefs, it was important for the therapist to support her in authentically reconnecting with her family. This would probably enable her to regain some of the self-control she lost during the assault.

Like Eva, Rochelle has cultural and family issues, coupled with strong religious values that also seem to complicate her recovery. For Eva and Rochelle, their identities as young women are connected to their families of origin. Both defined their personalities and self-concepts within the context of family. However, it is striking that Eurocentric definitions of individuation do not seem to apply to these women. Thus, a relational approach seems to be effective in helping them to decide whether to fully reveal the rape experiences. By doing so, Eva and Rochelle recovered some of the self-control lost during their assaults.

Without cultural competence, the therapist might have pushed these young women to fully disclose details of their assaults to their families, thereby robbing them of any sense of self-determination. Instead, the therapist allowed them to make their own choices about whether to reveal additional rape details. This conveyed a belief in their ability to choose the option that was best for them and respect for their families' honor and traditions.

Freda made an important connection with Rochelle when she acknowledged the relationship between the messages her own family had given her about dating White men and Rochelle's family's messages about her virginity. Familial and cultural messages influenced how both young women learned new ways to manage their feelings. Freda's recovery was predicated upon her acknowledgment that she believed racial myths about African American men. Both women faced painful acknowledgments about their families' cultural messages that had to be reconciled if they were to recover from their assaults.

In keeping with feminist and multicultural theories, group participants may achieve the developmental changes displayed by Eva, Rochelle, and Freda within cultural and relational contexts of connection and empowerment. De las Fuentes and Wright (1991) articulate three key assumptions concerning empowerment that are relevant to this discussion. First, survivors must be helped to reestablish their personal integrity. After all, assailants have robbed them of the personal ability to control most aspects of their lives; this includes their bodies, their surroundings, and their identities (e.g., racial, ethnic, familial).

In the rape recovery group, activities that were syntonic with the participants' cultural orientations reaffirmed their personal power, thereby helping them to reclaim it. As for Gloria, it is important for survivors to be taught to reexamine how they interpret the pervasive sexual violence that takes place in this society as well as in the world community. Furthermore, they must learn that sexual violence norms are culturally biased and filled with racial and culturally oppressive messages. Teaching survivors to recognize the sociocultural (e.g., gender, race, social class) determinants of sexual violence is essential to the overall quality of their intimate relationships as well as their recovery.

Second, in most instances, women's relationships with other women are best characterized by mutuality. In the rape recovery group, mutuality promoted the regaining of personal power among participants. It can be a source of freedom and security for participants to recognize that they are valued as much as the group therapist(s) or counselor(s).

The last assumption concerns survivors' relationships with the larger society. During session two, participants challenged rape myths and misconceptions. Freda's acknowledgment that she believed White men are safer to date than Black men was a painful admission. Working through this myth was difficult for her because she had to accept the reality that she held some beliefs about African American men that had racial overtones. Freda had to learn how to challenge such preconceptions and to distinguish between safety and risk cues more effectively than she had in the past.

Other participants in the group obviously benefited from Freda's awareness of racist myths and their link to messages about race and various ethnocultural groups in this society. Such new awareness has the capacity to influence new self-perceptions and healing. At a broader level, this vignette lends support to the perspective that standard group interventions must be modified before they can be effectively applied to the needs of women survivors of color.

## PSYCHOTHERAPY GROUP

The psychotherapy group was a heterogeneous, mixed race group with an African American woman and a Caucasian man as co-leaders. The participants, who were prescreened to determine their suitability for the group, presented with a variety of interpersonal difficulties. Three of the participants had received no prior therapy, while the others who had recently been in therapy were referred by their primary therapists.

## The Participants

Sam was a 22-year-old Caucasian male college senior who was experiencing depression and anxiety following the breakup of a relationship. He was referred to the group following an initial interview with another therapist.

Tony, a 20-year-old African American male college sophomore, was socially withdrawn and had few friends. He was referred to the counseling center by an African American professor. The group was Tony's first treatment experience.

Señor Miguel, a 23-year-old Mexican American man, feared his family's rejection if they learned about his homosexuality. He had been treated in individual therapy. Both he and his therapist agreed it was time for him to move on to a group.

Lee, a 24-year-old Chinese American fine arts graduate student, obsessed about his relationship with his father. The eldest of three children, Lee was concerned that father would not approve of the career he had chosen, since he had not decided to pursue law, the profession his father preferred for him. Two years prior, a friend had suggested therapy to him. The group was Lee's first treatment experience.

Anna, a 25-year-old Latina graduate student, ended a physically and verbally abusive relationship with an Hispanic man six weeks prior to her group prescreening interview. She wanted to learn how to have healthy dating relationships. Anna was referred to the group by a community counselor at a shelter for abused women. She had participated in both individual and group counseling periodically during the previous two years.

Sara, a 19-year-old Jewish first-year student, was experiencing family separation difficulties. She had moved away from home for the first time that year to begin her college studies. Sara was truant from school and saw a community counselor in her hometown.

Towanda, a 20-year-old African American junior, was having relationship difficulties with her live-in boyfriend. In addition, she described symptoms of depression. Towanda was referred to the group by another staff psychologist at the counseling center who she had seen for six sessions earlier the same year.

The psychotherapy group had been meeting for almost six weeks when a confrontation between Tony and Sara took place during a discussion about how participants get their needs met.

SARA: I feel hurt that Tony never says anything to me in the group. Tony, you seem selfish and insensitive to what I'm saying in this group.

Unusually quiet, Tony responded angrily to Sara's accusations by raising his voice in the group session.

TONY: You don't know anything about me! How can you say that about me? You privileged little White girls are all alike! You think the world revolves around you and that I must cater to your every wish. I am not your slave or servant! You aren't the only one in this group who's hurting and needs support. So, just be quiet and leave me alone! (pointing his finger at Sara)

SAM: (Interrupts their exchange by defending Sara.) Sara was just making a comment. Why are you jumping all over her? I think it's you [Tony] who should be quiet!

DR. JONES: There seems to be some misunderstanding here. Let's see how we can make sense of the confusion that is happening now. Sam, it seemed important to you to come to the aid of Sara during her exchange with Tony. What prompted you to help Sara?

SAM: I thought Tony might strike Sara and I feared for her safety.

DR. JONES: I'm not clear exactly what you observed [in Tony] that led you to draw that conclusion.

SAM: Well, sometimes Black men are aggressive.

MR. SMITH: Sara, did you feel threatened by Tony? Did you feel yourself at risk?

SARA: No, not really. I just thought he was not paying attention to me.

MR. SMITH: Sam, it seems your observations were inaccurate. Sara wasn't at risk, but you thought so. You thought it was your "role" to defend her from Tony, whom you saw as threatening her. Does this pattern sound familiar?

Sam: Yeah, my ex-girlfriend said the same thing to me. She said I'd always try to protect her. She said I was smothering her. I guess I did the same thing to Sara.

OTHER GROUP MEMBER: Possibly.

DR. JONES: And from whom (or what) are you trying to protect Sara? Someone or something bad? Your actions said you saw Tony as bad and you wanted to protect Sara from him. What led you to have that belief?

SAM: Well . . . I guess it's because I haven't interacted this closely with African American men. I guess I thought he could or might hurt her because that's what I learned as a child growing up in North Carolina. Black men will hurt White women unless you take care to protect them from harm.

MR. SMITH: Well, Sam, I certainly do appreciate your honesty in owning that belief. That wasn't easy. I'm sure you are not the only one who has ever had such preconceptions about a racial group different from your own. The important thing now is for you to decide if you want or need to hold onto that belief. In this instance, it seemed as if the belief caused you to act in a way that was hurtful to Tony and to yourself.

ANNA: Your actions seemed hurtful, in my opinion. I just ended a relationship with a man who said one thing and then acted totally differently. It makes me suspicious of your actions when you hold such biased and narrow-minded viewpoints. It's prejudiced and it makes me not trust you. Until this happened, I really liked you. But now, I don't know what to think about you.

SAM: I had no idea how powerful and hurtful those old beliefs could be. I thought I was doing something good by speaking up for Sara, but I was wrong. I hurt her and I hurt myself, also. I'm really sorry, Sara.

SARA: Yeah, Sam. I don't need that kind of help. I want something different from you and others here in the group. I want recognition and acknowledgment that I'm a worthwhile person.

DR. JONES: And now, do you feel recognized and valued by the group, Sara?

SARA: Well, sort of. I guess I have to take responsibility for asking for that kind of support from the group and from others in my life. I have to speak up if I want something. When you don't do that, I'm learning that miscommunication can happen and that can be disastrous as I have just experienced.

MR. SMITH: It's important for each of you to be honest and genuine with each other in this group. Perhaps of equal importance is the need for each of you to examine your own preconceptions and beliefs you have about each other, especially about those who are culturally or racially different from you. Otherwise, those preconceptions and beliefs can develop into prejudices which hurt you as well as others.

## Discussion

As this mixed race group addresses the confrontation that took place between Tony and Sara, the group leaders were challenged to help the group to confront some unexpected racial stereotyping that surfaced. Without social competence the group leaders might have simply ignored or minimized the racial theme embedded in Sam's admission to having negative assumptions about African American men. Instead, he was encouraged to examine his own bias without criticism. He was not labeled a racist or accused of prejudice. Rather, the group leaders addressed the racial issue directly and openly just as they confronted other issues. Racial prejudice was treated as a clinical issue rather than as an aberration of a "sick" or problematic participant. This enabled the members of the group to gain a new understanding of their own racial attitudes and beliefs. They recognized that racial attitudes and beliefs are learned early in life and that negative misconceptions are ever-present in daily interactions. Moreover, group participants learned how beliefs about racial differences that develop very early in life continued to influence and to restrict how they interacted with each other. Such beliefs and attitudes limited how Tony and Sara interacted with each other and influenced conflict between them. Most importantly, Tony, Sara, and the other group participants learned that race, culture, and racial attitudes provide a social context for developing and maintaining trust. Trust can be violated whenever racial misconceptions are acted upon. Perceptions of and feelings about others are influenced by such misperceptions unless these are challenged.

Tony and Sara's conflict enabled both of them to challenge and to modify their racial perceptions to prevent them from continuing to adversely affect their interactions with others. These revelations helped group participants to develop a multifaceted understanding of themselves and the realities they encountered as students. Moreover, they acquired new information about how race, cultural background, and racial attitudes influenced their perceptions of self and others. They also learned to relate to persons who are different from themselves. Such awareness promoted their relational growth and served as a powerful therapeutic intervention for all of the participants.

## THE AFRICAN AMERICAN WOMEN'S SUPPORT GROUP

The final case study for this chapter involves an African American women's support group that met once a week for two hours for twelve weeks. Co-led by a counseling center staff psychologist and a psychology professor, both African Americans, this support group was open to undergraduates and graduate students. As for the groups described previously, participants were required to undergo a screening interview. Five women participated in the group with a variety of presenting concerns. Participants were free to introduce new topics for discussion. Occasionally, group co-leaders structured sessions and suggested topics for discussion.

## The Participants

Sheronda, a 19-year-old first-year student, was interested in learning how to get along better with other African American women. She decided to join the group after seeing a flier in the residence hall. The middle child and only girl in a family of four children, Sheronda grew up in a neighborhood with a small number of women; therefore, her opportunities to develop friendships with women were limited. She was excited about the opportunity to participate in this group. This was Sheronda's first treatment experience.

Monique, a 21-year-old junior, wanted to learn more about herself and her "Blackness." She had been rejected for participation in a Black sorority and subsequently questioned whether she was "Black enough." An only child of middle-class professional parents, Monique had not received any prior counseling. She wanted to learn more about herself, including her African American identity, and to feel less hurt and sad about being rejected by the sorority.

Jari, a 25-year-old graduate student in chemical engineering, was the third participant. The youngest and only female of four siblings, Jari admitted she had not had many close African American women friends. She interviewed for the group at the suggestion of a therapist who had been treating her for stress-related concerns. Deeply Afrocentric in her demeanor, Jari had experienced conflict with a professor recently concerning her research. She was the only African American woman in a graduate program of 125, with only three African Americans and six women. Jari sought support and kinship with other African American women.

Nikki was a 21-year-old scholar and athlete. She was recruited as the first African American gymnast in the school's history. An attractive young woman, Nikki felt harassed constantly for dates by both African American and White men. She had been brought up by her single mother and often felt isolated and lonely. Because of a recent depressive episode, Nikki was referred to the counseling center by her coach. She was seeing a therapist individually and had been prescribed an antidepressant. At the time of her interview for the group, she was experiencing relationship difficulties with an African American male athlete she had dated for one year.

Kim was a 22-year-old first-year law student from Chicago. A survivor of childhood sexual abuse by a male cousin, Kim had sought counseling as an undergraduate student. Later, she saw a counselor for nearly two years for school-related stresses during her undergraduate years. While Kim had made progress on the abuse issue, she also recognized that counseling could be useful for prevention. Therefore, she wanted to use the group for support as she made the transition to law school.

During midterm exams, a campus-wide racial crisis occurred which was influenced by an incident in one of the resident halls. African American residents were upset by how the governance board handled the decision and filed a complaint with the Dean of Students, charging racism in their governing body's decision making. Several student protests occurred after the incident. The student newspapers were full of editorials about the incident and students' responses to it.

The group co-leaders were concerned that this racial crisis could cause additional distress for students. Therefore, they decided to elicit participants' reactions to the incident during the next group session. The following is an excerpt from that session:

NIKKI: It sort of makes me feel angry, because I live in that resident hall. If you can't trust the hall governance to make good decisions, then who can you trust? . . . I just don't feel safe in that residence hall or any place other on this campus now.

COUNSELOR B: Unsafe? Have there been times in your life when you didn't feel safe for similar reasons?

NIKKI: Sure, I've been a part of other racial incidents before . . . in high school. It makes me just not trust White people.

MONIQUE: I went to school with White kids in my Catholic high school. They seemed okay most of the time. I just don't understand what's happening here.

KIM: Come on, Monique. You aren't that naive. They have racism in [her hometown]. I know. I've been down there before. You just have your eyes closed to reality.

COUNSELOR B: It seems like you're coming down hard on Monique, Kim.

KIM: I just think you're a little naive, Monique. I know you understand about racism and bias. Wake up!

JARI: And what if she is young and naive. That's what's important about being in a group like this. You can talk about things and learn without being punished by White folks. I think that is just what Monique is trying to do now. This stuff on campus is hard on all of us. Even I have overheard racial comments in my department. And you know engineering students never get involved with anything.

COUNSELOR A: Well, it seems that the current campus issues are affecting each of us personally. For some, it's easier to handle than for others. It seems important that you each give yourself time to deal with these honestly. What do each of you need in order to deal with the event and take care of yourselves?

NIKKI: You know, the campus incident has made me think of something that happened to me several months ago. One night I was studying in the lounge late when I overheard two girls talking in their room with the door open. I had walked past the room earlier and they looked up at me, then resumed talking. As I studied, I heard one of the girls remark, "Yeah, the nigger bitch tried to talk to us at dinner. She tried to be our friend. Who does she think she is? How could we possibly be friends with a nigger?" Now, I know they knew I was out there. I jumped up and walked past the room. They looked up at me and smiled. Never did they offer an apology or at least an explanation.

I just left the room and went to bed. I really felt hurt by their comments, even though they weren't talking directly to me and didn't call me by name. It scared me, too. You know, I'm the only African American on the gymnastic team. Suppose something like this happened while away at a meet. I'd be there all alone with no one to support me.

COUNSELOR B: Nikki, I'll admit it's scary when people say racially offensive things. You felt hurt at that time and now it seems like that hurt is returning as we hear about the recent event. Your old pain is here in the middle of your current feelings about this incident. How is your reaction today different than before in the dorm?

NIKKI: Well, I'm angry now and I want to do something about it! Before, in the dorm, I couldn't do anything or say anything. I never got really angry about their comments either. I guess I'm getting angry at those girls now. I'm not hiding from it like I did then. I'm talking about it now. Overall, I guess I feel stronger now than I did after the earlier incident. I have something I can do about it other than just keep the feelings in and hidden.

JARI: I can tell that you are responding differently than you did in the other scenario. Hearing your story has made me realize that I, too, can do something in similar racial situations.

MONIQUE: Me, too. I see how important it is to speak up and tell someone. It's necessary for me to look carefully at the situation that you're in and ask yourself what you can do to improve it for yourself. When people say racially hurtful things to me, I don't have to internalize them and feel bad. It's really important for me to share this awareness with someone and be able to take some action to show care for myself.

## Discussion

Monique understood that she still felt hurt by the racial incident. She was also helped to recognize the connection between the larger campus racial incident and her own unexpressed anger and hurt. She learned a more productive way of managing related feelings, particularly the hurt that typically accompanies racial incidents. Instead of internalizing such feelings and blaming herself, Monique learned to express her feelings openly and directly. Her disclosure also led to her development of more productive coping strategies for dealing with racial encounters. At a broader level, the interpersonal learning that occurred in this group helped all of the participants learn effective ways of responding to racial incidents and other harmful interactions.

The co-leaders in this case anticipated that the campus racial crisis might have had an adverse effect on the participants. Less socially aware professionals might have viewed their anticipation as countertransference or as unwarranted intrusion into the group process. Rather, these co-leaders took the initiative to pay attention to the campus crisis to promote healing among the participants. The interpersonal modeling and learning that occurred within the group enabled each one of its participants to view such campus events in a different light; one which reinforces the importance of preserving a positive sense of self, despite adversity. A socially competent and pragmatic group leader will recognize that African Americans live on campuses where oppressive incidents can and do occur. A forum for acknowledgment of such oppression may be central to the process of pluralistic, sociocultural change (Chau, 1992). By allowing this group to address the racial crisis, the co-leaders minimized the psychological fallout from the incident (Gainor, 1992). Furthermore, they exhibited the diversity-inclusive foresight which epitomizes the spirit of multicultural group work.

## IMPLICATIONS FOR COLLEGE HELPING PROFESSIONALS

The three case studies that have been discussed offer useful examples of how racial and cultural issues may surface in counseling and psychotherapy groups. These cases also show how race, culture, and other social contextual variables (e.g., religion, gender) may influence group dynamics and processes. Group leaders who fail to acknowledge such realities overlook clinical material that is central to recovery and healing. Furthermore, it is important for group leaders to recognize the significance of social content (e.g., culture, race, gender, social class) and to accept ethical responsibility for managing it competently. This requires cultural and social competence, a sensitivity to such issues, and an understanding of how these affect group dynamics and processes. Group leaders must also recognize how various aspects and stages of identity development (e.g., racial, gender, ethnic) influence interpersonal learning so that group interventions can be applied accordingly.

Because the demand for multicultural groups is expected to increase in the near future, it will be important for group leaders to prepare to attend to the following:

1. PSYCHOLOGICAL AND SOCIAL DEVELOPMENT. Culturally homogeneous groups have been shown to promote students' psychological and social development, particularly racial identity development (Fukuyama & Coleman, 1992; Gainor, 1992; Merta, 1995). Therefore, racial identity development may be critical to the mastery of age-appropriate adult developmental tasks (Helms, 1990).

2. CULTURALLY HOMOGENEOUS GROUP SERVICES. Culturally homogeneous groups help students to define their roles as men and women of color and support the trial of new, more effective behaviors. For those like Nikki in the African American women's support group who have not yet developed sufficient trust in Caucasians to share feelings openly, such groups may be clinically indicated. Nikki gained comfort and support from not having questioned the legitimacy of the racial harassment she had previously experienced. Also, those who have been hurt or traumatized by racially oppressive incidents can benefit from the support of such a group. For example, this was demonstrated by Anna, the Latina from the psychotherapy group who had been battered by her male partner. Fortunately, she eventually regained much of her trust in Hispanic men.

3. CULTURALLY SENSITIVE AND COMPETENT CLIENT SATISFACTION MEASURES. Such measures can help group leaders to determine how satisfied group participants are with the outcome of their group. Such feedback also offers participants an opportunity to assess their own personal growth and development in the group. This approach was particularly valuable for members of the African American women's support group.

4. DETERMINATION OF APPROPRIATENESS FOR MIXED RACE GROUPS. Even though the demand for mixed race groups is expected to increase in the future, most practitioners are not trained sufficiently to determine a person's suitability for such a group. As mentioned previously, it is important for group practitioners to understand how human diversity affects group dynamics, group processes, and other interpersonal processes. The integration of these can only facilitate the transfer of learning to daily life group settings.

## CONCLUSION

The effective delivery of comprehensive group services to students of color satisfies ethical mandates of the American Psychological Association (1990) and the American Counseling Association. The material that has been presented in this chapter is intended to challenge group counselors and psychotherapists to examine their interventions from a socially progressive perspective to facilitate the empowerment and optimal growth of an increasingly diverse college student population.

## REFERENCES

American Psychological Association (APA). (1990). *Guidelines for providers of psychological services to ethnic, linguistic, and culturally diverse populations.* Washington, D.C.: APA.

Association for Specialists in Group Work (ASGW). (1990). *Ethical guidelines for group counselors and professional standards for the training of group workers* (p. 14). Alexandria, VA: Author.

Chau, K. L. (1992). Educating for effective group work practice in multicultural environments of the 1990's. *Journal of Multicultural Social Work, 1 (4),* 1–15.

de la Fuentes, C., & Wright, D. J. (1991). *Surviving rape.* Austin: The University of Texas at Austin Counseling and Mental Health Center.

Fukuyama, M. A., & Coleman, N. C. (1992). A model for bicultural assertion training with Asian-Pacific American college students: A pilot study. *Journal for Specialists in Group Work, 17 (4),* 210–217.

Gainor, K. A. (1992). Internalized oppression as a barrier to effective group work with Black women. *The Journal for Specialists in Group Work, 17 (4),* 235–242.

Helms, J. E. (1990). Generalizing racial identity interaction theory to groups. In J. E. Helms (Ed.), *Black and White racial identity: Theory, research, and practice* (pp. 187–204). New York: Plenum.

Ivey, A. E., Ivey, M. B., & Simek-Morgan, L. (1993). *Counseling and psychotherapy:*

*A multicultural perspective.* Boston, MA: Allyn and Bacon.

Merta, R. J. (1995). Group work. In J. Ponterotto, M. Casas, L. Suzuki, & C. Alexander (Eds.), *Handbook of multicultural counseling* (p. 569). Newbury Park, CA: Sage.

Ponterotto, J., Casas, M., Suzuki, L., & Alexander, C. (Eds.). (1995). *Handbook of multicultural counseling* (p. 18). Newbury Park, CA: Sage.

PART II

# UNDERRECOGNIZED AND EMERGING CHALLENGES

Yvonne M. Jenkins

**COMMENTARY**

Highly visible dimensions of social diversity, such as race, ethnicity, and culture are not the only sources of diversity in college settings. Learning problems, age, socioeconomic background, health status, and sexuality are also important sources of diversity. As for students who live with more visible types of diversity, those who live with less visible ones also develop unique strengths, are often isolated, and are sometimes relegated to the margins of college communities. Therefore, Part II of this book is included to draw attention to underrecognized and newly emerging challenges associated with diversity in academic settings and the risks these pose to the psychosocial and academic well-being of students.

Dinklage opens Part II with chapter 12, a vivid description of the world of a learning disordered student, with a special focus on students with dyslexia. This chapter is both unique and challenging because it provides an informed and empathic window on the internal experience of dyslexics based on many years of professional experience. From college counseling and mental health perspectives, Dinklage highlights the need for multilevel, situation-specific interventions for learning disordered students. Of particular relevance to college populations, he acknowledges the limitations of standard instruments for diagnosing learning disabilities for students of color and other nontraditional populations.

In chapter 13, Hansen focuses on nontraditional students, another less visible but diverse student population. These include undergraduates between the ages of 25 and 34, who have key roles (e.g., spouse, parent, employee) and responsibilities in addition to that of student. Many nontraditional students are from the most visible socially and economically disenfranchised groups in the U.S. Yet, others are from less visible groups and are challenged by learning problems and a variety of other issues (e.g., physical, psychological, familial). Many first-generation college students, commuters, and other students whose lifestyles differ from most undergraduates, are included in this population. Hansen suggests with proper intervention some nontraditional students respond to multiple roles, significant time constraints, and the pressures of reality problems with incredible resilience. She concludes by identifying some of the unique mental health needs of this population and recommends strategies for addressing these.

In chapter 14, Shin describes how cultural values influence career decision making for Asian American students through a series of case vignettes. Particularly evident are the centrality of harmony, interdependence, and family to this process. It is clear from Shin's observations that this collective cultural orientation is an important contrast to the more individualistic orientation of the dominant U.S. culture and may be a source of strength as well as complexity. More importantly, she emphasizes that effective career intervention with Asian American students must be guided by their cultural orientation. Toward this end, Shin shares a helpful perspective on what constitutes culturally competent career counseling with this population.

In the final chapter, Gould poignantly reveals some challenges of a relatively new minority on college campuses and the mental health practitioners who treat them. Written from a relational and humanistic perspective, the experiences of both client and therapist are especially moving in this case study. Gould describes the client's doubts and fears about entering therapy as he progresses from HIV positive status to full-blown AIDS status. Particularly moving is Gould's openness about her personal experience of treating this client, especially the powerfully transformative influence on her approach to practice. She challenges traditional approaches to establishing rapport with clients and calls for a more flexible needs-specific approach to treatment than traditional approaches allow. Gould's stance is supported elsewhere by Chin, De La Cancela, and Jenkins (1993).

CHAPTER 12

# THE WORLD OF THE SO-CALLED "LEARNING DISABLED" STUDENT

Kenneth T. Dinklage

## INTRODUCTION

To set the stage for this discussion of the world of the "learning disabled" college student, I believe that the oxymoronic flavor of this term should be dispelled. Instead of thinking of this highly diverse student population as one that is unable to learn, it seems more appropriate to think of it as having certain glitches in processing information which may cause a variety of academic difficulties. Yet, those who get to college are terrific learners. Therefore, it is worthwhile for colleges and universities to actively address this issue.

### Section 504 of the Rehabilitation Act, 1973

The seed for this position was planted by Section 504 of the Rehabilitation Act enacted by Congress in 1973 (Rothstein, 1986). The Act mandated that "no otherwise qualified handicapped individual shall solely by reason of his [or her] handicap be excluded from the participation in, be denied the benefits of, or be subjected to discrimination under any program or activity receiving federal financial assistance." Although learning disabilities were included in a list of "handicaps" to be covered, it took a while for this law to have much impact in college communities since, unlike handicaps involving sight, hearing, or physical mobility, clear and useful definitions and guidelines concerning learning disabilities emerged slowly from it.

### Definition of Learning Disability

In 1987, the Interagency Committee on Learning Disabilities recommended the following definition to Congress:

> Learning disabilities is a generic term that refers to a heterogeneous group of disorders manifested by significant difficulties in the

acquisition and use of listening, speaking, reading, writing, reasoning, or mathematical abilities, or of social skills. These disorders are intrinsic to the individual and presumed to be due to central nervous system dysfunction. Even though a learning disability may occur concomitantly with other handicapping conditions (e.g., sensory impairment, mental retardation, social and emotional disturbance), with socioenvironmental influence (e.g., cultural difference, insufficient or inappropriate instruction, psychogenic factors) and especially with attention deficit disorder, all of which may cause learning problems, a learning disability is not the direct result of those conditions or influences. (Kavanaugh & Truss, 1988, p. 4)

A key word here is *intrinsic*, that is, a characteristic one is born with. Learning disabilities seem to run in families. Relevant research indicates that the brain structure of those who have these disorders has some distinct features. As with neuroscience in general, hot new findings are emerging fast in the neurology and the neuropsychology of learning disorders. The brain findings certainly confirm the reality of these conditions, although most early researchers believed that cognitive difficulties were a brain-based syndrome (Geschwind, 1982). This means there is no cure for dyslexia, since the brain cannot be rewired. However, it is possible to develop ways to cope with these conditions.

A student with a learning disorder surely has a right to: (a) understand the disorder; (b) have it understood by professors and administrators; (c) have available special pedagogical support; and (d) receive reasonable academic accommodations designed to minimize the psychological and academic costs that are inherent to the condition. Section 504 of the 1973 Rehabilitation Act was designed to eliminate discrimination against all physically, psychologically, and intellectually challenged people, but application of that principle came slowly to college students with learning disorders. Prior to the inception of this Act, some of the more progressive school systems had been addressing the issue, but hardly any colleges were doing so. The substantial momentum eventually achieved by the Act was boosted a great deal by the clarification and force of the Americans with Disabilities Act (ADA) in 1990.

## The Americans with Disabilities Act (1990) and Other Relevant Legislation

The Americans with Disabilities Act (1990) was so named at the suggestion of disabled persons who testified during the development of the legislation. The term "disability" was much preferred over "handicap," which had been used in the 1973 Rehabilitation Act.

In remarkable detail and thoroughness, the ADA established a clear and comprehensive prohibition of discrimination on the basis of disability. Objective, enforceable standards were set up with clear implementation guidelines. ADA covers all physical and mental disabilities and is concerned with preventing discrimination in public and private employment, housing, public accommodations, education, and access to public services. The government's *ADA Handbook* highlights a key difference between this Act and the other major antidiscrimination statute, the Civil Rights Act of 1964.

Like the latter that prohibits discrimination on the basis of race, color, religion, national origin, and gender, the ADA seeks to ensure access to equal employment and educational opportunities based on merit. However, while the Civil Rights Act of 1964 prohibits any consideration of personal characteristics such as race or national origin, the ADA necessarily takes a different approach. When an individual's disability creates a barrier to employment or educational opportunities, the ADA requires institutions to consider whether reasonable accommodations could remove the barrier. The implementation of this latter requirement necessitates the identification of the disability and barriers encountered as a result of it. This has had a powerful impact on universities in the U.S. The mechanisms that slowly began to take effect in 1973 are presently given universal attention. Any university that ignores the ADA is now vulnerable to litigation.

Although the concept of a learning disability is now firmly embedded in law and must be invoked to obtain the benefits guaranteed by the law, I prefer to use the term *learning disorder*. This term is consistent with the diagnostic labels used in the *American Psychiatric Association's Diagnostic Manual of Mental Disorders* (1994), which outline the criteria for learning disorders and classify into the following categories: (a) reading disorder; (b) mathematics disorder; (c) disorder of written expression; and (d) learning disorder, not otherwise specified.

These four diagnoses comprise the current categorization of the same array of symptoms included in the considerably older terms, dyslexia and dyscalculia. The reason I prefer any of these terms over learning disability is twofold: to emphasize the specificity of the difficulties that are discussed, and to avoid the slightest hint that students with these difficulties have any general inability to learn. Learning disorders come in varied degrees of severity, from the slightest of limitations to the incapacitating. These conditions also vary in the array of symptoms a given individual might manifest.

### The Focus of this Chapter

Because the focus of this book is college students, those focused on in this chapter have mild to moderate learning disorders. In some instances, their conditions are complicated by social or cultural differences, but are not the direct result of these differences or the presence of a concurrent disorder (e.g., attention deficit disorder). A formal diagnosis is required by law to make such students eligible for "the level playing field" strategies required by law.

From this point on, those students who have a learning disorder will be referred to as LD students. In addition to the broad spectrum of diversity that is represented among this college population, it is also important to emphasize that the identities of students with learning disorders are not restricted to their conditions.

### The Incidence of Learning Disorders

Learning disorders are not a rare phenomenon. Various studies have reported the incidence of dyslexia in the U.S. and European populations to be approximately 10%. In the college population the percentage is smaller, but far from insignificant. The percentage differs at different colleges based on admissions criteria, self-selection factors, the availability of support programs, and so forth. Even at the most selective colleges and universities, it is believed that 2% or 3% of the student body might have a learning disorder. For this reason, it is worthwhile to pay attention to how institutions of higher learning have generally responded to students with learning disorders.

## INSTITUTIONAL RESPONSES TO COLLEGE STUDENTS WITH LEARNING DISORDERS

Even with all the changes in institutional responses to students with learning disorders that have been prompted by the antidiscrimination laws of 1973 and 1990, there is still considerable variation between college resources and institutionalized assumptions and practices. For example, even though there are colleges with extremely comprehensive programs designed to address the needs of LD students, only Landmark College is devoted entirely to students with these conditions. Some institutions still seem to ignore learning disorders or demonstrate other forms of resistance to the acknowledgment and inclusion of this population. However, even though most colleges and universities have put forth much effort to be in compliance with the laws, the range, style of responsiveness, and incidence of successful outcomes is broad.

Until federal and state laws forced some consciousness raising at colleges and universities, many faculty and administrators denied that dyslexia, for example, existed at all; others believed that there was no way for those with this disorder to be admitted to college. If by chance they did, then, of course it was assumed to be a mistake. It was also believed that addressing the needs of LD students was not within the purview of institutions of higher learning. Many college faculty members did not believe their mission included special remediation or the provision of accommodations such as extra time on exams, reduced course loads, note takers, and so on.

Not so long ago, any academic accommodations were thought to devalue the authenticity of a degree. That view has not altogether disappeared today. However, since the antidiscrimination laws were enacted and institutions of higher learning have had more experience with acknowledged LD students, accommodations are presently seen as providing a level playing field where performance for these students is judged by the same standards of excellence required for all students. In the rare instance where tutoring or extra time is insufficient, exemption from an expendable requirement might be considered.

## THE CASE OF HARVARD UNIVERSITY

One example of this latter point was provided by Harvard University many years before there were any laws to protect and to support those with learning disorders. In 1959, Harvard adopted a policy that acknowledged its LD students for whom a special academic accommodation seemed rational. There had always been a number of students who did not finish their degrees because they had not met the foreign language requirement. It did not seem to matter how smart they were or how hard they worked. While they were as talented as other Harvard students, they were peculiarly limited in their capacity to learn a second language because of difficulty in making sound-symbol associations and in grasping syntactical dynamics.

When a close look at such cases was finally taken, it became evident that this was not the first time these students had difficulty learning a language. Back in the first, second, and third grades they had difficulty with learning to read and to spell. By virtue of their intelligence and remedial help, they eventually became good readers. Faced with learning a second language and being without most of the advantages that were available to them while they learned their primary language, these students predictably had trouble learning a new language while keeping up with the normal course load.

Over time, it became evident that the students who were unable to learn a foreign language were dyslexic. This established that the problem was an intrinsic, built-in, diagnosable disorder that could not be cured. These students had an array of other problems for which they compensated as best they could. Even though today these are recognized as deserving of accommodation, at that moment in time failure to meet the college language requirement was the most dramatic and obvious consequence of the intrinsic cognitive glitches that are inherent to dyslexia. These students had poor reading and writing skills, thereby constituting a major ordeal for them.

The complexity of the foreign language problem forced administrators to confront this issue. The Harvard faculty eventually voted for a policy that permitted waivers of the language requirement for dyslexics. By sheer coincidence, as this policy was going into effect in 1959, I began working as a staff psychologist at the University Health Services. Shortly thereafter, I became the diagnostician involved in such cases. It is from 38 years in that vantage point that I have been given access to the spectrum of feelings that students with learning disorders must contend with. Even though most of the observations that follow are based on the experiences of Harvard students, they are relevant to LD students in all highly competitive college settings.

## THE CASE OF BROWN UNIVERSITY

Brown University was the first Ivy League institution to do a thorough and highly effective job of educating faculty about learning disorders. This can be attributed to Harriett Sheridan, Dean of the College and a board member of the Orton Dyslexia Society, who tailored existing supportive services and initiated others to meet the needs of students with dyslexia. Dean Sheridan also created a position for an assistant dean to handle the administrative aspects of services, policies, and accommodations for dyslexic students. Her initiatives made Brown a model for other colleges.

One of her most important initiatives was an annual note to all faculty members and academic advisors asking them to be on the lookout for dyslexic students, with instructions on how to do so. An excellent account of Brown's practices in this arena was published in a 1985 edition of the *Brown Alumni Monthly* (Hinds). The effectiveness of those initiatives was greatly enhanced by being developed at the administrative level. With such leadership, the attention of the faculty was assured.

### Other Consciousness-Raising Mechanisms

A group of dyslexic students at Brown subsequently wrote a pamphlet for students that outlined the signs of dyslexia; this allowed those who were not aware that their difficulties had a name to identify themselves as having dyslexia. This pamphlet even listed tips for coping with a variety of problems associated with dyslexia. It then indicated the campus resources where further advice and assistance were available. Such printed material has come to abound at colleges and universities now that all institutions of higher learning have designed coordinators of services for students with learning disorders and other special challenges.

One of the most impressive publications is a booklet entitled *Understanding Learning Disabilities: Guide for Faculty*, which was published by the Georgetown University Office of Student Affairs (1990). It is a thorough description of how learning disorders are manifested and how Georgetown is prepared to respond. This readily available booklet is a model for many institutions in the process of designing their own versions of such information. While this booklet was targeted for faculty, it would require little adaptation for the inclusion of students as intended readers.

Such widely circulated written material does much for consciousness raising about learning disorders. Furthermore, the discussion of such issues in departmental faculty meetings, administrative boards, and forums open to the college community will ensure that learning disorders are understood and that unexpected but necessary considerations and barriers within existing support systems can be worked out. However, a problem with open forums is that those who tend to be believers already attend. College-wide awareness and sensitivity to LD students will only be achieved by the universal dissemination of information which is initiated or endorsed by those in powerful positions at the institution. This can do much toward transforming the external world of the college LD student.

## THE EXTERNAL WORLD OF THE COLLEGE LD STUDENT
### Circumstances Associated with Awareness and Diagnosis

Many students with learning disorders were diagnosed in elementary school and have struggled with the challenges associated with their conditions since then. Others were not diagnosed until after they were admitted to college. The timetable of a diagnosis seems to be somewhat dependent on the severity of the problem, or how tuned into such matters the parents or the school system happen to be. Even in cases where the student knows he or she has a learning disorder, the choice may not be to disclose this information in the college application process. If a student was granted extra time to take the Scholastic Aptitude Test (SAT), then it is likely that this information would have been disclosed to the admissions committee. Others disclose this information in order to explain difficulties in their academic record.

At Harvard, the parents of all newly admitted students are asked by the dean's office if there are health matters, including learning disorders, for which care will be required or which should be taken into account. Those who disclose at this time are referred to the college's coordinator of services for disabled students who will determine what, if any, services or accommodations are needed or desired by the student. Many other LD students continue not to disclose. They managed to do well in high school despite their condition and rely on the same compensatory strategies used before to help them to manage their college courses. Under no circumstances do they want to be labeled. Then there are others who have used a variety of strategies to get through school prior to college without any awareness of their learning disorder until the college years.

## Personal and Academic Challenges Imposed by Learning Disorders

Regardless of whether or not one is aware of having a learning disorder or whether or not that condition is disclosed to the institution, the LD student who has succeeded up until that point tends to be in for new, more intense challenges associated with having a learning disorder. For example, the simple reality of living in a dormitory can be a painful experience. Dormitory living provides intimate exposure to how one's peers function. It can also be an eye opener, as the LD student's own idiosyncratic family and personal experiences are compared to those of others. Furthermore, the LD student's comparison of his or her own skills and learning styles with those of roommates or study groups who are not challenged by such conditions can highlight differences that might have only been dimly suspected before.

The foremost challenge for this population involves confronting academic difficulties influenced by the specific nature of the disorder. For example, the huge volume of reading required for college courses is overwhelming to the poor reader. Not only might the LD student spend twice as many hours as others on the material, but in some instances he or she might reach conclusions that are divergent from the rest of the class. The student who got by in the past on the basis of Cliffs notes, memorizing what the professor said, or pumping fellow students about what was in the textbook, will quickly discover the ineffectiveness of such strategies in college. Instead, he or she will have to read textbooks no matter how long it takes. Scary!

The LD student who is a poor writer is also challenged in important ways. The volume and performance standards for writing assignments will make the degree of impairment apparent in his or her struggle to communicate ideas on paper. Term papers are mountainous hurdles that often yield disappointing results. For example, one suburban woman dyslexic received a sympathetic note from the reader of her first term paper: "It must be so difficult starting out at Harvard when English is your second language." Of course, English was her native language, but her writing was so full of faults that it gave a poor impression. She felt embarrassed, to say the least.

Poor reading and writing can conspire to make exams an inadequate measure of an LD student's mastery of course material. Multiple choice questions can be daunting. Reading a case or other material which is to be discussed in an exam might take so long to complete that little time is left to write one's essay. And if one is a poor writer, any essay will take an inordinately long time to complete and may be so poorly organized that a coherent presentation of points to make the intended argument is not achieved. How frustrating it is to know that one is on top of course material but unable to demonstrate this very effectively on exams. It is not uncommon for such a student to describe what a particular course was all about to a roommate who is neglecting that same course, who then goes on to get an A on the exam while the same LD student achieved only a C. This feels infuriatingly unfair. Yet, when faced with the flaws in his or her essay, the anger might turn to confusion. If no perspective or help is obtained, not only could the persistence of the problem undermine one's grade point average, but also over time it could corrode the self-image to the point where little else is left but self-doubt.

The devastating impact of escalating academic demands on the LD student stands out starkly in relation to difficulties encountered with learning a foreign language. All Harvard students were successful in high school, including those with learning disorders. There are many ways for an LD student to survive a high school language course without recognizing the extent of his or her problem in that area. If the course is not very demanding, one can do work for extra credit (e.g., book reviews in English) or use a little rote memory to rely on for the next exam.

The LD student often begins college studies full of excitement and the expectation to continue an uninterrupted record of success, only to be ambushed by the requirement to learn a foreign language. The pace of a college level language course far exceeds that for high school courses and rapidly involves varied complexities of grammar and different levels of language material. Most LD students are left in the lurch somewhere. Unlike many courses where extra effort brings better results, extra effort does not always yield positive results in a language course. Imagine the pride of being accepted to the college of one's choice and all the expectations associated with that. Then imagine what it would feel like to try one's hardest, only to discover that nothing seems to work. Obviously the sense of helplessness and fear concerning the future such futility generates is enormous.

Furthermore, this sense of futility negatively affects performance in other courses as the student perceives his or her chances for acceptance into graduate school. But what it hurts most is the student's sense of self. The student begins to ask, "What is wrong with me?" The negative appraisal of the self rapidly expands to become a questioning of one's overall intellectual and psychological competence (e.g., "Maybe I really am stupid. I know I am not lazy, but maybe it is some kind of emotional block.").

Think now how humane it was of Harvard to figure out what was going on with these students and to offer relief from their ordeal via a waiver of the language requirement. In more recent years, some other colleges dealt with this issue by offering alternative or substitute courses. This clearly saved some students from wrecked college careers. Even though the waiver of the foreign language requirement made a huge difference for many students, several problems were still left unaddressed.

## Other Significant Considerations: Culture, Psychological Support, and Nonacademic Success

Although Harvard decided that under medically based circumstances the foreign language requirement for the bachelor's degree was expendable, waiving the reading and writing requirements of the curriculum was not considered. Neurologist Norman Geschwind, a pioneer researcher on dyslexia, frequently initiated his talks on the topic by stating that while dyslexia was neurologically based, it could also be seen as a culturally created disorder. He asserted that if our culture was not built around reading and writing, specific language disorders would never be noticed or perceived to cause specific difficulties. In contrast to the college students whose conditions are mild to moderate in severity, those who are most severely disabled by this disorder often become functionally illiterate and are pushed to the margins of society.

A variety of factors have been helpful to those with learning disorders. Most helpful to those who had substantial difficulties early on were understanding teachers and parents. Mastery of nonacademic skills (e.g., sports, music, art, social skills) is another characteristic of those who effectively overcome dyslexia, in particular. What is essential in this regard is that conditions that nurture self-esteem are vital to compensate for painful academic experiences. It is also important for helping professionals and others who support college students with learning disorders to be aware that some students have internalized an array of disturbing feelings concerning their conditions.

## THE INNER WORLD OF THE LEARNING DISORDERED COLLEGE STUDENT

College students with learning disorders have a wide range of feelings associated with their plight. In this section, I will discuss those feelings that have been disclosed to me, particularly those related to self-image. It would be misleading to believe that this discussion applies to all students with learning disabilities. It is also unlikely that any single student would have all of the feelings that are about to be discussed.

Most students with learning disorders cannot escape feeling at least some degree of humiliation and shame. After all, how can one let such a challenge roll off one's back when his or her expository writing essay is read to the class anonymously as an example of "*what not to do*"? Imagine how the public and personal humiliation might feel in a foreign language course where a student is totally lost and unable to respond to any of the assignments. The looks from classmates in such instances can easily remind the LD student of early ordeals in school that might have been repressed over the years.

Given the reality that most adolescents want to be like their peers, it is easy to understand that repressed humiliation and any signs of a continuing problem might be denied. But humiliation in the college classroom can breach those defenses, leaving one vulnerable to embarrassment and recurring feelings of inadequacy, shame, and humiliation. A common response to this unexpected breakthrough of feelings is, "Good grief, I thought I was out of all that stuff."

One student recalled a memory that was a composite of his early schooling; it had a nightmarish quality:

> I am being asked a question, a simple question . . . get lost in the words right away; I try to hold onto the first words I hear. . . . I don't understand the question. The rest of the words are lost as in the ocean; they have drifted away. I am drifting away. The words all together were a lifeboat, but I am left holding only flotsam, floating debris, and soon I sink out of sight. I can feel the teacher and my classmates looking at me, waiting for an answer, an answer everybody knows is easy . . . but for some reason I have heard only the first few words and now the dark water closes over me. What's wrong, it's so easy. Don't you get it? You're weird . . . stupid . . . lazy, and you are not trying hard enough. What's wrong with you?

Although this student had difficulty with concentration, it could just as well have been the ordeal of being the dunce of his reading class despite being in an advanced math group. The college experience highlights such discrepancies. After all, an Ivy League student with a learning disorder? It seems like such a paradox, yet it isn't really. College academic experiences often trigger old feelings of failure that were once overcome enough to permit a successful secondary school experience.

Of course, some students will not have to become reacquainted with shame or humiliation because these feelings have never left them. These feelings gradually take a toll on the self-image and trigger feelings of unworthiness, inadequacy, and illegitimacy. In addition, loneliness begins to set in for the student who does not fully understand his or her learning disorder and who is without a supportive network that is informed on this topic.

A particular ramification of the poor self-image few LD students escape is the fear of being "found out" and denounced in some way. The worst case of such fear that I have encountered was in my work with a young woman in her first year at another college. She recognized that her limited reading skills might prevent her from passing most of her courses. Typically, before any help could be given to her and before she could get a full perspective on her situation, she committed suicide. Solutions were, indeed, available. It did not have to mean the end of her college career and certainly not the end of her life. However, her shame, loneliness, and fear that everyone would find out she was an "imposter" ultimately drove her to end her life.

**Cover-up Strategies**

In order to avoid being found out or denounced, a panoply of cover-up strategies might be employed. Some common examples are: the use of a translation aid instead of relying on one's knowledge to translate a passage in Latin; reliance on Cliffs notes instead of reading the book; use of a word processor for a spelling or grammar check; pretending to read a Bible passage out loud when, instead, one has simply memorized it; submitting extra make-up projects, and so on. Of course, these strategies are also used by many non-LD students. However, the perceived need to resort to such strategies often leaves them feeling as though they are imposters.

The college student who becomes aware for the first time that he or she has a learning disorder might wonder if prior achievements were due to sheer luck or some halo effect of nonacademic accomplishments. Of course, the prior accomplishments were real. In fact, perhaps, in many instances those were greater than they appear because they were achieved despite challenges imposed by the learning disorder. Some LD students also contend with significant social challenges.

## STUDENTS OF COLOR AND LEARNING DISORDERS
**African Americans**

The diagnosis of a learning disorder may be no relief at all to the student from a racial group that is discriminated against. Some of the African American students with learning disorders I have talked to have been reluctant to acknowledge their conditions in fear of how these conditions might be perceived by others, or how these might be used as ammunition for bigotry. Research and laws make it clear that race has nothing to do with learning disorders. In fact, these conditions are known to be equally distributed across age, socioeconomic status, intellectual levels, and all literate cultures. The prevalence of inadequate reading skills can, of course, be attributed to any one of a variety of factors. However, inadequate reading skills do not constitute a learning disorder.

Despite the fact that no research has ever shown a connection between race and learning disorders, apparently some schools have automatically assumed poor readers to be learning disordered. This practice has potentially increased the amount of financial aid from the state a school system is eligible to receive. Because socioeconomic factors can contribute to poor reading skills, such premature and inaccurate labeling is likely to have a negative effect on African American youth from the inner city in particular. This also stigmatizes the group with rather serious and long-term consequences to self-confidence. Awareness of this practice and other discriminatory uses of diagnoses can certainly make an African American student apprehensive about the ramifications of being diagnosed with a learning disorder. For these reasons, students from this population have often declined accommodations.

Many LD students prefer not to ask for help. However, for those who are already reeling from the backlash from affirmative action while struggling to combat enduring stereotypes, such accommodations can take on a different and more negative parameter of meanings that do not hold for Caucasian students.

## Asian Americans

There is no reason to doubt that learning disorders are less prevalent among Asian American students than any other student population. But primarily drawing from the Japanese world view that any physical or mental defect is unacceptable would put the LD student at a significant social disadvantage. The presence of a learning disorder would negatively affect one's career and marriage prospects, social status, as well as status in one's own family. For these reasons, some students of Asian ancestry might never acknowledge the presence of a learning disorder to themselves or to others, thereby increasing their vulnerability to loneliness and isolation. Of course, shame about learning disorders is not nonexistent in the mainstream U.S. culture. However, unlike most Asian countries, there is legislation in the U.S. to diminish discrimination against physically and mentally challenged persons.

### Academic Accommodations: A Common Necessity

LD students from nontraditional groups are not the only ones in need of academic accommodations (e.g., oral instead of written exams, note takers, tutorials, permission to work at a reduced course rate). Some students may believe that the value of their degree is degraded by such accommodations. As accommodations are increasingly prevalent in colleges, there is a rising backlash among non-LD students who wonder if these represent a lowering of standards. Not only must the LD student contend with self-derogation, but also sometimes derogation from peers and faculty. This has important implications for improvement by institutions of higher learning.

### How Colleges and Universities Can Help

The previous discussion suggests that a multi-faceted approach to intervention is necessary to effectively confront troublesome issues in the external and internal worlds of the LD student. This would entail:

1. identification of the problem (i.e., diagnosis to determine if the student has a learning disorder and what areas of learning are affected);
2. insuring a supportive institutional climate by educating administrators, counselors, faculty, and students about learning disorders;
3. teaching academic strategies and techniques to improve or overcome impaired skills; and
4. the provision of psychological support to address the internal issues that have been discussed.

The strategies stated above primarily apply to the external world of the LD student. However, those external realities that have been previously discussed certainly have an impact on feelings. Therefore, there will be instances when the above strategies will not be sufficient in such instances and an LD support group or individual counseling/psychotherapy may be indicated. On the other hand, it is unlikely that psychotherapy alone will be sufficient to meet the needs of the LD student without implementation these strategies. It would be like giving someone artificial respiration while he or she was still in the lake. Obviously, the victim would have to be removed from the lake before he or she could be helped to breathe.

### 1. Diagnosis

A diagnosis can pave the way for major changes in the life of the LD student. If an evaluation was conducted prior to three years ago, current policy requires that a thorough evaluation is needed for formal documentation of a learning disorder. Depending on the nature and severity of the problem, such a diagnosis makes the student immediately eligible for the reasonable and appropriate accommodations mandated by law. Once a student has been admitted, the college must provide services that consider his or her learning disorder. For example, the language requirement might be waived or extended time on exams might be granted. The most valuable benefit of a diagnosis is that it explains that the student's difficulties are not caused by stupidity, laziness, or some kind of emotional block.

For years, there was an insidious complicated psychoanalytic theory that learning disabilities were caused by family dynamics. However, no LD student was ever cured by psychoanalytic psychotherapy. Instead, help was only provided when specific defects were identified and educational strategies were developed to address those deficits.

The key elements of an LD diagnosis are: (a) significant intracognitive discrepancies, or (b) aptitude-achievement discrepancies of similar magnitude. All of us have cognitive strengths and weaknesses, but generally within a normal range of variation. Intracognitive discrepancies far outside that range result in symptoms of learning disorders. Similarly, wide aptitude-achievement discrepancies indicate functioning well beyond normal variation. For instance, an LD student with an I.Q. of 120, a standard score measure of aptitude, might achieve a word recognition or spelling standard score of 90; that is, two standard deviation scores below his or her I.Q. score. Such an enormous discrepancy indicates that a strikingly inefficient learning process is operative. Therefore, one or more cognitive domains that contribute to the learning in question must be impaired or somehow compromised. Determining an LD diagnosis can be an expensive process, which can be difficult for a college to solve.

An even thornier and more complex issue is the questionable reliability and validity of common testing procedures for nontraditional students, populations that were not adequately represented in the norm groups used for standardizing such tests. Test findings in these instances might inappropriately suggest a learning disorder, or are more likely to yield muddled findings that fail to meet strict diagnostic criteria. Therefore, a deserving LD student would be denied accommodations and left to sink or swim. A detailed educational history and classroom observations are highly useful in such instances, even though it is important to recognize the limitations of test results. Since the findings of aptitude and achievement tests cannot yet be relied upon when assessing nontraditional students, the sensitivity and competence of the evaluator are essential.

## 2. Insuring a supportive institutional climate

The college environment affects every aspect of the LD student's world. If faculty are understanding about learning disorders, it is likely that LD students will become aware of their conditions sooner or later. Also, informed faculty members can be case finders. This is the usual way that students with a previously undiagnosed learning disorder are found.

Several years ago, there was a sophomore whose research in biology yielded some interesting findings which were worthy of a journal article. After the student discussed what should be included in the article with her professor, she began to write the first draft. The outcome was disorganized and failed to communicate coherently the information in writing that she seemed to have such a command of previously. A less understanding professor might have concluded that this student had overestimated her capabilities, rewritten the article, shipped it off, and forgotten about her. Coincidentally, however, this professor had two dyslexic children. Because of his familiarity with this pattern, he was reasonably sure that he could explain this brilliant young woman's writing problem.

The professor referred the student to me for testing, which made her diagnosis clear. The findings were also supported by her family and educational history. She was referred to an LD tutor and improved her writing skills to her appropriate capability level within one year. Without the professor's recognition of her difficulty, however, this young woman might have floundered throughout her college years. After all, she had struggled with writing and grades, which did not reflect her true ability for years. Unfortunately, most faculty are not knowledgeable about learning disorders. Therefore, education for faculty in this area is essential if a college is to be as sensitive and helpful to this student population as possible.

## 3. Teaching academic skills

Those students whose learning disorders were diagnosed in the early primary grades and who were fortunate enough to have had special educational resources available to them may begin their college studies reasonably ready to cope with the challenge. Others are likely to require help with basic academic skills. Relevant study skills and academic survival skills are commonly taught in workshops, noncredit courses, and through individual tutoring by professors who are interested and creative enough to discern what is needed inside and outside of the classroom.

An excellent outline of useful learning approaches is found in Sandra Crux's *Learning Strategies for Adults: Compensations for Learning Disabilities.* Yet, the greatest benefit is likely to come from individual tutorial assistance with writing. Most colleges have a writing center that is helpful to most students who write poorly. Students are usually asked to bring in a writing sample which will be analyzed, edited, and restructured. For the LD student, completing that first draft might be half the problem. Some interactive assistance is usually necessary for selecting a topic and organizing the approach to it that might be taken.

## 4. Accommodations

Reasonable and appropriate accommodations for students with learning disorders are mandated by law. Many colleges once offered such accommodations on an ad hoc basis long before there were any laws requiring them to do so because it was the fair and rational thing to do. But now all colleges are addressing this issue. While there is much variation in the ways this issue is administered, the most common structure is to have a coordinator of services for disabled students who has the administrative power to arrange for necessary accommodations. Such a person might be based at a dean's office, registrar's office, or in a separate administrative entity.

Although this administrator coordinates campus services for learning disordered students, he or she also needs to be aware of off-campus resources. With the exception of larger colleges or universities, few others are in a position to have full-time LD specialists on staff. In some instances, there are general purpose counselors who have a special interest in learning disorders. Even with such persons on staff, students with specialized tutorial needs will probably need to be referred to an off-campus private practitioner. Ideally, over time the coordinator of services might develop an annotated roster of tutors that includes their areas of expertise and evaluations by prior clients. This administrator's office would also access other services, such as taped books, classroom note takers, and so forth. In addition, he or she would be involved in educating the college community and general consciousness raising about learning disorders.

If the above strategies are implemented, then a great deal will have been done by the college to help students with learning disorders. Nonetheless, the peculiar stresses college imposes on LD students and any scars they might have suffered in the past may give rise to any of the difficulties which have been discussed and the need to address these effectively.

## 5. Psychological support

When perceived neglect of a learning disorder is compounded by early deprivation or resentment, psychotherapy may be indicated. Furthermore, when the diagnosis of a learning disorder lowers self-esteem, influences the perception of an added social burden, and generally causes distress for students of color, culturally competent clinical intervention could be beneficial.

Support groups can be remarkably helpful for students with learning disorders. Discussing one's feelings and experiences with others in the same or similar situations is a powerfully validating and supportive experience. Also, to have genuine empathy from others can alleviate isolation and loneliness. An ongoing open-ended group may evolve into a long-term psychotherapeutic experience. Other groups may be time-limited, with or without a leader, and focused on support rather than psychotherapy. Either type of group has the potential to have value. Both may also offer opportunities for pooling information and sharing creative coping strategies.

Finally, it is important to acknowledge that the presence of a learning disorder is not *all in one's mind*; there are some *real* limitations. The challenge is not to generalize from its limitations to the student's whole essence as a person. It is the whole person who needs attention. It is important to remember, however, that the student with a learning disorder does have more difficulty with some tasks than with others; sometimes such difficulty must be taken in consideration in choosing whether or not to pursue a particular career.

Replotting one's career path because of a learning disorder can be a painful experience. Deciding between alternative choices is difficult but possible, and can require sensitive and sophisticated career planning. The indomitable spirit of students with learning disorders is often remarkable.

Clearly, the cases that have been discussed suggest that having a learning disorder can "make or break" the student. Many succumb to the frustration and sense of futility generated by these conditions, as evidenced by precollege dropout rates, chronic depression, and delinquent and criminal behavior. Yet, those who make it to college are often resilient, motivated never to give up, and likely to capitalize on that indomitable will. Therefore, institutions of higher learning are challenged to provide the understanding and services that have been outlined in this chapter.

## REFERENCES

*Americans with Disabilities Act Handbook.* (1990). Washington, D.C.: U.S. Government Printing Office.
American Psychiatric Association. (1994). *Diagnostic and statistical manual of mental disorders* (4th ed.). Washington, D.C.: Author.
Brown University. (1985). *Dyslexics at Brown: A student perspective.* Providence, RI: Office of the Dean of the College, Brown University.
Crux, S. C. (1991). *Learning strategies for adults: Compensations for learning disabilities.* Middleton, OH: Wall & Emerson, Inc.

Georgetown University. (1990). *Understanding learning disabilities: Guide for faculty.* Washington, D.C.: Office of Student Affairs, Georgetown University.

Geschwind, N. (1982). Why Orto was right. *Annals of dyslexia, 32,* 13–20.

Hinds, K. (1985). Dyslexics at Brown. *Brown Alumni Monthly.*

Kavanaugh, F., & Truss, T. J., Jr. (Eds.). (1988). *Learning Disabilities: Proceedings of the National Conference.* Timonium, MD: York Press.

Rothstein, L. F. (1986). Section 504 of the Rehabilitation Act: Emerging issues for colleges and universities. *Journal of College and University Law, 13 (3),* 229–260.

## SUGGESTED READING

Dinklage, K. T. (1971). Inability to learn a foreign language. In Blaine, G., & McArthur, C. (Eds.), *Emotional problems of the student.* New York: Appleton-Century Crofts.

Dinklage, K. T. (1991). Counseling the learning disabled college student. *Journal of College Student Psychotherapy, 5 (3),* 3–27.

Pennington, B. (1991). *Diagnosing learning disorders: A neuropsychological framework.* New York: Guilford.

# CHAPTER 13

# KEY FACTORS THAT DIFFERENTIATE NONTRADITIONAL FROM TRADITIONAL STUDENTS

Diane G. Hansen

## WHO IS THE NONTRADITIONAL STUDENT?

Nontraditional students differ from traditional students in terms of age, life stage, and daily life pressures encountered. The majority of nontraditional students are between the ages of 25 and 34. However, according to the United States Bureau of Labor Statistics, the numbers of adult learners over the age of 34 is increasing. In 1986, 13% of the adults enrolled in formal educational programs were over the age of 54. Given the increasing length of the life span and the fact that many individuals are working well into their 70s and 80s, this trend can be expected to continue.

In addition, the changing economy, the downsizing of companies, and rapid technological advancements are also influencing greater numbers of adults to return to school to prepare for career changes and to facilitate career advancement. Brockett (1987) views education and reeducation as standard practice for the future. Adults may return to school for other reasons as well, such as self-fulfillment or changes in life circumstances. Aslanian and Brickell (1980, 1988) found in their interviews of 2000 adults that while 87% returned to school due to life transitions, 56% of those were due to a career-related event. Harriger (1994) also cited job-related factors as the major motivator for adults returning to college.

Given the age and life stage of the majority of nontraditional students, managing multiple roles is also part of the challenge related to returning to school. The primary role traditional students identify with is the student role. However, for the nontraditional student, how one negotiates the potential conflict between the student role and the roles of worker or parent or both has implications for academic adjustment and completion.

## Rationale for This Chapter

For the purposes of this chapter, a broader definition of nontraditional will be used than that encompassed by age, life stage, and multiple roles. The following definition more accurately reflects my professional experience with this population at a large, urban university in the northeast. The thesaurus of ERIC (Houston, 1990) defines the *nontraditional student* as an adult "beyond traditional school age (i.e., beyond the mid-20s), ethnic minorities, women with dependent children, underprepared students and other special groups who have historically been underrepresented in postsecondary education." (p. 175). Even this definition is limited. Because of the passing of the American with Disabilities Act (1990) we will see increasing numbers of students who are physically or learning challenged and those with psychiatric histories. Another neglected group includes those who postpone college because of substance abuse problems, or other issues such as childhood sexual or physical abuse which may have affected their identity development and overall readiness for college.

Clearly nontraditional students constitute a diverse group with a broad spectrum of needs. Their numbers at U.S. colleges and universities are increasing rapidly and will continue to do so into the next century. It is therefore important to have an understanding of some of the particular concerns and strengths this population might bring to a college mental health facility.

Via a case study and highlighting relevant research, I will provide an overview of some important needs of nontraditional students and factors to consider in treating them. Although I have chosen to focus only on students enrolled in an undergraduate degree program, nontraditional students are also often enrolled in graduate or certificate programs and enrolled on full-time or part-time bases.

## CASE STUDY

Jennifer represents a composite of several nontraditional students I have treated at a university counseling center. Many of the issues Jennifer is contending with reflect some of the commonalities among nontraditional students, irrespective of race, ethnicity or gender. However, it is important to acknowledge the impact of these variables on the nontraditional student's college experience.

### Background Information

Jennifer was a 26-year-old Caucasian woman of mixed ethnicity, predominantly Irish and French Canadian. She was a single parent on Aid to Families with Dependent Children and had a 4-year-old daughter. Jennifer lived with her daughter in a two-bedroom unit of a public housing development in a predominantly working-class neighborhood. She was not currently in a relationship. Jennifer was in the second quarter of her freshman year, majoring in computer technology. She had no close ties to her family who lived 10 miles away from the university. Jennifer came to the counseling center at the suggestion of her academic advisor with whom she had discussed her academic difficulties.

## Presenting Problem

In the initial interview, Jennifer reported feelings of depression and anxiety. These involved irritability much of the time, low motivation, and difficulty in falling asleep. In addition, she felt uncertain about being in college and her choice of major, and felt overwhelmed by the dual demands of being a student and a single parent. Her appetite was normal and she had no physical complaints. In fact, she had always enjoyed good health. Jennifer also denied alcohol or drug use. She stated that her feelings of depression and anxiety intensified during the winter quarter after missing a number of classes over a two-week period. This was attributed to the illness of her daughter which prevented her from attending day care. As a result, Jennifer fell behind in two of her most difficult courses. She was barely passing physics and was feeling overwhelmed by the amount of work she had to do to catch up. She was also having difficulty understanding the material.

## Family History

Jennifer had no support from her family. Her mother was described as alcoholic and emotionally unavailable. Jennifer didn't remember her father, who left when she was three, never to be heard from again. She had a 24-year-old brother in the service in Texas. A maternal aunt was supportive and they spoke twice a month by phone. Jennifer also had a couple of close friends from high school whom she kept in touch with by phone but didn't see very often. She had recently met other single mothers in her housing complex, but found it difficult to speak with them about the pressure that she felt from school, since they had never been to college. However, she did talk with them about the pressures of parenting. When asked whether she had made any friends in her classes, Jennifer told me that she had not in part because when she was not in class she was studying, taking care of her daughter, or doing errands.

## Academic History

In high school she achieved A's and B's. In the fall quarter of her first year of college, her grade point average was 2.5. Jennifer had taken a couple of computer courses at a local community college when she was employed and did well in those. The primary impetus for her current enrollment was the availability of grant money. Otherwise, she would not have been able to afford the tuition. One of her dreams had always been to attend college. Jennifer was the first member of her family to attend college.

## Treatment Goals

Jennifer's goals were: (a) to be able to get things under control so she could remain in school; (b) to manage effectively her parenting responsibilities simultaneously; and (c) to become sure she had chosen the right major.

## Treatment Considerations

Several questions were raised by the information gathered in the initial session. Did Jennifer have the ability to do college work? Had she chosen the appropriate major? How was she managing multiple roles? What supports did she have? How did she deal with stress? While these questions could certainly be raised with traditional students, they took on a special character given Jennifer's status as a nontraditional student. We might also have questioned what effect growing up in her troubled family had on all of the previous questions and whether or not her earlier experiences needed to be considered during the treatment process.

Based on our initial meeting, some factors were already significant. Jennifer's academic performance declined during the second quarter, which may have been attributed to her daughter's illness and Jennifer's subsequent absenteeism. She did not speak to her professors about her absences nor did she ask anyone for the notes from any of her classes. Furthermore, she did not seek help with any of her more difficult courses. Perhaps this was influenced by time pressures or not having an understanding of how to negotiate the system. Or it could have been related to not feeing entitled to ask for help due to adult child issues combined with early ethnocultural messages about asking for help. The literature on adult children of alcoholics speaks to the difficulty that this group has in asking for help or even knowing what to ask for (Seixas & Youcha, 1985). McGoldrick et al. (1982) and Langelier (1982) also address the tendency in Irish and French Canadian families to try to resolve difficulties through means other than mental health services. These issues may or may not have needed to be explored in order to assist her.

As Jennifer felt increasingly discouraged and began to question whether she was capable of doing the work, she began to fall further behind in her courses. Exploration of her past performance in high school and in the community college courses she had taken suggested that she was capable of doing college work. However, her weak background in the sciences seemed to contribute to current difficulties in this area.

It was important to help Jennifer to get her academic situation under control since this was her priority. Therefore, it was important to assist her with obtaining the support she needed to increase her chances of academic success. Jennifer and I agreed that the first thing she should do was to speak with her professors about her situation and to ask for extra help in her science classes. She also identified persons in each of her classes that might be of help to her with class notes. Together we were able to agree that Jennifer's past academic performance suggested she probably had the ability to do the work. Another important issue we addressed was the lack of support in Jennifer's life. Some of this was related directly to being a nontraditional student in that she was older than her peers and a single parent, which added to her sense of isolation. In addition, she was one of only four women in most of her computer technology courses. Even though Jennifer's aunt was supportive, they had limited contact.

As Jennifer applied some of the strategies we discussed and as she felt more supported both in the therapy and outside, her self-esteem and confidence grew stronger, as evidenced by the expression of a more hopeful attitude. In view of this and her limited time available for sessions, it did not seem necessary to explore the effect of earlier family issues.

## SPECIAL TREATMENT CONSIDERATIONS FOR NONTRADITIONAL STUDENTS
### The Significance of Psychological Support

For nontraditional students, the availability of psychological support for being a student can be essential to their adjustment and continuation in school. As illustrated by Jennifer's situation, many nontraditional students experience feelings of isolation due to age differences and life experiences that differ from those that are typical for traditional students. This is more pronounced for adult learners in day programs than those enrolled in part-time evening programs, where they are likely to encounter more of their cohorts.

Chartrand (1992) and Hoetler (1983) found a relationship between positive evaluation of one's self as a student and one's commitment to the student role. These findings suggest that feeling unsuccessful as a student or entering college with a negative evaluation of oneself as a student could lower commitment to the student role and persistence with academic tasks. In Jennifer's case, her early experience of herself as a student was fairly positive. It appears that her self-doubts about being successful in college had more to do with external pressures than with perceptions of herself as a student. Academics was one of the main sources of her self-esteem when she was younger.

The research suggests that it is critical to evaluate the level of support a nontraditional student has for being a student. According to Chartrand (1992), "support from family and friends influences both psychological distress and intentions to continue" (p. 199). One of Jennifer's goals in therapy was to develop more of a support network by identifying people like her aunt and a former teacher with whom she was still in contact, who might be willing to actively support her as a student. I encouraged her to be explicit with them about how they could support her (e.g., checking in with her weekly to see how she was doing, expressing confidence in her ability to meet her goals). We also discussed ways in which she might connect with other students by forming a study group that would meet during the day. Jennifer was able to make effective use of these interventions without too much difficulty. Her motivation was high, which is often true for nontraditional students.

## Career Choice

Since certainty of career choice and perceived study skills may be predictive of a student's intent to continue (Chartrand, 1992), it is important to assist nontraditional students in their educational and career planning as necessary. Both of these areas were addressed in my work with Jennifer. We examined her study habits, reinforced what she was already doing effectively, and suggested some strategies for note taking. We also developed a study plan. This helped her to feel more confident about her skills in these areas.

An exploration of Jennifer's career considerations revealed that she was clear about wanting a degree, but was less certain about her choice of a major. It was difficult to determine the source of her uncertainty. To what extent was her sense of discouragement caused by the added stress of parenting? How much was it related to computer technology not being an appropriate choice for her? Jennifer said that she had chosen computer technology because she had liked her computer courses and did well in them. She had also displayed an aptitude for math earlier in her education. Her other considerations included a desire for financial and job security. As Jennifer felt more supported and less overwhelmed and discouraged about her ability to manage school and parenting, I referred her to the *Occupational Outlook Handbook* for information about various career opportunities within the computer field. Thereafter, we discussed career testing to evaluate her career direction further.

## Role Overload

Helping nontraditional students find ways of coping with multiple roles and role conflict can be an important contribution to their adjustment. Butell and O'Hare (1986) found that selectively attending to role demands as well as changing attitudes and beliefs about particular roles can reduce role conflict. They also found that eliminating some roles and prioritizing others was helpful in reducing the pressure of conflicting roles.

Clearly the roles of student and parent influenced Jennifer to feel pressured and overwhelmed. In addition to her parental and student roles, she had other competing responsibilities, including housekeeping and grocery shopping. It was difficult for her to find time for herself, let alone to spend with others. Therefore, the next stage of our work explored how she felt about her parental role and how she managed conflict related to the competing demands of being a full-time student and a parent. Jennifer's daughter was very important to her and she worried about whether she was spending enough time with her. Clearly this is a concern for many mothers who go to school and work. How well they resolve this concern and how much support they have access to for the student or worker role will affect how successful they are in those roles.

Much of the work with Jennifer entailed helping her to form realistic expectations of herself as a single parent and mother. We also addressed some of her feelings related to the perceived stigma of being a single mother. As Jennifer became more accepting of herself as a single mother and began to be more open about this with some of her classmates, she felt less isolated. She also joined a single parents group which was offered through the grant program in which she participated. In addition, she was encouraged to explore whether she and the single mothers she had met at the housing development might exchange babysitting duties with each other to have time for themselves and other things.

As a result of the new coping strategies Jennifer developed in therapy, she developed a higher level of self-esteem and overall self-satisfaction. Furthermore, she developed a greater sense of control over her academic work and began to feel more confident in her abilities to manage school and single parenting simultaneously.

In view of Jennifer's previous personal and academic experiences, there is no doubt that other issues might have been addressed. However, the busy pace of her life was such that she had limited time available for counseling sessions. In fact, in many instances she had to cancel or reschedule due to child care difficulties or unscheduled class-related meetings. Limited time availability is a common theme for nontraditional students due to their multiple role responsibilities. It is therefore an important reality factor for consideration in treatment planning.

## SUMMARY

Nontraditional students are becoming a more visible presence on university and college campuses. This is particularly true for institutions of higher learning in urban settings and for community colleges. With shrinking enrollments and the increasing need for continued training for career purposes, more and more colleges and universities will be encountering nontraditional students. How they respond will determine their success in recruiting and retaining these students.

It is important to have mental health and counseling services which are sensitive to the particular needs of this diverse group. This means paying attention to just how much the psychological distress of nontraditional students may be related to the demands of multiple roles and role conflict. In addition, helping this population set realistic expectations of themselves in managing their varied role responsibilities can provide significant support and relief. Also assisting this population with developing support networks can be beneficial. Furthermore, enhancing study skills, when necessary, may also be supportive.

The other task that nontraditional students may need assistance with is examining their educational and career goals, particularly when they are experiencing difficulty in a chosen major or academic program. Given the time constraints for most of these students, it is incumbent upon institutions of higher learning to offer academic and supportive services at times which are conducive to the schedule of adult learners (e.g., late afternoon, evening). Finally, since ethnicity, race, and gender play a role in self-perceptions, world view, and help-seeking behavior, these factors also need to be considered as part of any evaluation of nontraditional students.

## REFERENCES

*Americans with Disabilities Act.* (1990). Pub. L. No. 101-336 (42 U.S.C. 12101-12213). Washington, D.C.: US Government Printing Office.

Aslanian, C., & Brickell, H. M. (1980). *Americans in transition.* New York: College Entrance Examination Board.

Aslanian, C., & Brickell, H. M. (1988). *How Americans in transition study for credit.* New York: College Entrance Examination Board.

Brockett, R. (Ed.) (1987). Continuing education in the year 2000. *New Directions*

*for Continuing Education Series, (36)* San Francisco: Jossey-Bass.
Butell, N. J., & O'Hare, M. M. (1986). Coping with role conflict among returning students: Professional versus nonprofessional women. *Journal of College Student Personnel,* 141–145.
Chartrand, J. M. (1992). An empirical test of a model of nontraditional student adjustment. *Journal of Counseling Psychology, 39 (2),* 193–202.
Harringer, C. (1994). Adults in College. H. J. Sinnott (Eds.), *Interdisciplinary Handbook of Adult Lifespan Learning,* 171–185. Westport, CT: Greenwood Press.
Hoetler, J. W. (1983). The effects of role evaluation and commitment on identity salience. *Social Psychology Quarterly, (46),* 140–147.
Houston, J. E. (1990). (Ed./Lexicographer). *Thesaurus of Eric Descriptors* (p. 175). Phoenix: Oryx Press.
Langelier, R. (1982). French families. In M. McGoldrick, J. K. Pearce, & J. Giordano (Eds.), *Ethnicity and family therapy* (pp. 229–346). New York: Guilford.
McGoldrick, M., Pearce, J. K., and Giordano, J. (Eds.) (1982). *Ethnicity and family therapy.* New York: Guilford.
Seixas, H., & Youcha, G. (1985). *Children of alcoholism: A survivors manual.* New York: Harper and Row.

CHAPTER 14

# CONTEXTUALIZING CAREER CONCERNS OF ASIAN AMERICAN STUDENTS

SungLim A. Shin

**INTRODUCTION**

East Asian cultures value group harmony and interdependence, collectivistic values that organize society, community, and family relations. As recipients of these traditions, Asian Americans of East Asian ancestry (i.e., China, Japan, Korea, Taiwan, and Vietnam) internalize traditional cultural values that have a significant impact on their behavior. In contrast, the dominant U.S. culture values individualism where autonomy of the individual is preferred over group harmony. The impact of this value orientation on Asian Americans is commonly overlooked. Asian Americans are wedged between their own complex historical and cultural realities and the pressure of the dominant U.S. cultural context of individualism. Therefore, the process of choosing a career sharply evokes the dynamic tension between individual well-being and family well-being, which is valued so highly in Asian cultures.

The fact that comprehensive career assessment and counseling focuses on the individual (Lowman, 1991) is consistent with the cultural orientation and values of the dominant culture of the United States. However, this approach can be problematic for Asian American students because of its inconsistency with their value for interdependence. For many Asian American students, the impact of career choice may involve the family in its expression of familial identity by contributing to the image it projects to the outside world (i.e., "face"), economic well-being that secures survival, prestige, and family continuity.

The career concerns of Asian Americans must be understood within the context of their cultural values. Therefore, culturally competent career counseling requires acknowledgment that it is unlikely that many Asian American students will readily respond favorably to traditional U.S. models of career intervention. The potential for this conflict can be elusive because many Asian American students appear well assimilated and acculturated on the basis of manner of dress, speech, interests, social skills, and academic performance. Yet, the latest fashion in dress and speech or the lack of an accent should not be assumed to represent complete internalization of the dominant U.S. value orientation, since these adaptations do not reflect the Asian influence of family and culture.

This chapter will focus on how career consideration for Asian American students can involve both Asian and dominant U.S. values. Three case composites are used to explore how assimilation and acculturation, which are often taken for granted or at face value, may hide complexities associated with the bicultural influence of Asian and U.S. values.

## THE ASIAN FAMILY

East Asian family organization and functioning reflect Confucian principles in its hierarchical, patriarchal system with specific role designation and responsibilities (Yum, 1988). The system values family well-being over individual well-being, and self-sacrifice over individual assertiveness. It also demands respect for authority and values individual modesty. These values reinforce proper hierarchical relationships with others and have the effect of emphasizing group harmony over individual need. This assertion of interdependence over independence ensures stability and continuity of the family and community, since the individual is important as a contributing member of a larger group. Values and behaviors that contribute to "the face" of the family encourage a sense of embeddedness and maintain group harmony and integrity. The Asian sense of identity and well-being, then, is closely intertwined with being a member of a meaningful group, such as the family, since the individual derives a significant sense of belonging, acceptance, support, and importance from the group. On the other hand, the possibility of disappointing the family jeopardizes one's esteem in the group and sense of belonging, since group harmony will be disturbed.

Power differences in the hierarchy are moderated by the overarching concept of being an indivisible member of the group. This perpetuates a sense of interdependence and is further maintained through mutual and reciprocal, although unequal obligations. For example, even though a parent possesses more power than the child, the group's needs emphasize the parent's obligation to family members (e.g., to make sacrifices to give one's children a high quality of education to insure future success). This duty carries the implicit and explicit expectation that the family's future social and economic position will be enhanced by children's success. Therefore, academic and career accomplishments are often the central foci of role expectations for children (Kim, 1993). Strong emphasis on contributing to and not shaming the group connects the individual's action to the group's well-being. This also influences the pressure that many Asian American students feel to comply with their parents' expectations of them.

## CASE COMPOSITES

Obviously, Asian American students struggle with confusion and conflict when faced with career decisions that potentially neglect cultural and familial expectations. Three case composites follow that explore how acculturation, overt assimilation, and efforts to assimilate are often taken for granted and at face value. These composites also show how assimilation and efforts to do so may mask the complex interaction between an individual's needs or goals, as influenced by Asian values, and dominant culture U.S. values.

The first composite explores how the cultural values of an Asian American student can lead to internal conflict and an impasse despite overt assimilation. It also highlights how differences in cultural values may become masked when two cultures share a similar regard for academic and career achievements. Furthermore, this composite shows how internal conflict often arises when the goals of an individual and the group diverge.

## SABRINA

Sabrina was a 26-year-old Korean American graduate student. Five years old when her family immigrated from Korea, she was considered "one and a half generation" by the Korean community.[1] She was the second of three children with an older brother and a younger sister. Her parents owned a stationery business that had supported the family and college education of all the children. Sabrina's brother was a medical resident and her younger sister was a college student majoring in premedical studies. Sabrina and her siblings had always performed well academically and all of them attended Ivy League schools.

Upon graduating from college, Sabrina entered the financial services sector of business. Although she had returned to school to complete an MBA degree, she wondered about pursuing social work. One of her issues concerned her disenchantment with the business world. Sabrina recognized that she would like to pursue a career which would have a counseling component. The situation was complicated by the fact that her parents were enamored with her potential financial analyst career for its security and prestige, even though they did not understand what her work involved. Another complication was Sabrina's parents' wish that she would marry and settle down. Sabrina sought career counseling to inquire about vocational testing.

## Cultural Considerations for Intervention

Different cultural reasons undergirded the family's esteem for Sabrina's "successful" academic and career achievements. High educational and career attainment were consistent with parental expectations and justified the sacrifices Sabrina's parents had made as immigrants. Further, the Korean community holds similar values and Sabrina's achievements reflected positively on her parents and family within the community. Ironically, her non-Korean peers respected and understood her achievements as statements of individual aspiration and personal success (i.e., she did it for herself). Sabrina had avoided directly confronting the bicultural conflict of norms and expectations because her actions had been approved of by both Korean and U.S. cultures, although for different reasons.

The importance she attached to maintaining goodwill and harmony by her actions was unlikely to be displayed in work and social settings that emphasize individualism. In the MBA program, competitive drive, self-motivation, and direction to pursue personal aspirations are valued. The power of these values influenced Sabrina to decide on an individual goal, even though it conflicted with her deep sense of loyalty and obligation to her parents. She felt guilty, disloyal, selfish, and anxious about disappointing her parents. Caught in this dilemma, Sabrina experienced herself as nonassertive, immature, dependent, and, therefore, weak for not pursuing her individual aspiration. All of this influenced considerable internal conflict which seemed to be a personal dilemma, a forced choice or no-win situation.

Despite Sabrina's high levels of acculturation and assimilation, she showed the profound influence of traditional Asian cultural values. Her serious concern about the impact her decision would have on her family was consistent with the valuing of interdependence. Chin (1993) elaborates on how the practice of this value reflects a desirable developmental quality:

> Asian cultures emphasize mutual interdependence as the criteria of maturity, that is, caring for one's family. . . . Maturity is defined not as separation from the family, but rather as integration into the extended family network. This contrasts with the goal of achieving independence, defined in western cultures as the ability to leave family. (p. 87)

The practice of interdependence obliges the suppression of individual needs in deference to those of the group. This obligation incurs personal sacrifice which may be unacceptable to the individual whose identity revolves around "I" rather than "we." Friction arises when family members behave according to a different value orientation or associated identity, as in this case study of a young man named Ethan and his father.

The following composite explores how an interpersonal conflict between a son and his father can encompass and reflect cultural disparities.

## ETHAN

Ethan was a 27-year-old gay *Sansei* (third-generation) Japanese American man with an MBA. He was the youngest of three siblings and the second son. His father was "very Japanese" even by *Nisei* (second-generation) standards. Ethan's brother was a nuclear engineer and his sister an advertising executive. Even though he had come out to some people and did not try to hide his sexual orientation from his family, he was not certain his siblings were aware of his sexual orientation. Ethan was closest to his mother who was aware of his homosexuality. She urged him not to bring up the topic in their family or in public. In contrast, his father did not acknowledge his sexual orientation.

Ethan wanted to decide whether to join the family business, which he thought he could run successfully, or to pursue a different career. While he was keenly interested in and familiar with the family's business, Ethan was concerned about working in a traditional Japanese environment that was strongly influenced by his father. He had definite ideas about how the company should be run more "professionally" in contrast to his father's more traditional "family"-oriented style. Ethan was also concerned that his older brother was the designated successor after their father retired. He wondered whether testing could aid his decision making.

Ethan identified himself as a gay male and an American who happens to be of Japanese heritage. His sexual orientation was an important source of identity for him, with his Japanese heritage as a secondary source of identity. In contrast, his Nisei father identified himself as Japanese, despite being born and raised in the U.S. This identification extended to his expectations of filial piety, family loyalty, and harmony from both his family and the company.

Another cultural disparity between Ethan and his father was the difference in their perceptions of public and private matters. In Japanese culture, public knowledge of a gay or lesbian sexual orientation is considered a breach of an unspoken behavioral contract. Thus, although Japanese culture does not have moral or religious sanctions against homosexuality, it does have a bias: "Japanese society has never known religious homophobia, but the Confucian emphasis on marriage and procreating the family line continues to exert a dominant influence" (Dynes, 1992).

Therefore, despite Ethan's views on the subject, his sexual orientation was viewed within the culture as a private behavior that should not have any bearing on the company and should be concealed from public presentation. From this perspective, Ethan would be seen as failing and shaming the family by putting his own needs before those of the family and company. Ethan equated any requirement to suppress his sexual orientation with a lack of personal affirmation, rejection, and a failure to be assertive enough. This particular perception reflected an individualistic rather than group orientation.

### Cultural Considerations for Intervention

It was important to help Ethan to become aware of cultural disparities reflected by attitudinal and behavioral expectations. This proved vital to initiating the process of understanding his experiences at the margins of the dominant U.S. culture, and how he perceived responses to his sexuality within the company. This also permitted the significance of his sexual orientation to be understood within U.S. and Japanese cultural contexts, as well as an opportunity to explore whether or not there were any ways in which the views of his family and the company on this issue converged in a way that was advantageous to him. It was important to consider homophobia as an explanation for his father's attitude in view of his exposure for many years to the politics concerning gay males in the U.S. In addition, a Japanese cultural explanation was important to consider.

The next composite explores a young Asian immigrant's experience with marginalization. His stressful life circumstances set up a no-win situation due to limited resources and a clash of cultural values.

### TOM

Tom was a 23-year-old first-generation Vietnamese man concerned about his ability to find a job after graduation. Although his major was engineering, he considered the possibility of consulting work. Yet, Tom wondered whether he should abandon the possibility of pursuing consulting and simply get a job as an engineer, since the probability of being hired for an engineering position seemed more likely. His interest in consulting happened by chance when he learned from a classmate that consulting was a good stepping stone toward an MBA degree and learning about businesses. Tom thought about starting his own business after he accrued the necessary experience.

Tom initially sought counseling for stress associated with finding employment. This resulted in a sleep disturbance, poor concentration, and rumination.

At the age of 12, Tom left Vietnam for the U.S. with an aunt while his parents and siblings were left behind. This separation occurred because of his family's fear that he might be drafted. Some years later, Tom's family immigrated and joined him. He was the only one of his siblings to have attended college; his family took menial jobs to support themselves and his education. Tom majored in engineering because it required less reading and writing in English, which always had proved to be difficult for him.

Survival was a theme that gave urgency to Tom's career decision-making process. He felt caught between his family's economic welfare and a personal desire to pursue his own interest. Tom also equated pursuing his career interest with jeopardizing family security due to uncertainty about consulting as a viable professional option. Because his family was unfamiliar with consulting, they equated the career with risk and instability. On the other hand, they accepted engineering as a respectable profession with a stable income.

Compounding the dilemma was Tom's sense of inadequacy about his academic performance and preparation for a professional career, since others around him seemed to "know" what to do and to not have difficulty finding jobs. Self-blame, a sense of failure, and shame were the products of his reasoning that if he was as smart and motivated as the others, he would not experience such difficulties.

## Cultural Considerations for Intervention

This mix of responsibility and blame incorporated Tom's self-imposed pressure to do the right thing for the group. It also incorporated his assumption that he, alone, was ultimately responsible for his predicament. This perspective unconditionally equated unfulfilled hope and failure with insufficient effort and individual inadequacy rather than lending itself to a broader contextual explanation.

With the latter perspective in mind, Tom could be helped to broaden his view of this dilemma beyond individual characteristics to include broader culturally based realities which reveal significant sources of marginality (e.g., economic scarcity, cultural unfamiliarity, the language barrier) and inaccessibility to appropriate resources. This would explain his difficulties more fully and more accurately.

When the focus of career counseling with Asians and Asian Americans is on survival, consideration of the attainment of material goods and assurance of upward mobility are primary. It may seem self-centered to both Asian parents and Asian American students to pursue "individual" interests. Several professions including medicine, dentistry, engineering, and accounting have a great appeal to immigrant and first-generation Asians, since these offer economic stability and prestige. Meanwhile, careers that are less familiar to these groups are discouraged when the path to social recognition and economic mobility is unclear or indirect.

Individualism attributes success to individual initiative, innate ability, and motivation. Strikingly absent from this value standard is the reality of unequal privilege, resources, and opportunities associated with social and cultural variables (e.g., race, ethnicity, class, education, language barrier, trauma). Tom's unique life expectations provided a more appropriate context for understanding his difficulties. Such information also reframed his anxiety and pressure to achieve as challenges, indications of success, and strengths rather than inadequacies or failures.

## Implications for Career Counseling with Asians and Asian Americans

Effective career counseling recognizes the influence of significant people and life experiences on career development. Counseling Asian Americans requires cultural competence and sensitivity, as well as awareness of the full range of effects that biculturality may have on career decision making. Effective intervention also requires the counselor's self-understanding concerning internalized assumptions and biases that might serve as barriers to the counseling process.

College students often appreciate it when areas of difference are explicitly raised for exploration. This is usually a validating and creativity-enhancing experience that is commonly responded to with some level of relief, recognition, and anxiety-free curiosity about their situation. Moreover, such intervention can be empowering and liberating to students who initially find themselves bound by traditional or culturally conflicting perceptions of their options.

## CONCLUSION

The case composites illustrate how, despite overt assimilation, cultural and familial expectations shape career concerns of Asian American students. Impact of these influences on career concerns remain invisible when career counseling reflects the dominant U.S. values. Culturally competent and sensitive counseling require awareness of the full range of effects biculturality have on Asian American students' career concerns and the counselor's awareness of his or her own assumptions and biases which may serve as barriers.

## NOTE

1. The Korean community uses decimals to designate children who came to the U.S. at an early age from Korea. The birth order of these children, who are offspring of immigrants, is between the immigrant and second generations who are born in the United States.

## REFERENCES

Chin, J. L. (1993). Toward a psychology of difference: Psychotherapy for a culturally diverse population. In J. L. Chin, V. De La Cancela, & Y. M. Jenkins, *Diversity in psychotherapy: The politics of race, ethnicity, and gender* (p. 87). Westport, CT: Praeger.

Dynes, W. R. (1992). Introduction. In W. R. Dynes & S. Donaldson (Eds.), *Asian homosexuality*. New York: Garland Publishing, Inc.

Kim, E. Y. (1993). Career choice among second-generation Korean-Americans: Reflections of a cultural model of success. *Anthropology and Education Quarterly, 24 (3),* 224–248.

Lowman, R. L. (1991). *The clinical practice of career assessment: Interests, abilities, and personality*. Washington, D.C.: American Psychological Association.

Yum, J. O. (1988). The impact of Confucianism on interpersonal relationship and communication patterns in East Asia. *Communication Monograph, 55 (4),* 374–388.

CHAPTER 15

# PSYCHOTHERAPY IN THE SHADOW OF DEATH
A Graduate Student with AIDS

Nadja B. Gould

## INTRODUCTION

This case focuses on the complex therapeutic management of a young graduate student with AIDS. The conflicts between patient and family involving sexual orientation are interwoven with the depression arising from a life-threatening illness. The therapist is called on to work creatively in a situation markedly different from the usual college health service scenario.

## SAM

Sam was a 26-year-old graduate student in anthropology who first sought therapy in 1990 at Harvard University Health Services. He had been referred by his internist to the AIDS support group, which I lead, and therefore had a chance to "look me over," as he put it.

In our first session, Sam made it clear that he was not the "therapy type," and that his recent illness precipitated his calling for an appointment. He was well aware that his symptoms marked the transition from being a healthy person who was HIV positive to a person with AIDS (PWA). At the same time he was numbed by this realization, "in shock," and quite depressed.

### Background of the Problem

Six weeks earlier, Sam had been hospitalized at the university infirmary with his first bout of pneumocystis pneumonia. His doctor had recommended the AIDS Support Group and also suggested individual counseling, having learned that Sam had not yet told his family about his HIV status. Dreading the thought of that phone call home, Sam was thrown into a state of anxiety which he had not experienced since his undergraduate years when he "came out" to his family and a few friends. He had known he was HIV positive for about three years, having been tested in San Francisco during his senior year at another university. He had only told his boyfriend at the time. Sam's partner at the time of his therapy, Jason, also knew that he was HIV positive and had thus far tested negative himself.

**Family Background**

Sam grew up in a city in the western U.S., the youngest of three children and the only boy, in an intact middle-class family. He described his parents as "basically good people, just a little clueless" when it came to understanding their gay son. Sam's father ran a successful car dealership, and his mother taught music in the local school system. He said his parents probably cared about him "too much," having seen him as the son they had waited for, with high hopes for him, both academically and personally. Sam described little conflict between himself and his parents during his adolescence.

As our work in therapy progressed, he began to refer to himself during high school as "that former good boy" who, unlike his older sisters, had not rebelled in any overt way. Sam's academic success, editorial positions on the school paper, and intense involvement in a church youth group kept his family, and to some extent himself, distracted from his emerging sense that he was "different," a difference which he came to identify as being gay. However, it was not until he had left home to begin his freshman year in college that he cautiously began to seek out gay-affiliated groups and gay-centered social activities on campus. Many months of highs and lows followed: elation over his first relationship with a classmate (this was the first sexual experience for both); devastation when it ended, and excitement at being part of a new community that included meetings of gay and lesbian political and social groups, rallies, dances, crushes, flirtations, and flings.

In his sophomore year, at Thanksgiving, Sam came out to his entire family during the four-day weekend. He talked first with his mother, who, while not entirely surprised, became tearful and needed to be reassured by Sam that neither she nor other members of his immediate family had done anything wrong to cause his sexual orientation. His mother worried that there "had been too many women in the family" and "not enough rough and tumble boy activities."

When Sam told me his "coming out to family story" in our third or fourth session, he cried openly for the first time, feeling that now he would have to bring "even more shameful news" to his family, which was likely to cause them "even more pain." I spoke directly about the connection between his internal experience of shame at being gay and his feeling about the stigma of having AIDS. In other words, the virus, which does not discriminate between gender, race, sexual orientation, or economic status, becomes stigmatized in the minds of many people, including PWAs. This is because of its sexual transmission and the reality that AIDS is a disease which is ultimately fatal. In Sam's case, the stigma was so powerful and the shame so great that he had not been able to tell his parents immediately after testing positive during his senior year. Therefore, his wish to inform his family of his illness, along with his shame and fear of telling them, would become the major focus of our work together.

## Building A Therapeutic Alliance

When Sam first came out to his family at age 19, his parents had suggested counseling. This suggestion was partly influenced by their feeling of helplessness, not knowing what to say to him about being gay, and partly because they hoped a professional would confirm that his homosexuality was "just a phase . . . temporary." He was terrified that he would have to "spill his guts" to "some shrink" at his college counseling service and so never went, although some of his friends were in therapy. Sam's doubts and fears about therapy as a process and about me as a trustworthy person emerged in the initial months of our work. It became clear that many of his fears grew out of his experience of feeling "different" and being part of a marginalized, stigmatized group. I would need to gain his respect and confidence while giving him reason to feel that the experience of therapy could be helpful to him. I decided that the traditional "therapist neutrality" would not be helpful toward engaging him in the treatment, and that building trust as quickly and smoothly as possible was my first order of business. The clock was ticking. We didn't know how much time we had together. I decided to answer his questions honestly and directly:

1. no, I did not think being gay was a psychological disease or aberration;
2. yes, I had worked with gay students and PWAs before;
3. yes, I would see him with his family or with his partner if he felt that would be helpful; and
4. no, I would not make judgments about his past sexual activities or his occasional lapses in safer sexual practices, which he felt were responsible for his having been infected.

I responded to his initial fears about the therapeutic process by acknowledging that had it not been for his HIV disease, he would not have wanted or needed to be in therapy now; I neither heard nor interpreted his comments as resistance.

Because I was willing to respond directly to Sam's initial concerns, we moved rather quickly to the important process of establishing his goals for therapy. These seemed to fall into two categories which we labeled "internal" and "external." Internal referred to his many feelings. He wanted not just to talk about and analyze them, but also to *feel* them. Sam had no trouble generating a list. Fear, anger, guilt, shame, embarrassment, envy, rage, panic, grief, and despair all emerged in the early weeks of the therapy, and then returned over and over again, like variations on a musical theme.

The second issue he wanted to work on was more pragmatic and related to his external world. Sam struggled with questions such as:

1. When and how should he tell his parents about his recent hospitalization and its meaning?
2. How could he negotiate his relationship with Jason especially in light of Jason's seronegativity?
3. Would I advocate for him by being in touch with his internist on a regular basis?
4. Could I help him make difficult medical/legal decisions (e.g., living will, health care proxy)?

As we started our work together with these internal and external goals in mind, I began to feel my own version of helplessness and despair. How would I manage my own anger at this horrible disease, my own anticipatory grief that this wonderful, vibrant young man who could have been my son would probably live only a few more years? Having worked with hospice and cancer patients, I knew that peer support and consultation were indispensable. I also knew that I was fortunate to be working closely with two internists, one an AIDS specialist, the other a hospice medical director, both of whom gave generously of their time and moral support.

After approximately six sessions, Sam asked if Jason could join us, so that they could spend a session or two preparing for Sam's planned phone call to his parents. Sam felt that if Jason were "part of the team" along with me, he would have more courage and feel more supported in this difficult task. In retrospect, this request does not seem strange. However, at the time it meant a departure from my usual practice of therapy. I had been trained in the days when one was either the client's individual therapist or the couple's therapist, but not both. So I needed to discard old theories and reconceptualize my role so that the therapy would be most helpful to Sam.

I found myself able to be more flexible by focusing on the real therapeutic goal, which was to help Sam find ways to feel more powerful and less marginalized. Making this shift and working with Sam and Jason together turned out to be enormously helpful and did not compromise the therapeutic alliance. During the first year or two of treatment, Jason joined us only a few times, always at Sam's request and to address a specific concern. But, as Sam became sicker in the third and final year of treatment, they always came together. Jason, having known me, was comfortable in my office, accepted my offer to make occasional house calls, and ultimately became Sam's spokesperson and advocate to the medical caregivers and family.

Another departure from the traditional therapeutic stance was the attention Sam and I paid to spiritual issues, to Sam's particular religious beliefs, and my proactive involvement of the campus chaplain. Sam had grown up in a liberal Protestant church, had been active in his high school youth group, and still attended services occasionally. Fortunately, his particular denomination did not condemn homosexuality. We discussed the importance of prayer to him, his belief in an afterlife, and the spiritual comfort he derived from these beliefs. One day I asked him if he would like to meet with the campus chaplain of his denomination. Hesitant at first, Sam was relieved that I knew the chaplain personally, had worked with her before, and asked if the first meeting could take place in my office with the three of us together. I saw this as an appropriate request and possible bridge to their subsequent meetings, so it took place, was successful, and never became a question of turf or property.

## Therapeutic Challenges and Tasks

Psychotherapy with a college student with AIDS has challenged me to redefine my role as a therapist and to address two fundamental and overlapping therapeutic tasks. The first is how to approach the developmental issues of young adulthood against the expectation of a premature and untimely death. We know that early adulthood is a time when men and women become increasingly independent, develop a more stable professional and personal identity, make commitments to long-term intimate relationships, and consolidate career choices. Thoughts of physical illness, deterioration, and dependence are anathema. The physical body is healthy, energetic, attractive, taken for granted. Considerations of mortality go largely unheeded.

Suddenly and brutally, young people with AIDS are forced to deal with issues which would not normally be confronted until old age. The second task of this therapy was to confront these issues. In the normal process of reaching old age, people are in a position to look back on a lifetime of opportunities and achievements. They have raised their families, experienced the deaths of their parents, planned for retirement, and learned to accommodate in small increments to the biological slowing down process. These two life stages ordinarily occur sequentially, with a long and productive mid-life period between them.

With AIDS, the forced compression of these stages takes place. With the premature realization of mortality, depression is inevitable. In the second year of our work together, Sam became increasingly depressed. Being part of the AIDS support group was an antidote to isolation. At one point I suggested a medication consult, and one of my psychiatric colleagues prescribed a low-dose antidepressant which proved helpful. As time passed, Sam began to trust me. As his physical condition deteriorated, he asked if I would be with him during the final stages of his disease, and at his dying. I promised that to the best of my ability I would.

## WHEN TERMINATION MEANS DEATH

AIDS itself was perhaps the most difficult challenge for me as a therapist and as a person. I realized that the "termination" of this therapy would not be the usual termination but would be the final chapter of Sam's short life. Sam had a fine mind, a promising academic future, and a loving partner. Yet, his body became increasingly cachectic, wracked with disease. I also observed that his mind became increasingly clouded and confused.

The witnessing of such deterioration is more often the experience of an oncology social worker, not a therapist in a college health service! Of course, we as therapists are accustomed to dealing with loss, trying to help clients come to terms with a variety of losses and changes in their lives. However, we have much less experience dealing with terminal illness and death, especially in the college student population.

When Sam died in August, 1993, after working with me for almost three years, and as I counseled other young men with AIDS, I became aware that a different kind of therapy had taken place. Instead of launching another graduating senior or doctoral student out into the "real world," I was holding the hands of the dying, sitting with grieving families, and going to funerals. The implications for training and education of mental health professionals are many and clear. The AIDS epidemic has brought an enormous challenge to the doors of our college health services, which requires us to respond in new and creative ways.

CHAPTER 16

# SALIENT THEMES AND DIRECTIVES FOR COLLEGE HELPING PROFESSIONALS

Yvonne M. Jenkins

In the previous chapters, the authors have presented a realistic window on the lives of college students of color and other students from diverse populations. The insights they have provided via this window confirm that diversity is a fascinating and complex reality that contextualizes the life experiences and problems of these populations in meaningful, consequential, and, perhaps, even predictable ways.

What was once a projection has since come to pass: The population of the U.S. *has become* more diverse than ever before. This reality is expected to expand beyond the millennium. Current attention to delivery of culturally competent counseling and mental health services is a very positive outcome of this transition, which is being increasingly practiced in college settings. Even so, much of the intervention with college students still fails to attend adequately to underlying social and cultural contexts for their concerns and experiences in college settings. Neither is the value of these contexts to guiding treatment planning and evaluation of outcomes always appreciated.

With these remaining challenges in mind, the authors have included a timely, intriguing, and challenging variety of case studies that are rich in content and instructive for helping professionals and trainees who treat these promising populations. In addition, the case studies are of value to educators, college personnel workers, health providers, and others concerned with understanding and promoting the overall well-being of this population.

Obviously, it is beyond the scope of this book to attend adequately to the full range of concerns presented by these populations in counseling and psychotherapy. However, in this chapter salient themes drawn from the previous case studies are identified. Furthermore, the authors' and editor's perspectives on what actually constitutes competent practice with students of color and other diverse student populations are framed as directives for practice.

The content of this book is intended to generate thoughtful discussions that will enhance the personal and professional development of those who work with college students and those who aspire to do so in the future. It is my hope that other counseling and mental health practitioners will add to the literature on intervention with students of color and other nontraditional college populations.

## SALIENT THEMES

### 1. The group is the primary organizing unit for pluralistic populations

In contrast to the dominant U.S. culture value orientation, the group (e.g., family, ethnocultural), rather than the individual, is primary to pluralistic populations. However, the extent to which the group is valued and guides an individual's behavior may vary according to the social history of a particular reference group in the U.S., individual factors, and degrees of acculturation or assimilation to U.S. culture.

### 2. Biculturality

The complexity of biculturality has been highlighted by Simms, Hansen, Hart-Webb, and Shin. In chapter 2, Simms described the pain of not belonging to the White or Indian worlds as experienced by a Native American Indian woman student who had spent several years in White middle-class foster homes. Her pain was partly associated with being the target of White prejudice. As a child and adolescent, she had also suffered alienation, humiliation, and restriction from acknowledging her cultural identity by Caucasians who considered their race and cultural practices to be superior to her own. As if this wasn't enough, she was also alienated by other Native American Indian peers because she was placed with a White family, attended their schools, and spoke their language.

In chapter 9, Hart-Webb's case study of a young man of African American and Caucasian ancestries focused on other important dimensions of biculturality. Revealed were shifts in identification associated with belonging to two races and cultures, the conflict between power and powerlessness imposed by dual racial identities, the complex influence of two conflicting ethnocultural value systems, and the fear of "selling out" associated with conflicting loyalties. Hart-Webb also elaborated on how mixed race identity is a highly conflictual experience for some students that may (a) complicate the development of a cohesive, well-integrated self-concept; (b) threaten the self-concept; (c) complicate developmental conflicts; and (d) influence the perception that one's life is a "reversal."

Shin expanded the focus on biculturality to include its impact on the career decision making of Asian students. She emphasized that two conflicting sets of loyalties are imposed: the Asian expectation that one's career choice must promote the well-being of the family, and the U.S. value for the well-being of the individual. At times, being torn between two sets of loyalties leads to a psychological impasse, which can be difficult for the counselor to recognize immediately because of assimilation and a similar value for academic and career achievements by both cultures. Shin also emphasized that cultural and intergenerational disparities concerning attitudinal and behavioral expectations frame perceptions of sexual preference for some Asian Americans as well.

Economic disparities constitute another important aspect of biculturality that is not typically thought of as such. For example, a bicultural dissonance sometimes develops between students from backgrounds of privilege and those from working-class or economically impoverished origins based on lifestyle differences influenced by family income level. This is a powerful yet often invisible and understated difference that can be divisive along racial and ethnic lines. Students from working-class or economically impoverished backgrounds often feel isolated, as though they don't belong, and insecure about their personal competence and intellectual abilities. Several of the authors have suggested that for students, biculturality encompasses the coexistence of traditional versus nontraditional perceptions of culture, race, ethnicity, and economic realities which significantly affect their psychosocial, academic, and career development experiences.

## 3. Oppression is hazardous to self-perceptions, identity development, and relational development

Oppression involves domination, colonialization, exploitation, devaluation, annihilation, and the restriction of liberty reinforced by sexism, ethnocentrism, and classism (Bulhan, 1985; Chin, De La Cancela, & Jenkins, 1993). Oppression may be inflicted in response to any dimension of diversity, and is insidious, demoralizing, and systematic. Much of the mental health literature on oppression indicates that less understood differences and difficulties associated with competition on the part of persons from a less dominant group with a dominant or privileged group are assumed by the latter to be both evidence of inferiority and justification for a group's subordinate position in society (Bowen, 1978; Bulhan, 1985; Greene & Sanchez-

Hucles, 1994). Despite the inherently negative nature of oppression, some students respond to it with incredible resilience and unwavering determination to succeed. Yet, others struggle with its hazardous effects.

In chapters 2, 3, and 5, Simms, Allen, and Wu called attention to the powerful influences of oppression on self-perceptions, identity development, and relational development. Simms emphasized how cultural identification, linguistics, and the world view of a student of color may be compromised as early as childhood just to survive on the margins of this society. As a consequence, the student may grow up finding it difficult to feel at ease in the world. This was Alita's experience, the young Native American co-ed who struggled with personal insecurities during her college years after experiencing significant familial and economic problems for much of her life.

Allen expanded our understanding of how oppression affects identity development, relational development, and self-perceptions via his case studies of two African American students. The seldom acknowledged reality that many students from this group eventually recognize that they are not valued as highly as Caucasian students lends an important context for understanding what influences internalization of oppression. It also lends an important context for understanding what underlies the tendency of some African American students to seemingly isolate themselves from other groups of students by staying together. This is usually motivated by needs for connection, belonging, and social esteem (Jenkins, 1993), which can be difficult to fulfill elsewhere in the predominantly White college setting. Shared cultural values, social position in the U.S., and experience in daily living generated by oppression also strengthen the ties between African American students.

Wu's case study of an Asian American woman from a background of gender oppression and identification with a culturally negative mother made evident the complex impact of internalized oppression on self-esteem development, relational development, and achievement.

### 4. Oppression is associated with trauma, inadequate self-caretaking, and blaming the victim

Obviously, the lens through which the concepts of trauma and recovery in women are viewed must be expanded to include the effects of racism, colonization, and political and economic oppression (Daniel, 1994). In chapters 2, 4, and 8, Simms's, Walker's, and Alvarez's case studies suggest that trauma is inherent to the psychosocial experience of oppression. Simms describes how Alita was forced to relinquish prematurely her childhood because her mother suffered from alcoholism and her father from diabetes and heart disease. These disorders are common among Native American Indians and are often linked to poverty, persistent distress, and substandard health education and health care. Simms' analysis suggests that oppression limits economic resources for educating Native American Indians and increases the likelihood that youth from this population will be exposed to significant trauma and loss prior to the college years. Therefore, this population is at high risk for underfunctioning without timely and appropriate support.

In another compelling case study, Walker expands the concept of oppression to include "dual traumatization." She contends that for African American women, sexual and racial violations influence a dual trauma informed by the individual, familial, and sociocultural history of the survivor's reference group. The historical dimension involves a sociocultural context that implicitly devalues women as well as people of color. As a consequence, the dissociation, disempowerment, and shame commonly associated with trauma are frequently experienced by African American women survivors of sexual abuse. Walker argues that a set of defensively organized behaviors may have adaptive value for the survivor, the therapist, and her work organization. She also explains that the survivor's strengths and competencies become potential sources of further violation on personal and professional levels via complex relational patterns that reenact the trauma and lead to relational disconnection for the client.

At yet another level, Alvarez reminds us that for some Latinas, oppression has involved the trauma of exposure to political unrest and military terrorism. It is this editor's impression that the psychological aftermath of such trauma plus culture shock and pressures to succeed in the U.S. are significant to the incidence of suicide among international students without adequate culturally syntonic interventions and support systems on campus or in the community. Of course, cultural, developmental, and a variety of other personal factors also play a role in these tragedies. Finally, in chapter 6 Chan suggests that trauma involves loss and adjustment issues associated with translocation/immigration.

Beyond the association between oppression and trauma, Walker's attention to Tulani's post-graduation obligation to her sister highlights another outcome of oppression that can be a strength or a liability, depending on what motivates such action. In some situations, kin sponsorship is a measure of success, while in others it is indicative of conflict associated with goal achievement and survivor's guilt. Such conflict is often associated with optimism and survival, as well as internalization of a lack of permission to care for the self while taking care of others. The latter involves low self-esteem, a distorted perspective on self-caretaking, and poor self-caretaking practices characterized by discomfort with asking for help and a high tolerance for neglect and abuse. Women of color are particularly vulnerable to disturbances in self-caretaking due to the impact of societal problems and their nodal role in this society (Pinderhughes, 1982).

The oppression of women has often been based on biased and distorted perceptions that have resulted in blaming the victim for injustices suffered. In chapter 11, it is evident that this mindset, along with Asian cultural values and beliefs, influenced Eva's slightly different account of what *really* happened to her out of fear that if her family learned the truth, it would bring them shame and dishonor. Rochelle's fear of expulsion by school officials and rejection by her family, if they learned of her rape, was powerful enough for her to maintain her silence about the assault. These fears had an ethnic component, her religious beliefs, and included the expectation that she, rather than her male assailant, would be blamed and punished because of traditional perceptions of women rape victims. Gloria's sense of responsibility for having been raped by her boyfriend, and her decision to not reveal the incident out of fear of losing her student visa, wish to protect her family from harassment, and an expectation that she would be blamed and punished, also suggest that biased perceptions of the role of women in their victimization are still quite prevalent and powerful.

Biased and distorted perceptions of men have also been destructive. For example, Freda's choice to date a Caucasian man after several unsuccessful relationships with African American men was influenced by mythical and stereotypical images of Black men *and* White men.

### 5. Race, culture, ethnicity, and social class

RACE. Allen acknowledges that racial identity and society's negative responses to racial differences are likely to surface in the therapy of African Americans. He also acknowledges the complex interplay between racial identity issues, maturation tasks, and psychosocial experiences of clients. Hart-Webb echoes this in her case study of a mixed race student of African American and Caucasian backgrounds. In addition, Hart-Webb and Wright acknowledge that negative responses to racial differences are a significant source of polarization between groups. Such polarization seems to be particularly pronounced between the dominant culture and peoples of African ancestry, and the former and some Hispanic groups.

It is common for African American students to struggle to maintain or salvage self-esteem as a result of micro- and macroaggressions they are subjected to during the college years (Jenkins, 1993). Many also struggle to achieve success without adequate psychological support, despite racism and other social problems that consistently convey that they are tolerated rather than valued or welcome.

As stated previously, themes concerning race also surface in mythical assumptions, stereotypes, and fears. The degree of insight exhibited in relation to these may vary from one client to another. Two relevant examples were described in chapter 3. Like Ahmed, some students initiate psychotherapy with considerable insight into the racial overlay for their concerns, while others like Maya only develop such awareness via exposure to culturally competent intervention.

Allen's case study of Maya is rich with several racial themes: denial of the significance of race to her concerns; resistance to being confined by racial boundaries; social exclusion; minimization of her feelings about the racial slights she has encountered; estrangement from African American peers; and internalized oppression reflected in the role she assumed with the Caucasian woman roommate who eventually betrayed her trust. This role was a poignant reminder of "Jemima," the selfless stereotypical "Mammy" or caretaker. Collins (1991) contends that stereotypes are controlling images predesigned to make racism and other social problems seem "natural, normal, an inevitable part of everyday life" (p. 68).

Among racial themes that surfaced in Allen's case study of Ahmed were colorism, negative assumptions about intellectual capacity, fear of subjective evaluations by professors that could threaten his academic success, and his efforts to avoid "his father's failings," a reality that was perceived as "typical" for Black males.

In chapter 11, Wright's vignette from an African American women's support group revealed how a campus racial crisis caused psychic pain and reminded participants of other racial traumas they had experienced in the past. Unfortunately, all of the negative responses to racial differences that have been described in this collection are common in U.S. culture.

CULTURE. Culture plays a significant role in the student's relationship with academic and career decision making. In chapter 10, De Leon, Stefanisko, and Corteza argued that culture is among those factors that influence college enrollment, academic success, and positive career development for Puerto Rican women. In chapter 7, Vogel revealed how family expectations influenced by the Japanese culture affected a young woman's approach to problem solving concerning academic difficulties. In chapter 14, Shin emphasized the prominence of culture and familial expectations to career decision making for Asian Americans. In her case study of a Korean American student, she illustrates that culturally based realities are often significant sources of marginality (e.g., economic scarcity, cultural unfamiliarity, the language barrier) and inaccessibility to appropriate resources. Shin emphasizes that the East Asian cultural orientation, which values group harmony and interdependence, conflicts with the individualism and competition that are valued in the U.S. Vogel and Shin agree that intervention based on the latter can be a source of conflict for students of Asian ancestry.

In chapter 8, Alvarez suggested that cultural differences are a source of complexity for Latinas. In Latin America, professional roles for women are traditional, which can be difficult to negotiate with less traditional gender role expectations. Thus significant loss (e.g., family, cultural identity) may result from Latinas studying in the U.S., pursuing a career, and developing a professional identity.

Another important theme concerning culture is "culture shock." Some students who are less familiar with U.S. culture do not know how to interpret or respond to everyday language and social cues in this country. Vogel reported that even though culture shock is underreported, international students from Japan and other countries are commonly affected by this condition. Because of pride, many international students suffer in silence with feelings of insecurity, anxiety, helplessness, and distrust. However, culture shock is not confined to students from outside of the U.S.

Many students from the U.S. who are in the numerical or psychological minority (i.e., on the basis of race or social class or both) are not familiar with how to interpret or respond to everyday social cues in the college setting; neither do some have the economic resources or background experiences such resources have typically afforded their peers from economically privileged backgrounds. The isolation, alienation, and marginalization associated with such differences can be both overwhelming and stressful. Hansen's case study of a nontraditional student in chapter 13 and Hart-Webb's case study of a bicultural/mixed race student from a blue collar background in chapter 9 offered instructive examples of effective intervention with students from the U.S. who experience culture shock associated with economic differences.

Culture also determines how emotion is expressed or managed. In chapter 5, Wu emphasized that specific communication patterns and styles of affective expression are influenced by culture. These affect the therapist's ability initially to engage the client and to maintain a connection. In chapter 2, Simms used the case study of Alita to reveal that among Native American Indians, "the expression of the depth of a feeling can be limited to simply naming or recognizing [the emotion] as well as subtle displays of such" (p. 31).

In chapter 6, Chan called attention to how powerful cultural norms and expectations contained and defended the emotional turmoil of a quiet Korean American woman student who used considerable emotional restraint. This author also described this client's complex emotional struggle with respecting a father who had neglected her and the painful process of coming to terms with the reality that she had been raped by a fatherlike employer she admired and trusted who was from her ethnocultural group. After all, a dutiful Korean daughter was expected to respect authority, never to reveal her shame. Chan framed the young woman's shame, intense need for privacy, style of affective expression, and her stance on sexual expression within an informative cultural context.

In chapter 11, Wright's vignette from a rape recovery group highlighted how internalization of cultural and familial messages (e.g., myths, stereotypes, misconceptions) interact to influence to what extent some survivors feel free to disclose their assaults, who they choose for partners, and complexities of their recovery process. For example, a young Japanese American woman chose not to disclose the full details of her rape to her family out of respect for their sense of pride and honor. Therefore, prior to her participation in the group she tried to deal with her trauma alone.

For Rochelle, a Catholic Caribbean student, religious beliefs fueled the fear of rejection that prevented her from telling her parents the truth about having been raped. On the other hand, Freda, a young African woman survivor of date rape, chose not to disclose to her mother that her assailant was a White man she had dated; her mother had always given her negative messages about White men. For Gloria, who was studying in Israel at the time of her assault, it was fear that her family would suffer racial and ethnic harassment, or that she would have her student visa rescinded if she were to disclose that her assailant was an Israeli citizen.

Because race and ethnocultural issues shape interpersonal dynamics and group process, Wright argued that these issues must be acknowledged and attended to in treatment to promote the total well-being of group participants.

Alvarez's focus on Latinas acknowledged the connection between culture, politics, and emotional expression. In chapter 8, she acknowledged that there may be diverse and distinct interpersonal styles of relating in one country. Furthermore, she called attention to the reality that internalization of painful feelings is sometimes a protective mechanism against political unrest. This bears a connection to how social trauma is responded to by some U.S. ethnocultural groups (e.g., Native American Indians, African Americans, Japanese Americans) cognitively, emotionally, and behaviorally.

Behavior may have very different meaning from one culture to another. In chapter 7, Vogel attributes a contrast in the "feel" of Japanese families from White middle-class families to a difference in cultural orientations. For Japanese families, this contrast is influenced by a value for group harmony, deference to the needs of family, and achievement along expected academic and occupational dimensions. Whereas, in dominant U.S. culture, there is an orientation toward individuality, self-expression, and competition. Japanese parents have a central role in guiding their children's social and educational development. Thus, a young Japanese woman's decision not to immediately tell her parents about her academic difficulties had a timely cultural basis, in view of her father's illness, and was not indicative of a serious parent-child schism.

However, some students become immobilized by an inability to tell their parents of an impending failure or the wish to change a major. Vogel has observed that being in the U.S. may enable Japanese students to feel less shame about seeking help than if they were in their own country. Any reluctance on their part to work with a therapist from the U.S. tends to be associated with anxiety about the possibility of not being understood because of cultural and linguistic differences.

In chapter 12, Dinklage revealed that culture is also central to perceptions of learning ability in the U.S. Therefore, "learning disability" is acknowledged as a culture-bound concept.

**ETHNICITY.** Ethnicity, according to Pinderhughes (1989), refers to connection based on commonalities (e.g., religion, nationality, region, and so on) where specific aspects of cultural patterns are shared and where transmission over time creates a common history. Therefore, ethnicity is a significant source of heterogeneity in diverse populations. However, as for Miriam, a Mexican American Catholic woman, whose parents grew up in different parts of Mexico and whose older sisters were born in Mexico, ethnicity imposes conflicting loyalties for some students. These may be further complicated by the impact of biculturalism, linguistics, and sexism as Alvarez has indicated in chapter 8. Those who feel such conflict may not feel a sense of belonging to their ethnic group, country of origin *or* the U.S. In addition, they may feel a sense of estrangement in familial and love relationships.

**SOCIAL CLASS.** On the surface, social class, as determined by economic factors and value orientation, can be a relatively invisible source of difference. However, it can be a powerful determinant of a student's aspirations, savvy, or lack of sophistication in negotiating the college environment, and whether or not one generally feels "at home" in the college setting. Social class is also a relatively invisible but powerful source of intraracial and intraethnic difference between students which influences whether or not they interact with one another and the quality of level of comfort with such interactions. Even though social class can serve as a comfortable source of connection for some students, for others it can influence isolation and alienation. Hart-Webb alludes to this dynamic in chapter 9. Furthermore, in chapter 13, Hansen acknowledges the potential for isolation social class differences can lead to when the student contends with multiple roles and pressures.

## 6. Relationships

In counseling and psychotherapy, students from pluralistic backgrounds present with many of the same issues that students from the dominant culture present. However, social background variables (e.g., race, ethnicity, culture, social class) provide essential contexts for understanding their difficulties. Those themes associated with negative perceptions of diversity that have been highlighted by the authors are:

1. the reenactment of internalized oppression;
2. attempts to have relational needs met through work competence;
3. anxiety associated with possible reenactment of internalized oppression;
4. reluctance to seek help;
5. a lack of social esteem; and
6. social isolation and humiliation associated with not fitting in with primary reference groups and nontraditional roles of students.

**WHEN VISIBILITY OF SOME STUDENTS THREATENS.** The visibility of a group of African American or Latino/a students on some campuses is viewed as a threat by members of the dominant culture. Of course, this perception has historical and political bases. In addition to developmental factors that influence such group behavior for most students, those that feel threatened by these groups often lack awareness of their own internalized oppression as well as the primary role of the group in peoples of African ancestry and Latin American cultures. The value for the group over the individual also extends to many other cultural and ethnic groups.

**SILENCE AND THE CHILLY CLIMATE.** Silence between students in the numerical or psychological minority and the institutions in which they study is another key dynamic of many relationships. Such silence is often evident in a very diversified population including: students of color; international students; those from blue collar or low-income backgrounds; and those with learning disorders. Self-perceptions of intellectual or personal inadequacy and expectations that one will not be taken seriously or valued often accompany such silence. Because some professors, administrators, and others in authority fail to acknowledge and value diversity, a silent tension may be evident when related issues do surface, resulting in what Greene and Sanchez-Hucles (1994) refer to as the "chilling" of the climate. Social distance rather than collaboration is promoted by this climate. The same authors contend that such silence may reflect a need for less polarized language (e.g., good and bad, superior and inferior, normal or abnormal) to describe difference.

Students who do dare to acknowledge diversity issues, particularly problematic ones, are sometimes responded to with silence or chilling disdain that may result in their alienation or other negative attention. These students also tend to be perceived as troublemakers, psychologically unstable, or "the problem." Many of the challenges they encounter are not understood within a larger societal or systemic context. To add insult to injury, the same students are sometimes expected to educate and even comfort those in authority as well as peers whose self-development is still threatened by the challenge of embracing diversity. For example, some helping professionals and other college personnel workers rely on students for information that could more appropriately be gained through relationships with peers or friends from diverse backgrounds and culturally competent educational and training opportunities.

Furthermore, it is evident that some members of oppressed groups assume "that oppressions are interchangeable" (Greene & Sanchez-Hucles, 1994, p. 26). For example, some assume that the experiences of racism and homophobia are interchangeable. This frequently results in the projection of anger onto those who challenge this perspective, rather than introspection and an openness to other points of view. Responses to this anger by students who are the targets of such treatment often involve anxiety, helplessness, or dysfunctional caretaking, which may involve the perceived expectation to forgive, soothe or assuage White guilt. It may also involve psychological numbness or a gradual build up of rage.

### 7. Religiosity and spirituality

Religious beliefs and spirituality are common sources of support for pluralistic populations. Even when students of color are not actively involved with organized religion, their world views might be shaped by previous exposure to religious doctrine or religious communities. In chapter 10, De Leon, Stefanisko and Corteza found the practice of religious beliefs and connections to religious communities to be among those factors associated with the success of Puerto Rican women college students.

On the other hand, Hines and Boyd-Franklin (1996) remind us that "there are healthy and unhealthy forms of religiosity" and "some interpretations of religious doctrine can have a harmful impact" (p. 75). In chapter 4, Walker argued that there are instances when religiosity is associated with developmental vulnerability and may serve as a buffer against painful experiences. Yet, in chapter 11, Wright suggested that religious taboos may impose barriers to self-caretaking, growth-fostering relationships, and healing.

Several cultural healing approaches have a spiritual component, such as the talking circle, a supportive community highlighted by Simms in chapter 2, that Alita, a Native American Indian woman was invited to join. The talking circle provided Alita with support for her spiritual needs and affirmed her Indian identity. A more detailed account of religiosity and spirituality among people of color and other pluralistic populations is offered elsewhere (Comas-Díaz, & Griffith, 1988; McGoldrick, Giordano, & Pierce, 1996).

## 8. Generalizations are destructive

In chapter 2, Simms called attention to how "packaged judgments" concerning the use of alcohol serve as barriers to effective intervention with the Native American Indian population. In chapter 12, Dinklage defined the disturbing impact of negative expectations of achievement for African Americans, as these affect students from this population with learning disorders. This author also suggested that positive expectations of achievement for Asian American students has troubling effects. In both situations, requests for essential help are often delayed or postponed. Furthermore, several other authors acknowledged ways in which other forms of internalized oppression, based on generalizations, interfere with healthy self-perceptions, relational development, and effective self-caretaking.

## DIRECTIVES FOR COLLEGE HELPING PROFESSIONALS

Current demographics for college populations require more diversity-inclusive forms of intervention than standard practice has allowed. This must include culturally syntonic and socially responsible approaches to intervention guided by those key cultural and social variables that have been highlighted in previous chapters. Ethical and responsible practice in college settings is dependent on the ability of professionals to make this essential adjustment. This is not an easy task, in view of the complexity of diversity and the undeniable reality that the counseling and mental health professionals have generally supported and benefited from the "form or process of organized society, with its specific government and economic interests and power struggles" (Chin, De La Cancela, & Jenkins, 1993, p. 9).

Thus, traditional Western approaches to intervention have assumed Western interventions to be superior to traditional healing methods. Such interventions have also claimed to be "apolitical, scientifically neutral, and bias free (De La Cancela, Chin, & Jenkins, 1993, p. 9). It is unlikely that this claim has proved true with any degree of certainty for any particular population. It has no basis in reality for peoples of color and other nontraditional populations. Instead, it has minimized social inequities while overlooking problems in our society and economy while emphasizing psychological and psychiatric explanations (De La Cancela, Chin, & Jenkins, 1993).

With these disturbing truths in mind, the following directives are intended for counselors and mental health professionals to promote diversity-inclusive intervention in college settings.

## SELF-UNDERSTANDING AND DEVELOPMENT

A prerequisite to embracing diversity in others is the process of embracing one's own social identity. Therefore, in order to embrace diverse client populations, the helping professional is challenged to embrace his or her social identity. This requires exploring and gaining clarity about one's ethnic and cultural background, and tolerating the anxiety of defining and understanding one's experiences of difference. The latter involves becoming aware of any diversity-affirmative perceptions and attitudes one has internalized over the course of a lifetime, and any internalizations of oppression that might shape one's current perspectives of self and others.

In addition, embracing diversity involves assuming responsibility for sorting out and working through any personal barriers to embracing diversity outside of the helping relationship, and learning to value all of who one is as well as difference in others. This very personal process of self-development requires a lifelong commitment. Without progressive movement in this direction, it is virtually impossible to embrace diversity in others beyond a superficial level.

## PROFESSIONAL DEVELOPMENT

The professional development of counselors and mental health professionals must include training and continuing education that broadens understanding of how differential social and cultural realities influence ways that college students perceive and respond to the environment. It is also important for helping professionals to be aware of current events as they affect the global community in view of the connections that students may have to various parts of the world.

## DIRECTIVES FOR PRACTICE

As alternatives to the purely psychological and psychiatric explanations emphasized by traditional approaches to intervention, what follows are common themes that have appeared throughout the book concerning culturally competent practice with college populations; these are defined according to a synthesis of the authors' and the editor's perspectives. In addition, some other key directives for practice for specific client populations are highlighted based on the authors' perspectives.

## COMMON THEMES

1. Cultural competence is absolutely necessary for effective intervention with college populations. Achieving cultural competence

> begins with acknowledging that there have been systematic attempts to ignore, incapacitate, or destroy diverse cultures, and that one can become culturally proficient by integrating cultural knowledge into practice and theory. This requires a participatory process between the [helping professional] and the client, not just the ability of the therapist to know and understand the culture. (De La Cancela, Chin, & Jenkins, 1993, p. 11)

Cross et al. (1989) emphasize that culturally competent care implies the least restrictive or invasive interventions, coordinated care, and outreach to the home base of clients if necessary. In academic communities, cultural competence involves: acknowledging sociocultural and political contexts for problems and strengths; advocacy to eliminate those problems encountered; supporting the student's connection to natural support systems (e.g., ethnocentric organizations, ethnocultural organizations, churches and spiritual organizations); being prepared to work collaboratively with these, when indicated, on the student's behalf; and adhering to appropriate confidentiality guidelines despite the collaborative involvement of others in the student's care.

Cultural competence also involves supporting the self-determination of students within culturally syntonic parameters. Furthermore, it may involve recognizing the power of cultural and social content and accepting responsibility for addressing it competently. Achieving the latter can be as complex as the human diversity that requires it. Therefore, college helping professionals must think in practical terms about how diversity needs to shape the development of a therapeutic alliance, assessment of the problem, what approach is taken to the problem, and evaluating the outcome of intervention.

2. It is important to be aware of how race, ethnicity, and other social variables influence self-perceptions, identity development, relational development, academic performance, and career development.

3. Students' responses to diversity may involve strengths as well as vulnerabilities.

4. The influence of generalizations or universalism is antithetical to the process of embracing diversity. Greene and Sanchez-Hucles (1994) caution that "to reduce diversity to a simplistic analysis of human conditions, such as similarities and differences, produces reductionistic and erroneous theories, politics and practices that overgeneralize and universalize people's experiences." They remind us that "human beings are complex and that many aspects of reality interact, overlap, conflict with and complement each other" (p.21).

5. Growth fostering helping relationships acknowledge diversity and integrate its significance into the context of the intervention. Such relationships are essential to promoting the identity, relational, academic, and career development of students from diverse and nontraditional populations. The forms that the expression of personal qualities that promote such relationships and the sociocultural circumstances that contextualize these vary from one reference group to another. Therefore, the college helping professional must approach intervention from a flexible stance to truly enter the world of the client.

6. Effective intervention may require the helping professional to "wear multiple hats." Therefore, the role of counselor or therapist may be expanded to include educator, mentor, intermediary, and advocate. As such, the professional's use of self is vital to helping processes.

7. Become prepared to recognize signs of culture shock and to attend to these in international students, immigrants, and students from the U.S. who might be exposed to less familiar social and economic realities from those they are accustomed to.

8. Become prepared to recognize and attend to signs of shifting identities in relation to nationality and culture, socioeconomic class, and sexual preference.

9. Since the work of other college personnel is interdependent with that of college helping professionals, they too must strive toward cultural competence.

10. Know the factors that are associated with academic success for specific populations. Facilitate a connection between the student and such.
11. Make culturally homogeneous group services available.
12. Use culturally competent assessment measures for counseling, psychotherapy, intellectual functioning, and suspected learning disorders.

## OTHER KEY PRACTICE DIRECTIVES FOR SPECIFIC POPULATIONS
### Native American Indians

1. Explore the status and meaning of cultural values within historical and political contexts.
2. Be aware of the shortage of Native American Indian helping professionals.
3. Let your work with members of this population, as well as with others, offer the kind of example that will inspire Native American Indian students to become interested in pursuing a career in your field.
4. Don't apply "packaged judgments" regarding alcohol dependence. Assess each client's situation openly and objectively.

### Students of African Ancestry

1. Look for strengths of Black students; convey positive expectations of performance.
2. Be prepared to address adjustment and developmental problems associated with race to prevent highly complicated entanglements between racial issues and other psychological conflicts.
3. The "sorting out" and "working through" of racial identity issues that is required of some for success at predominantly White institutions involves coming to terms with societal and self-perceptions of what it means to be Black and achieving any resolution indicated.
4. Help students to learn productive ways to manage racism and discrimination.
5. Pay attention to the social climate on campus; acknowledging this preserves the positive identity of students despite adversity.

### Asians and Asian Americans

1. Insufficient information about shame and loyalty issues may interfere with treatment planning.
2. The career concerns of Asian Americans must be understood within the context of cultural values.

3. Recognize cultural disparities and help clients to become aware of how their attitudes and behavior express these.
4. The appearance of total assimilation should not be assumed to represent complete internalization of dominant U.S. values.

## Bicultural and Mixed Race Students

1. Work toward positive and cohesive identity integration.

## First-Generation College Students

1. Facilitate awareness of the benefits and psychological costs of getting an education.
2. Address conflict associated with social class transition.

## Nontraditional Students

1. These students may need concrete help negotiating multiple pressures and the college system.
2. Address role overload. Help students to find ways to reduce role conflict and to prioritize necessary tasks.

## Trauma Survivors of Color

1. Recognize when aspects of personal and professional functioning are compartmentalized. Work toward cohesive integration of the two when indicated, so that defensively organized behaviors that were once adaptive will not become sabotaging agents.
2. Be aware that traditional psychological nomenclature is inadequate to explain the more complex and nuanced phenomenology of the survivor's experience. In order to prevent the possibilities of unnecessarily pathologizing the client or viewing him/her within a context of deficiency, it is important to consider the political and sociocultural contexts that generate adaptations to trauma.
3. Attention to class and ethnicity, gender and race are important, even when the client and therapist share some aspects of social identity. This prevents reenactment of wounded relationships.

## International Students

1. A variety of problems presented by international students, recent immigrants, or numerical and psychological minorities may be related to ongoing stress associated with adapting to a new culture. Therefore, it is important to recognize and attend to the signs of anxiety associated with culture shock.

2. Do recognize limits of your knowledge about other countries. Do not generalize.
3. Be aware of what the choice to study in the U.S. represents for the student.
4. International students may needs to have a support person or host family to aid with transitioning into this culture.
5. It can be important to help students to reconnect with whomever they are disconnected from (e.g., family, friends) and to decide how to manage academic problems.
6. It is important to recognize the impact of migration, displacement, and exile on mental and social status.

## "Learning Disordered" Students

1. Institutions must take a multifaceted approach to the needs of this population that includes: problem identification; education; appropriate accommodations; and emotional support.

## Students Faced with Life-Threatening Illnesses

1. Be prepared to be flexible and to depart from the traditional. This may involve including others close to the student in the intervention, paying attention to spiritual issues, and collaboration with other professionals.
2. Two fundamental therapeutic tasks: (a) approach developmental issues of young adulthood against the expectation of a premature and untimely death; and (b) confront issues not normally confronted until old age.
3. Know that management of intense counter transference is indicated.

## TOWARD CULTURALLY COMPETENT SYSTEMS OF CARE
### Training and Continuing Education

College mental health services and counseling centers that serve as sites for practice, internships, and residencies, have a responsibility to offer culturally competent training. Therefore, culturally competent seminars and supervision must be offered. Furthermore, college helping professionals must take advantage of continuing education opportunities that promote an understanding of common adolescent and young adult development issues within appropriate cultural and social contexts and opportunities that promote diversity-syntonic skills development. Finally, since much of the work of college helping professionals is interdependent with that of other college personnel, college helping professionals could play a central role in promoting the cultural competence of this group by offering relevant diversity-inclusive training opportunities.

## Staffing

The staffing of college counseling and mental health services needs to be as reflective of the actual student population as possible. This applies to administrative and practitioner levels. The visibility of staff of color and awareness of the presence of other practitioners with interests in students of color and nontraditional populations are quite effective in enabling students from these populations to feel welcome and assured that their needs can be met. The presence of interested and competent practitioners can be made known via college media, printed brochures that include biographical sketches of counselors and therapists, and their special interest areas that can be made available to prospective clients, collaborative efforts with other college personnel, and the participation of staff members in various student forums concerning mental and social health issues.

## Research and Publication

Obviously, more research is needed on students of color and nontraditional students if relevant service delivery is to continue to be achieved. New research can aid with identifying changing trends in demographics of the college population, early intervention for students at risk, and meeting the particular intervention needs of specific populations. At a broader level, new research could aid with shaping relevant professional policy development in the fields of college counseling and college mental health.

Many college helping professionals have valuable insights and skills that could benefit other professionals as well as those in training. Such expertise could be shared easily with others if more professionals were encouraged to publish and provided with necessary resources (e.g., funding, time) for accomplishing this important task.

## CONCLUSION

Current demographic trends in college populations require college helping professionals to redefine their concepts of effective intervention with students of color and nontraditional populations. At the core of this task must be a commitment to self-understanding and self-development in relation to cultural and social realities. Such redefinition also requires progression beyond standard practice to culturally competent service delivery. Finally, culturally relevant research efforts and publications, as well as participation in relevant policy development, are necessary to achieve such redefinition.

## REFERENCES

Bowen, M. (1978). *Family therapy in clinical practice.* New York: Jason Aronson.
Bulhan, H. (1985). *Frantz Fanon and the psychology of oppression.* New York: Plenum.
Chin, J. L., De La Cancela, V., & Jenkins, Y. M. (1993). *Diversity in psychotherapy: The politics of race, ethnicity, and gender.* Westport, CT: Praeger.
Collins, P. H. (1991). *Black feminist thought.* New York: Routledge.
Comas-Díaz, L., & Griffith, E. H. (Eds). (1988). *Clinical guidelines in cross-cultural mental health.* New York: John Wiley & Sons.
Cross, T. L., Bazron, B. J., Dennis, K. W., & Isaacs, M. R. (1989). *Towards a culturally competent system of care.* Washington, D.C.: CASSP Technical Assistance Center, Georgetown University Child Development Center.
Daniel, J. H. (1994). Exclusion and emphasis reframed as a matter of ethics. *Ethics and behavior, 4 (3),* 229–235.
De La Cancela, V., Chin, J. L., & Jenkins, Y. M. (1993). Diversity in psychotherapy. Examination of racial, ethnic, gender, and political issues. In J. L. Chin, V. De La Cancela, & Y. M. Jenkins, *Diversity in psychotherapy: The politics of race, ethnicity and gender,* 5–15. Westport, CT: Praeger.
Greene, B., & Sanchez-Hucles, J. (1994). Diversity: Advancing an inclusive feminist psychology. In J. Worell & N. Johnson (Eds.), *Feminist visions: New directions in education and training for feminist psychology practice.*
Hines, P., & Boyd-Franklin, N. (1996). African American families. In M. McGoldrick, J. Pearce, & J. Giordano. (Eds.), *Ethnicity and family therapy* (p, 75). New York: Guilford.
Jenkins, Y. M. (1993). Diversity and social esteem. In J. L. Chin, V. De La Cancela, & Y. M. Jenkins. *Diversity in psychotherapy: The politics of race, ethnicity, and gender* (pp. 45–64). Westport CT: Praeger.
McGoldrick, M., Giordano, T., and Pearce, J. (Eds.) (1996). *Ethnicity and family therapy.* New York: Guilford.
Pinderhughes, E. B. (1982). Minority women: A nodal position in the functioning of the social system. In M. Ault-Riche (Ed.), *Women and family therapy,* 51–63.
Pinderhughes, E. B. (1989). *Understanding race, ethnicity, and power: The key to efficacy in clinical practice.* New York: The Free Press.

# AFTERWORD

# DIVERSITY AND THE HELPING PROFESSIONS
## Lessons in Understanding, Advocacy, and Sensitivity

Thomas A. Parham

> "All book sense, and no common sense, makes an educated fool."
> (African American Proverb)

The desire to increase levels of multicultural competence is compelling many clinicians and academicians to seek opportunities to train and learn more effective ways of delivering mental health services to diverse populations. Those who navigate the waters of training in the helping professions are generally greeted with an assortment of journals, periodicals, textbooks, videotapes, and other resources which promise to aid them in the development of competent and effective professional skills. However, despite the increasing number of resources available, questions remain about how to enhance one's learning experience with real case studies. Yvonne M. Jenkins, in this text entitled *Diversity in College Settings: Directives for Helping Professionals* may have just solved your problem.

What you have just been exposed to is what White and Parham (1990) and White (1984) before them refer to as the value of learning from direct experience. People from all walks of life have espoused the newfound theories of their respective disciplines, only to be surprised, frustrated, and, in some cases, disillusioned by personal situations and circumstances which conflict with their book knowledge theories. It is my belief that true personal and psychological growth emerges out of the discoveries instigated by situational phenomena. Indeed, many clinicians and academicians have come to learn that the dictates of their own experience are often more compelling than those we tangentially touch through our studies.

As we focus then on lessons learned, what should we take from this text as our challenges for the future? Certainly, one of those lessons should be a more profound awareness of the changing faces entering our colleges and universities across this country.

## Preparing for Demographic Changes

The growing numbers of culturally different students (i.e., students from other than White middle-class backgrounds) in this country are forcing many people to ask the question of how to best prepare for a diverse society. And like the society they mirror, educational institutions and the helping professionals who serve them are also confronted with issues of how to best address the counseling and mental health needs of persons who are culturally different from traditional populations, who for too long have been unaccounted for in our theories and models of counseling and therapeutic intervention.

Yet, the question of how to prepare seems irrelevant on one level, since increasing diversity has become a reality and is no longer just a prediction. In several states, for example, the majority of youngsters attending public schools at primary and secondary levels are children of color, and the numbers are steadily increasing. Soon, these youngsters will apply to colleges and universities nationwide, thereby presenting higher education with a formidable challenge: educating and providing counseling and mental health services to a culturally diverse student body. Clearly, counseling and mental health professionals at the higher education level need to respond swiftly and decisively to these changing demographics.

Despite the present urgency to respond to cultural pluralism, the efforts of a few committed individuals are being stifled by many in the mental health profession who seem less than willing to: (a) recognize our changing demographics, and (b) endorse programmatic initiatives which are designed for and aimed at true diversification. My observations of the counseling and mental health professions as a whole lead me to conclude, unfortunately, that those in our field of psychology, who should be most qualified to assist society in examining biases, prejudices, stereotypes, and defensive behavior, may be resistant themselves to change. Now, I should also acknowledge that a lack of movement toward real diversification and multiculturalism on the part of some may have to do with their inability to determine what to do or how to make a difference.

Indeed, the counseling and mental health professions and the institutions where we practice our trade should become the forums in which issues of ethnicity, gender, culture, social class, ability level, and so forth are topics of critical discourse and analysis. Yet, instead of providing decisive leadership, many helping professionals are passively waiting for social phenomena to dictate our next move. As a consequence, academic administrators are quickly relearning that students are tired of waiting for change. Ethnic student protests have continued with regularity on campuses throughout this nation in recent years with curriculum, faculty composition, and quality of campus life issues becoming the targets of their frustration and anger. And who can blame them?

Most culturally different students come to college expecting a "universal" education, but leave having only been taught by culturally sterile or U.S. dominant culture perspectives. For many culturally different students, their dreams of academic excellence and educational enrichment are shattered by experiences of alienation, overt hostility, and harassment, all of which are usually a part of such students' experiences on predominantly White campuses. Counselors and mental health professionals in higher education as well as those who treat college students in private practice, hospitals, and community agencies must be prepared to respond to these issues that students present.

**Endorsement versus Advocacy**

That "comfort with passivity" posture, or perhaps resistance to change, which seems to characterize some individuals in the counseling and mental health professions has forced many practitioners to assume a posture of reactivity and defensiveness when confronted with new demands. Consequently, institutional mechanisms for implementing change have become reactions to student unrest or student crises, rather than clear, systematic, comprehensive, proactive strategies for diversification.

While many in the helping professions and the institutions they occupy are quick to endorse verbally the principles of multiculturalism and diversity, operationalizing changes in professional practices, curriculum design, training, hiring and promotion criteria, and general quality of campus life issues have proved to be a much more difficult enterprise. I believe that it is important for helping professionals to recognize that there is a qualitative difference between endorsement and advocacy. When one endorses an idea, this involves giving credence to that issue or verbally suggesting that an issue may have some merit. Advocacy, on the other hand, not only requires that an individual endorse the concept, but that he or she actively work toward its full implementation. What I am really suggesting here is that if we as helping professionals want to make a true commitment to diversity and multiculturalism in college settings, then we must begin to value and accept diversity in ways which allow *our own behaviors* to move from endorsement to advocacy.

### Lessons Learned

What then have we learned from this text about what our challenges are for the future? Central to answering this question is another important question. That is, how do we make diversity in college settings real and substantial as opposed to superficially "interesting and exotic"? In this context, *Diversity in College Settings* suggests the following implications for helping professionals who intervene with college populations:

### LESSON 1: DEFINITION OF CULTURE

Operationalizing diversity in college settings requires a better understanding of culture. Too often, culture is simplistically defined through celebrations on campus where food, ethnic clothing, music, and sporadic holidays are the tools of incorporation. Clearly, culture is a complex constellation of values, mores, customs, and traditions which help inform and shape each person's experience. In that context, I would invite us to consider, as Nobles (1986) has before me, that culture provides a general design for living and a pattern for interpreting reality. Consequently, operationalizing diversity in college settings requires a more in-depth understanding of what the designs for living and patterns for interpreting reality are which culturally different students bring with them into educational settings.

### LESSON 2: UNDERSTANDING DESEGREGATION VERSUS INTEGRATION

In many of our college settings and other institutions across this country, diversity as a construct has been perceived as synonymous with demographics. Demographics in this regard include those attributes which distinguish people by race, age, physical ability, ethnicity, gender, and sexual orientation, as well as a host of other attributes (e.g., education, work experience, social class, religious beliefs, marital status, socioeconomic status, geographic location) which one acquires over a lifetime (Loden & Rosener, 1991). The fundamental problem with reducing diversity to demographics is that institutions believe that diversity goals have been achieved to the degree that the percentage of people in each of the above categories increases.

My analysis of college and university settings leads me to believe that we do not have integrated or diverse environments but rather desegregated ones. A desegregated environment assumes that each of us has the right to occupy the same geographical space. And so, the yardstick by which we measure progress in embracing diversity is often related to the degree to which our frequency distributions match whatever targeted goals have been set. True diversity, in my mind, is only partially a function of increases in the demographics. I would argue that *true diversity is not a question of whether or not the environment is desegregated, but if the policies and practices of that institution have changed as a function of changes in the demographic makeup.* If our institutions are 10% African American, 10% Chicano/Latino, 8% Asian, 2% Native American Indian, and 48% women, but continue to function in a culture which is Eurocentrically oriented and male dominated, then the diversity of that institution must be questioned.

## LESSON 3: YARDSTICK TO MEASURE PROGRESS IN VALUING DIVERSITY

Those of us concerned with valuing and operationalizing diversity are prepared to move from the endorsement stage to the advocacy stage. However, I believe that progress is often stifled by good intentions that have little direction. Many of us know what we want to do (i.e., promote and value diversity), but few of us have developed specific tools which enable us to accomplish that end. In my opinion, valuing and operationalizing diversity in college settings requires three factors: (a) a cognitive, emotional, behavioral, and spiritual pledge of support; (b) sound programmatic planning; and (c) some measure of accountability. Thus, the valuing of diversity must be trumpeted among senior administration, faculty, staff, and students. Each of those segments of the university population must develop specific programmatic initiatives designed to achieve diversity objectives. Furthermore, someone must be held accountable for diversity progress or a lack thereof.

With each of these factors in mind, I invite you to consider methods of intervention which can be made at both systemic and individual levels. In constructing a three (i.e., pledge of support, programmatic planning, accountability) by two (i.e., systemic versus individual intervention strategies) model of operationalizing diversity, we can plan strategies for embracing diversity in a more pragmatic way. Systemic interventions which correspond to pledges of support include: the development and analysis of mission statements which embrace the value of diversity; an analysis of public information which communicates the institution's commitment to diversity; or even an analysis of minutes/notes taken at staff and campus-wide meetings. For example, at a preliminary meeting it should be easy to tell how much people value diversity by how and how much they talk about it.

Systemic interventions which correspond to the programmatic initiatives category include recruiting and hiring more diverse administrators, faculty, staff, and students, and developing strategies to retain those who currently occupy these segments of the university population. Other programmatic initiatives include: training and professional development opportunities which speak to specific diversity objectives; orientation of new workers to the institutional culture; modifying the work environment to be more sensitive to the needs of diverse people; and providing mentoring programs for individuals reflected at every level of the institution's population.

Systemic strategies that correspond to the accountability factor involve the development of job descriptions which include functional tasks related to operationalizing diversity goals. Furthermore, accountability requires the development and setting of performance objectives, evaluation of the degree to which those objectives have been met, the provision of incentives for those who achieve substantial progress, and providing disincentives for those whose progress is lacking or otherwise unsatisfactory.

Ultimately, each of us must realize that institutions are composed of individuals. Consequently, each individual must set for himself or herself specific goals as well. Individual goals which correspond to the pledge of support factor include, for example, a commitment to take risks. Often times, diversity progress in institutions is stifled because individuals are rarely invited to think differently, are often afraid to speak up, and are typically anxious about engaging in behavior which is in some way different or unconventional. Achieving diversity goals in this area requires that individuals take cognitive risks (i.e., the willingness to stretch one's thinking beyond its current levels); verbal risks (i.e., the willingness to express different or unconventional ideas); and behavioral risks (i.e., the willingness to respond to institutional realities in ways which are different from the status quo). Clearly, college helping professionals can assist administrators, faculty, and staff with managing their anxiety and discomfort about risk taking. Furthermore, individuals must also examine their own biases and assumptions concerning diversity to more fully understand themselves and their relationships to a diversity commitment.

Individual interventions which correspond to programmatic initiatives include individual commitments to attend specific seminars or training institutes which focus on the development of awareness and sensitivity, increasing knowledge about different populations, and enhancing skills in working more effectively with diverse populations. Practitioners may also want to consider reading books and periodicals which increase their knowledge and understanding of different cultural groups. In this regard, practitioners must also take seriously the challenge of supplementing the knowledge and information gained from seminars and books with real life experiences. Each of us must find ways to develop avenues for more direct contact and experience with diverse populations.

Individual interventions related to the accountability factor involve the need to set personal goals, to hold one's self accountable for achieving those goals, and the need to hold others accountable for achieving their goals as well.

Obviously, I feel very strongly about the need to better operationalize diversity in our institutions of higher learning, and I believe that helping professionals have a key role to play in helping to realize this goal. Institutions of higher learning are in need of mental health professionals who understand that desegregating our profession is a far cry from true integration, and diversity defined by mere demographics is light-years away from genuine multiculturalism. Institutions of higher learning are in need of more mental health researchers who can design culturally relevant research studies which further our knowledge in culturally sensitive ways. In addition, such institutions are in need of helping professionals who must do more to validate client responses to societal oppression and must work toward its eradication.

Therefore, it is important for us to understand that many traditional psychological theories fail to recognize systemic factors in the assessment of the etiology of psychopathology and client dysfunction. Consequently, many clients from culturally different backgrounds are treated with therapeutic or counseling approaches inadvertently designed to help them adjust to oppression because underlying theories assume that the individual rather than the environment is responsible for their distress or concerns. Mental health professionals must recognize that what many presenting clients disclose may provide us with evidence of structural defects in the foundation of social policies and practices. As counselors and mental health professionals committed to social engineering, we must use client concerns as a barometer for social change and to advocate to the larger institutional powers-that-be on their behalf. Client concerns demand our immediate advocacy, while our ethical responsibility mandates that we consider this.

Our institutions are also in need of mental health academicians who not only teach culturally relevant courses, but join their practitioner counterparts in lobbying licensing boards and professional associations to require those who seek licensure or certification, or who offer services to clientele training in multicultural interventions and culturally specific psychology. Our institutions are also in need of more department chairpersons who advocate for and implement a meaningful level of diversity among faculty and hold themselves and their faculty accountable for achieving diversity objectives.

In conclusion, I would like to share a personal perspective as a note of hope and encouragement. My 43+ years on this planet and my 15 years as a professional psychologist have taught me much. I now know that helping professionals must be sensitive enough to listen, compassionate enough to care, personally secure enough to confront inconsistencies, and experienced enough to empathize. But my time on this planet has also taught me that if counseling and mental health professionals are to be successful in promoting the valuing of and operationalization of diversity in college settings, we must be bold enough to challenge inequality, brave enough to speak out against social injustice, and visionary enough to believe that we can change our institutions if we put our individual and collective energies forward.

## REFERENCES

Loden, M., & Rosener, J. (1991). *Workforce America.* Homewood, IL: Business One Irwin.

Nobles, W. (1986). *African psychology: Towards its reclamation, revitalization, and reascension.* Oakland, CA: Black Family Institute.

White, J. L. (1984). *The psychology of Blacks.* Englewood Cliffs, NJ: Prentice-Hall.

White, J. L., & Parham, T. A. (1990). *The psychology of Blacks: An African American perspective.* Englewood Cliffs, NJ: Prentice-Hall.

## CONTRIBUTORS

IRVING M. ALLEN, M.D., is a psychiatrist at Harvard University Health Services and in private practice in Brookline, Massachusetts. He is also a consultant to the New England Home for Little Wanderers and on the faculty of the Stanley H. King Counseling Institute for private secondary school educators. Prior to 1984, Dr. Allen was employed by the Veterans Administration for 15 years where he acquired an interest in post-traumatic stress disorder. His more recent interest involves the effects of trauma on the history and current plight of African Americans. In 1997, Dr. Allen published a book chapter entitled Post-traumatic stress disorder among African Americans, in Anthony J. Marcella et al. (Eds.), *Ethnocultural Aspects of Post-Traumatic Stress Disorder.*

MARGARITA ALVAREZ, Ph.D., is a licensed clinical psychologist at the Stone Center Counseling Service, Wellesley College and the Latino Mental Health Program, Cambridge Hospital, Department of Psychiatry, Harvard Medical School. Dr. Alvarez's primary interest is immigration as it is influenced by loss, identifications, and trauma. She also specializes in the psychology of women as determined by the interplay of ethnicity, social class, gender, and race. Dr. Alvarez has presented on these topics at numerous professional meetings. She has also published several papers on related topics.

CONNIE S. CHAN, Ph.D., is Associate Professor of Human Services at the College of Public and Community Service at the University of Massachusetts, Boston. At UMASS, she is also Co-Director of the Institute for Asian-American Studies. Dr. Chan, a licensed psychologist, is author of *If It Runs in the Family: At Risk for Depression* and numerous other publications that focus on how the interplay of gender, culture, and sexuality affects Asian American women. In 1993, Dr. Chan was awarded an Achievement Award for "Innovations in Treatment of Ethnic Minority Populations" by the American Psychological Association's Minority Fellowship Program.

BELINDA LOPEZ CORTEZA, M.A., is a Ph.D. candidate and research assistant in the School and Counseling Psychology Program at the University of Massachusetts, Amherst. She has presented papers on multicultural issues in career development and counseling at professional conferences. Ms. Corteza is also a member of Psi-Chi National Honor Society in Psychology.

BRUNILDA DE LEON, Ed.D., is an educational psychologist who is licensed in Puerto Rico and Massachusetts. She is an Assistant Professor in the School and Counseling Psychology Program at the University of Massachusetts, Amherst. Dr. De Leon has also worked in public schools, health care facilities, and community agencies. She is the author of numerous journal articles on Puerto Rican women. Her publications and research have focused on social and cultural adaptation, gender roles, education and career development of college students, and culturally competent mental health service delivery. Dr. De Leon has presented at numerous professional meetings in the U.S. and abroad.

KENNETH T. DINKLAGE, Ph.D., is a clinical psychologist with a strong interest in neuropsychology who has worked as a psychotherapist and diagnostician at the Harvard University Health Services since January of 1959. After his B.A. at Yale and his Ph.D. at Harvard, he worked briefly in the student health services at Dartmouth and Cornell. Shortly after coming to Harvard he began evaluating students for possible learning disorders and arranging for academic accommodations many years before these were mandated by law. Publications include: *Inability to Learn a Foreign Language* (1971), *Counseling the Learning Disabled College Student* (1991), and *The Evolution of the Harvard University Mental Health Service* (1992).

NADJA B. GOULD, L.I.C.S.W., is a clinical social worker who has been with the Harvard University Health Services since 1978. Her areas of professional focus include crisis intervention (pregnancy counseling, rape counseling), supervision of several undergraduate peer counseling groups, and psychotherapy with persons living with life-threatening illness. She developed the first AIDS support group at Harvard, which she has led for the past six years, and has worked individually with a number of persons with AIDS.

DIANE G. HANSEN, Ed.D., is a licensed psychologist with more than 18 years of experience at the Counseling and Testing Center at Northeastern University in Boston where she is Assistant Director of Clinical Services. In addition to the delivery of counseling and mental health services to students, she has taught counseling courses and has trained and supervised graduate students and professionals.

DIANE HART-WEBB, M.S.W., L.I.C.S.W., is a former trainee in clinical social work at Harvard University Health Services. Mrs. Hart-Webb is currently a clinical social worker at MetroWest Medical Center in Natick, Massachusetts. She has several years of experience in the hospice field and in hospital settings. Ms. Hart-Webb is interested in research on eating disorders and the developmental issues of ethnically diverse adolescents.

**YVONNE M. JENKINS, Ph.D.**, is a licensed psychologist at Harvard University Health Services, faculty member of the Jean Baker Miller Institute at Wellesley College, network member of the Center for Multicultural Training in Psychology (Boston, MA), and in private practice with Brookline Psychological Associates, formerly Frauenhofer Psychological Associates (Brookline, MA) and has recently joined VISIONS, a non-profit organization that provides antiracism training, and consultation on multiculturalism and diversity. Her recent publications include *Diversity in Psychotherapy: The Politics of Race, Ethnicity, and Gender* and *Community Health Psychology: Empowerment for Diverse Communities*. Dr. Jenkins's professional interests include mental health issues associated with cultural and social diversity, college mental health, and women's mental health. She has also lectured, published articles, and presented on these topics at numerous professional meetings.

**THOMAS A. PARHAM, Ph.D.**, is Assistant Vice Chancellor for Counseling and Health Services and Director of the Counseling Center, as well as an adjunct faculty member at the University of California, Irvine. Previously, he served as Director of the Career and Life Planning Center and the Counseling Center at UCI. Dr. Parham is also licensed to practice psychology in California. He is a past President of the National Association for Multicultural Counseling and Development, a division of the American Counseling Association. Dr. Parham has served on the editorial boards for the *Journal of Multicultural Counseling and Development* and the *Journal of Counseling and Development*. Currently he is an ad hoc reviewer for the *Journal of Black Psychology*. His research interests include psychological nigrescence and racial identity development. Dr. Parham is the co-author of *The Psychology of Blacks: An African-American Perspective* (Prentice-Hall, 1990) and the author of *Psychological Storms: The African-American Struggle for Identity* (African-American Images, 1993). He is currently co-authoring a book with his brother, Dr. William Parham, entitled *Therapeutic Approaches with African-American Populations*.

**CHESTER M. PIERCE, M.D.**, is Professor of Education and Psychiatry in the Medical School, the Graduate School of Education, and the School of Public Health at Harvard University. Dr. Pierce is also a psychiatrist at the Massachusetts General Hospital in Boston. For nearly 25 years he was also psychiatrist at the Massachusetts Institute of Technology. He was Founding President of the Black Psychiatrists of America, is a former President of the American Orthopsychiatric Association, and has chaired committees for the National Institute of Mental Health. Dr. Pierce has published widely on racism and a variety of other topics.

SUNGLIM A. SHIN, Ph.D., is a licensed clinical psychologist at the Bureau of Study Counsel at Harvard University. She is also in private practice. Dr. Shin was previously a staff psychologist at the MBA Counseling Services of the Harvard Business School. Her professional interests include the influence of social adaptation on Asian Americans and international students, and the "Self-in-relation" theory of the Stone Center at Wellesley College.

WINONA F. SIMMS, Ph.D., is Assistant Dean of Students and Director of American Indian and Alaskan Native Programs at Stanford University. Previously she was an Assistant Professor in the Department of Counseling at the University of North Dakota. She has authored several papers and book chapters on cultural and mental health issues of Native American Indians. Dr. Simms has also been awarded several research grants for projects associated with the achievement of Native American Indians and career counseling with this population. She is interested in the psychosocial experiences of Native American Indian college students and effective healing modalities for this population.

MICHELLE C. STEFANISKO, M.S., is a Ph.D. candidate and research assistant in the Counseling Psychology Program at the University of Massachusetts at Amherst.

SUZANNE H. VOGEL, L.I.C.S.W., is a clinical social worker/psychotherapist at the Harvard University Health Services and maintains a private practice in Cambridge, MA. Her long-term interest in cross-cultural sociology and mental health began with intensive family research in Japan in 1958–60. She continues this interest currently as a consultant/supervisor at Hasegawa Hospital, a private psychiatric hospital in Tokyo.

M. MAUREEN WALKER, Ph.D., is a psychologist at the Harvard Business School, where she provides consultation in the areas of career management, academic advisement, and personal development. She is also on the faculty of the Jean Baker Miller Institute at Wellesley College. In addition to her private psychology practice, her professional experience includes antiracism leadership training in business and religious communities. Dr. Walker's current research focuses on racial identity development and relational competence. Dr. Walker is licensed in Massachusetts.

DORIS J. WRIGHT, Ph.D., is an Associate Professor in the Department of Counseling and Psychological Services at Georgia State University. Previously she held positions as staff psychologist and Program Director for Consultation Services at the University of Texas-Austin. A prolific writer on cultural diversity and college student development, Dr. Wright edited *Meeting the Needs of Today's Minority Students* in Jossey-Bass' *New Directions for Student Services* series. She also co-edited the 1988 NASPA monograph, *From Survival to Success: Promoting Minority Student Retention* and authored a chapter in the 1992 monograph, *Diversity, Disunity and Campus Community*. During the nearly 20-year period she has worked in college settings, Dr. Wright has designed and facilitated more than 50 types of groups and workshops.

JENAI WU, Ph.D., is a licensed clinical psychologist. She is also a candidate at the Boston Psychoanalytic Society and Institute. Dr. Wu is in private practice, a clinical consultant to the Stone Center at Wellesley College, and a staff psychologist at Massachusetts General Hospital where she is on the supervising faculty of the Psychiatry Residency and Psychology Internship programs. She has lectured, published articles, and presented papers at numerous professional meetings on mental health issues concerning Asians, Asian American women, and various other clinical issues.

# INDEX

## A
abuse, 58, 69, 100, 192, 222
acculturation, 7, 110, 203–4, 218
*ADA Handbook,* 173
advocacy, xiii, 10, 231, 239–46
affirmative action, 12, 14, 48, 183
African American(s), 15, 37–49, 55, 117, 136, 155, 164, 225, 229; and dual traumatization, 51–65; and learning disorders, 182–3; men, 155, 156, 222; students, xii, 37–49; therapists, 45–6
AIDS, ix, xiii, xiv, 170, 211–16; person with (PWA), 211, 213, 215
Allen, I.M., 2, 220, 222–3
Alvarez, M., 3, 220, 221, 224
*American Psychiatric Association's Diagnostic Manual of Mental Disorders,* 173
Americans with Disabilities Act 1990, 172–3, 192
anger, 121, 151, 214, 228; politics of, 58–9
antidiscrimination laws, 174–5
anxiety, 8–9, 88, 107, 111, 193, 227
Asian American(s), 77, 82, 201–9, 219, 233–4
Asian(s), 67–75, 77–85, 94, 206–8; cultural perspective, 82, 222; cultures, 74, 77, 201, 204; families, 74, 202–3, 207; values, 203–4
Aslanian, C., & Brickell, H.M., 191
assertiveness, 94–5
assimilation, 203–4, 218–19, 234
authenticity, 18–19
autonomy, 104, 112, 201

## B
barriers, 33, 131, 139–40, 173, 208, 229; language, 136, 207, 208, 223
Beatrie, M., 61, 64.
belief systems, 31, 105, 109, 112
Bem Sex Role Inventory (BSRI), 133–5
Betz, N., & Fitzgerald, L.F., 132
biculturality, 208, 218–19, 224, 226, 234
biracial, 122; bind, 117–27; children, 118; identity, 121; individuals, 123, 151
Black: culture, 46, 124; identity development, 2, 44–5, 120; males, 43–4, 120, 156, 223; universities, 16; women. *See* women, Black
Black Identity Scale, 39, 45
blaming the victim, 220–2
Boesch, R., & Cimbolic, P., 46
Bowser, B.P., Auletta, G., & Jones, T., 17, 47
Brandi, E., 51
Brandi, E., & Walker, M., 58
Brice-Baker, J.R., 59
Brockett, R., 191
Brown University, 176
Butell, N.J., & O'Hare, M.M., 197

## C
career(s), 52, 110, 201; choices, 103, 144, 170, 196, 203, 215, 219, 223; concerns of Asian American students, 201–9, 223; counseling, 202, 208; development, 132, 144, 219, 232; intervention, 170, 202
Catholic Church, 103–4, 109
Caucasian(s), 37, 39, 44, 117, 121, 151, 222; helping professionals, 11, 45
Chan, C.S., 2, 3, 221, 224–5
Chartrand, J.M., 195

Chin, J.L., 204
Chin, J.L., De La Cancela, V., & Jenkins, Y.M., 38, 170
Civil Rights Act of 1964, 173
class, ix, 63, 99, 208, 232, 234. *See also* social class
Collins, P.H., 223
color, ix, 5, 7, 173; people of, 5, 11, 12, 14, 55, 57, 62, 130, 221, 229–30, 239; professionals of, 11, 16; skin, 17, 41, 102; students of. *See* students of color; survivors of, 51–65; therapists of, 45, 236; women of, 16, 130, 151, 222. *See also* women
Comas-Díaz, L., & Jacobsen, F.M., 45
competence, 112; cultural, xvi, 12, 239; social, ix, xvi, 12
conflict, 101, 221; identity, 103–6; of loyalty, 102, 125
Confucian philosophy, 74, 202
connection, 19, 75, 97, 132, 155
counseling and mental health professionals, xv, 30, 113; African American, 46, 57; Asian American, 77; college, 38, 217–37; Japanese, 87; Native American, 32–4; of color, 45
counseling and mental health services, xiii, 5–6, 198, 239; college, xv, 13–16, 45–8, 99, 149, 169; culturally competent, 99, 129, 235–7
countertransference issues, 45, 63–4, 235
Creek/Yuchi, 34
Cross, W.E., Jr., 57, 133–4, 231
cross-cultural: experience, 87, 105; interventions, 113; therapy, 87–97, 105–6
Crux, S., 186
cultural: assumptions, 27, 89; competence, 154, 165, 208, 231–3, 235; differences, 30, 67, 87, 99, 110, 174, 206, 224; expectations, 113, 122, 203, 208, 223–4; factors, 6, 89, 133; identity, 102, 109, 113, 220; issues, 77, 149–50, 155, 164; orientation, 156, 170, 201, 225; patterns, 132–3, 226; sensitivity, 132, 165, 208; values, 1, 31, 70, 137, 170, 201–2, 220, 233
culture, ix, xiv, 2, 4, 6, 7, 9, 17, 46, 67, 75, 77–85, 102, 105–6, 110, 132, 144, 150, 160, 164, 202, 219, 222, 223–7, 232, 241–3; dominant, 5, 14, 15, 27, 31, 44, 51, 57, 60, 62, 222, 227; Korean American, 81, 83; of origin, 110, 113; patriarchal, 104
culture shock, 11, 24, 221, 232, 234; and cross-cultural therapy, 87–97

**D**

De las Fuentes, C., & Wright, D.J., 156
De Leon, B., 132, 223
De Leon, B., Stefanisko, M., and Corteza, B.L., 4, 223, 228
depression, 34, 37, 39, 91, 111, 157, 188, 193, 211, 216
desegregation, 242–3
Dinklage, K.T., 169, 226, 229
disabled persons, 172–3
disconnection, 51, 60, 62, 102, 112
discrimination, 14, 113, 120, 136, 144–5, 172–3, 183, 233
disempowerment, 46, 51, 221
dishonor, 151, 154, 222
displacement, 113, 235
dissociation, 51, 221
diversity, xi, xiii, xiv, xvi, 2, 6, 9–10, 19, 48, 99, 105, 110, 142, 149, 169, 219, 228–9, 232, 239, 241–3; among Latinas, 99–115; and the

helping professions, 239–46; embracing, 228, 232, 243–6
dominant culture. *See* culture, dominant
domination, 14, 219
dual traumatization, 51–65, 221
dyslexia, ix, xiv, 169, 172–4, 176, 180
dyslexics, xiii, 175–6

**E**

Edwards, A., & Polite, C., 38
ego integrity, 121–2
empathy, 9, 18–19, 93
empowerment, xiii, 114, 155–6
Encounter Stage, 44, 57, 134, 144–5
engagement, 18–19
Erikson, E., 117
Espín, O.M., 106, 109
ethnicity, ix, xi, xvi, 1, 2, 9, 14, 17, 19, 30, 44–6, 60, 63, 99, 102, 110, 129, 132, 145, 150, 156, 192, 198, 207, 219, 226–7, 232, 234, 241–2
exoticism, 13, 62
exploitation, 113, 219

**F**

face, 202; losing, 82, 85n 1; saving, 85n 1, 94, 96
Family Environmental Scale (FES), 134–5
family(ies), 132, 145, 152, 202, 225; characteristics of, 134, 155; continuity, 201–2; dynamics, 110, 154; dysfunction in, 54; extended, 137, 145–6; female-headed, 130; harmony, 93–4; loyalty, 75, 101, 205; of origin, 112; orientation, 132; relations, 60, 70, 74, 140–1; roles, 105, 141; secrets, 70, 74; traditions, 155; White, 225

fear, 151, 214
feminine qualities, 134–5
filial piety, 205
Fitzgerald, L.F. & Crites, J.O., 132
Fleming, J., 37
folklore, 105
Forrest, L., & Mikolaitis, N., 132

**G**

gay and lesbian groups, 212
Gehrie, M., 7
gender, ix, xi, xiv, xvi, 1, 5, 10, 14, 19, 63, 99, 102, 129, 132, 142, 156, 165, 173, 192, 198, 213, 234, 241–2; identity, 74, 122; oppression, 2, 220; role issues, 3, 44, 74–5, 96, 102, 103, 109, 111, 132, 133–4, 144
Geschwind, N., 180
Gibbs, J.T., & Moskowitz-Sweet, G., 120–1
Gould, N.B., 170
Greene, B., & Sanchez-Hucles, J., 228, 232
grief, 113, 214
group harmony, 201–2, 205, 223, 225
group services for students of color, 149–67
guilt, 91, 94, 111–12, 214

**H**

Hacker, A., 37–8
Hackett, G., & Betz, N.E., 131
Hansen, D.G., 169–70, 218, 224
Harrigan, C., 191
Hart-Webb, 3, 4, 218, 222, 224, 227
Harvard University, 174–6, 177; Health Service, 211
health care systems, 5, 235–7
Helms, J.E., 57
help seeking, 10; anxiety about, 11–12

Herman, J., 52
Hines, P. & Boyd-Franklin, N., 228–9
Hispanic(s), 130, 132, 165, 222; communities, 138–9, 145; families, 131, 136, 140–1
HIV infection, ix, xiv, 170, 211–16
Hoetler, J.W., 195
homophobia, 9, 108–9, 206, 228
homosexuality, 157, 205–6, 213, 215

**I**

identity, xi, 27, 34, 105–6, 108–9, 113, 118, 121, 126, 202, 205; African American, 161; and sexuality, 77; conflicted, 103–6, 111; consolidation, 108–9; development, 2, 7, 45, 57, 109, 111, 118, 133, 144–5, 165, 192, 219–20, 232; dilemma, 117–27; dual social, 102–3; ethnocultural, 101–2; familial, 201; formation, 2, 63; lesbian, 109, 111; mixed race, 117, 218; multicultural, 111; of Asian women, 74; personal, 19n 1, 45; racial. *See* racial identity; social. *See* social identity; struggles, 102, 108
Identity Development Model, 134
Imes, S.A., & Clance, P.R., 54
Immersion/Emersion Stage, 44, 57, 134, 145
immigrants, ix, 3, 5, 204, 206–8, 232, 234; experience of, 77
immigration, xvi, 2, 11, 70, 99, 113, 221
inadequacy, 111–12
independence, 88, 95, 135, 202
individualism, 88, 93, 95, 117, 155, 170, 201, 208, 224, 226
*inipi*, 28, 34
integration, 242–3
Interagency Committee on Learning Disabilities, 171
interdependence, 170, 201–2, 204, 224
Internalization/Commitment Stage, 45, 134, 144–5
interventions, xi, xv, 6, 16, 29, 33–4, 60, 93, 106–7, 113, 169, 170, 196, 208, 224, 229–32, 235; countertransferential, 63; cross-cultural, 31, 113; cultural considerations for, 204–6; culturally competent, 1, 149–67, 187, 221, 223, 231; group, 149–67; psychospiritual, 61; with diverse populations, 1–5, 18–19, 230
isolation, 224, 227

**J**

Japanese: culture, 205–6, 223; family life of, 87, 93; society, 87, 89, 93–4, 97, 205
Japanese Americans, 225
Jenkins, Y.M., 239
Jenkins, Y.M., De La Cancela, V., & Chin, J.L., 105
Johnson, S.M. & Mapp, K.L., 6
Jones, E.E., 45
Judaism, 104
Judeo-Christians, 120

**K**

Kaplan, A.G., 8
Kerwin, C., Ponterotto, J.G., Jackson, B.L., Harris, A., 118
kin sponsorship, 59, 221

**L**

Lakota, 34
Landmark College, 174
Langelier, R., 194
Latin American(s): culture of, 109–10, 112–13; gender roles of, 103

Latinas, 3, 221, 224–5; diversity among, 99–115; in the U.S., 111–12
Latinos, 130
learning disorders, 172–81, 183–8, 226–7, 229; academic accomodations for, 184–8; diagnosis of, 184–5; psychological support for, 187–8
lesbians, 109; identity, 109, 111; rights of, 109
Lewis, S., 61
Lipsky, S., 60
loyalty issues, 73–4, 111, 125, 204, 219, 233

## M

Mahler, M., 7–8
marginalized groups, xi, xiii, 14–15, 206–7, 223–4
masculine qualities, 134–5
McGoldrick, M., et al, 194
mental health services. *See* counseling and mental health services
Merta, R.J., 150
migration, 99, 102–3, 105, 109–10, 113, 235
Miller, J.B., 19, 108
Minority Identity Scale, 134
Minority Status Survey (MSS), 133
mixed race, 3, 117, 218, 222; therapy groups, 156–60, 166
mother-daughter relationships, 67, 112
multicultural: counseling, 150; group services, 149–67; theories, 155
multiculturalism, 142, 241, 245
Muskogee, 35
mutuality, xiii, 14, 18, 19, 156

## N

Native American Indians, 21–35, 221, 224, 225, 233; and alcohol, 33; cultural values of, 29, 31; healing approaches, 27, 34, 230; identity of, 34
Nickerson, K.J., Helms, J.E., & Terrell, F., 46
*Nisei*, 205
Nobles, W., 242

## O

Oberg, K., 88
*Occupational Outlook Handbook*, 196
Ochberg, R.L., 106
oppression, xvi, 1, 2, 3, 14, 15, 17, 37, 47, 51, 102, 156, 219–22, 228; internalized, 60–1, 223, 227, 229
"Oreo," 126n 1
Orton Dyslexia Society, 176

## P

parenting, 193
parents: expectations of, 94; influence of, 136–9, 145–6; Japanese, 226; single, 195, 197
Pentecostal churches, 145
personal: agency, 62; growth, 132; integrity, 156
Pinderhughes, E.B., 6–9, 226
pluralistic populations. *See* populations, pluralistic
Ponterotto, J., et al, 150
poor, the, 5
populations: college, 117, 169, 229; disenfranchised, 13, 16–17; diverse, ix, 1–5, 12, 16–17, 149–50, 226–7, 239, 243; diverse college, 4, 5–20, 169, 171, 217–18; indigenous, 31; Latin American, 130; marginalized, xi, xiii, xv, 5, 6, 11, 12, 14, 16–17; Native American, 21–35, 229, 233; nontraditional,

17, 169, 230, 236; pluralistic, xii, 17, 18–19, 31, 130, 218, 228–9; student, xv, 102, 166, 174; under-served, xiii
post-traumatic stress disorder, 81–2, 84
poverty, 112, 130, 221
Pow Wow, 35
Pre-Encounter Stage, 44, 57, 134
prejudice, 1, 9, 14, 38, 48, 120, 160, 239
Protestant churches, 145
psychocultural borders, 100–3
Puerto Rican(s), 130, 139–44, 146

## R

race, ix, xi, xvi, 1–6, 10, 14, 17, 19, 30, 39–40, 44–6, 48, 63, 99, 132, 142, 145, 150, 156, 160, 164–5, 169, 173, 183, 192, 198, 208, 213, 222–4, 227, 232, 234, 242; relations, 12
racial: attitudes, 42, 160; boundaries, 223; concerns, 43; crisis, 161, 164, 223; differences, 222; encounters, 164; groups, 51, 182; identity, 12, 37–8, 43–4, 46, 48, 57, 118, 133, 165, 218, 222; issues, 39–40, 46, 48, 63, 155, 160, 164, 223, 225; socializtion, 57
racism, 1, 9, 11, 37, 46, 144, 156, 161, 220, 222–3, 228, 233
rape, 82–3, 150–6, 222, 225; date, 225; recovery group for, 155, 225; trauma symptoms of, 151
relational: connection, 59–62; development, 2, 63, 219–20, 229, 232; disconnections, 56; growth, 63–4; patterns, 112; processes, 62; theory of women's development, 105
religion, 173, 226, 228
religiosity, 62, 228–9
religious: beliefs, 61, 225, 228–9, 242; orientation, 132, 155
role models, 136–7, 143, 164

## S

Sanford, L., 51
*Sansei*, 205, 207
Section 504 of the Rehabilitation Act, 1973, 171–2
self: -acceptance, 93; -blame, 151, 207; -caretaking, 220–22, 229; -concept formation, 7, 117, 219; -determinism, 95, 155, 231; -differentiation, 59–62; -efficacy, 62, 132, 133; -esteem, 15, 48, 82, 111, 155, 180, 187, 195, 197, 220–2; -expression, 93, 226; -in-diversity, 8–9; -perceptions, 219–20, 232
Self-Efficacy Scale (SES), 133–4, 135
sensitivity training, 48, 239–46
separation, 112–14, 157
service delivery: culturally competent, 113–14
sexism, 11, 219, 226
sexual: expression, 84, 225; orientation, 111, 122, 205–6, 211, 213, 242; preference, xvi, 219, 232; trauma, 51; victimization, 55; violence, 156, 221
sexual abuse, 11, 51, 54, 161, 192; survivors of, 51, 221
sexuality, xiv, xvi, 77–85, 104, 109–10, 122, 169, 206, 219
shame, 51, 63, 71, 73, 77–85, 94, 108, 111, 121, 151, 152, 181, 183, 207, 213–14, 221–2, 225, 233
Sheridan, H., 176
Shin, S.A., 170, 218–19, 223–4
Simms, W.F., 1, 218, 220–1, 224, 229
social: ambiance, 12–13; class, ix, xi, xiv, 1, 10, 110, 132, 142, 156,

165, 222, 224, 226–7, 234, 241–2; competence, 160, 165; esteem, 13, 14, 18, 220, 227; factors, 6, 133, 149–50; identity, 1, 8, 9, 17, 19n 1; injustice, 102–3, 142, 230, 245; status, 17, 19
socialization, 7, 57, 131
society, 106; hierarchical, 92, 202
sociocultural factors, 138–40, 144, 156
socioeconomic status, xvi, 102, 129, 169
sociopolitical issues, 129, 142–4
spirituality, 30, 34, 62, 228–9, 235
Steele, C., 48
stereotypes, 2, 9, 14, 15, 29, 38, 48, 100, 160, 183, 223, 225, 239
Stiver, I.P., 56
students: African American, xii, 2, 37–49, 149, 220, 222, 227; Asian, 77, 149, 219; Asian American, 67–75, 77–85, 170, 183, 201–9, 229; Caucasian, 2, 183, 220; culturally different, 240–2; first-generation college, 170, 234; gay, 213; Harvard, 175, 179; Hispanic, 129–48, 149, 227; international, 6, 87–9, 94–5, 97, 113, 221, 224, 232, 234–5; Japanese, 3, 87–97, 226; Korean American, 2, 223; Latina, 129–48, 149, 227; learning disabled, 119, 169, 171–90, 235; mixed race, 3, 222, 224, 234; Native American Indian, 1, 21–35, 149, 218, 233; nontraditional, 169–70, 184–5, 191–9, 224, 227, 234, 236; of color, xii, xiii, xiv, xv, 1–4, 6, 11, 12, 13, 15–17, 130, 142, 149–67, 182–8, 217–18, 220, 227–8, 236; populations of, xv, 166; Puerto Rican women, 4, 129–48, 228; role, 191, 195; traditional, 191–99; White, 38; with AIDS, 211–16, 235; with dyslexia, 176; with HIV, xiv, 235
substance abuse, 10, 37, 120, 192
suicide, 10, 221
Surrey, J.L., 8
survivors, 52, 234; abuse, 51; African American, 56, 58; guilt, 60; of rape, 150–6
sweat lodge, 28, 34

**T**

talking circle, 27, 28, 34, 35, 229
Tarpley, N., 38
therapeutic relationship, 67, 70–1, 74, 105
therapy: cross-cultural, 87–97; group, ix, 149–67; individual, ix, 28–9
traditional healing practices. *See also* Native American Indians, 28
trauma, 11, 220–22, 225, 234; rape and assault, 83; survivor, 123
treatment: cultural context for, 95–7; goals, 92, 123
tribal community colleges, 21, 22, 25
Trimble, J.E., 31
Tyler, F.B., Brome, D.R., & Williams, J.E., 19

**U**

U.S. dominant cultural values, 7, 32, 88–9, 93, 143, 170, 183, 201, 203, 206, 208, 218, 223–4, 226, 234, 241
*Understanding Learning Disabilities: Guide for Faculty:* Georgetown University Office of Student Affairs, 177

**V**

values: personal, 105, 134, 141, 218

victimization, 123, 222
violation: racial, 51, 221; sexual, 51, 221
Vogel, S.H., 3, 223–4

**W**
Walker, M.M., 2, 220–1, 229
Wasicu, 35
West, C., 39
White: guilt, 228; institutions, 16, 37–49, 57, 220, 241; men, 155, 156, 225; society, 121, 124–5; values, 126n 1
White, J.L., 239
White, J.L., & Parham, T.A., 239
women, 3, 51, 55, 109, 144; African American, 51–67, 151, 160–4, 221; African Caribbean American, 59; and relational theory of development, 105; Asian American, 39, 67–75; Black, 44, 61; career development of, 132, 224; Cuban, 110; ethnic minority, 132; gender roles of, 2, 44, 67, 140, 222; growth and development of, 111; Hispanic, 129–48; immigrant, 106; Japanese, 87–97; Korean American, 77–85; Latin American, 99–115, 131; lesbian, 109; Mexican, 110; Native, 32, 33; of color. *See* color, women of; oppressed, 102, 222; Puerto Rican, 110, 129–48, 228; role models, 143, 145; White, 40; with dependent children, 192
Wright, D.J., 4, 222–3, 225
Wu, J., 2, 220, 224

**Y**
Yuen, L.M., & Depper, D.S., 75

CPSIA information can be obtained
at www.ICGtesting.com
Printed in the USA
LVHW082331211019
634939LV00006B/102/P